In Pursuit of Peace in Israel and Palestine

In Pursuit of Peace in Israel and Palestine

GERSHON BASKIN

VANDERBILT UNIVERSITY PRESS

Nashville

© 2017 by Gershon Baskin
Published by Vanderbilt University Press
Nashville, Tennessee 37235

First printing 2017
This book is printed on acid-free paper.
Manufactured in the United States of America

Library of Congress Cataloging-in-Publication Data on file
LC control number 2017000459
LC classification number DS119.7.B2918 2017
Dewey classification number 956.9405—dc23
LC record available at lccn.loc.gov/2017000459

ISBN 978-0-8265-2181-1 (cloth)
ISBN 978-0-8265-2183-5 (ebook)

This book is dedicated to all the innocent victims of the Israeli-Palestinian conflict. It is written with the hope that more innocent lives will not be lost because of the inability of leaders to return to the table to negotiate peace. It is dedicated to all those Israeli and Palestinian heroes who dedicate their lives, day in and out, to work for peace. Peace is made by the actions people take to change attitudes and behaviors and to create hope for a much brighter tomorrow.

Contents

Acknowledgments

Many people have influenced me and impacted my life and my work over the past six decades. Amongst those there is one constant shining light of intelligence, principle, integrity, and action—my mother, the late Rita Geller Baskin, who was killed in a car accident in Florida nine years ago. Her spirit and guidance is always with me.

My unending appreciation is also given to my family—my wife Edna, who has tolerated and suffered my too many hours away from home and the anxiety of my travels to dangerous places, and my three children, Elisha, Ben, and Amit who have grown up into extraordinary adults living the values of our home and each making their own significant impact on the world that we share.

Preface

On October 18, 2011, Israeli soldier Gilad Schalit returned home after five years and four months in captivity in Gaza, held by Hamas's military wing, Ezzedin al-Qassam. Schalit was exchanged for 1027 Palestinian prisoners in Israeli jails. The deal made between the government of Israel and Hamas that ended this painful saga was facilitated through the development of a secret direct back channel of negotiations between me and several Hamas leaders. My first direct contact with a Hamas leader began in April 2005 while attending a UN Conference in Cairo. A friend from Gaza, Prof. Mohammed Samhouri, an economist, was attending that conference. During the first day of meetings, Prof. Samhouri approached me with someone whom he described as a former student and now a professor of economics at the Islamic University of Gaza. Prof. Mohammed Migdad had traveled from Gaza to Cairo via Sinai because he heard that there might be some Israelis at this conference. He had never spoken with an Israeli before, and he was interested in asking some serious questions. In more than two decades of working with Palestinians, I had not yet spoken to anyone from Hamas. This was a golden opportunity for both of us.

Prof. Migdad and I spent about six hours together during the next two days in deep debate and exploration. For me the biggest challenge in our conversations was in trying to explain that my self-definition as a Jew did not solely consist of an identification with a religion. I tried very hard to explain that although very secular, I am also very Jewish. The complexities of defining "Jewish" were, not surprisingly, beyond his comprehension as a believer in the ideology of the Muslim Brotherhood and Hamas, a refugee living in the impoverished Gaza Strip, growing up with the consciousness of placing blame on Israel and the Jews for all of his people's problems and sufferings. Much of our conversation reminded me of similar conversations I have had with many Palestinians and other Arabs over the past decades. Nevertheless, I proposed to Prof. Migdad that our dialogue, being both interesting and important, should be continued and expanded to include other friends from both sides. Prof. Migdad agreed.

Over the next months, we attempted to organize the dialogue. I found four non-EU countries that were willing to host and sponsor our talks: Russia, Norway, Switzerland, and Turkey. Prof. Migdad organized a group of his colleagues from the Islamic University. I organized a group of senior

Israeli academics and experts. In the end, the dialogue did not take place. The Palestinian participants had cold feet and would only participate if they had the explicit green light from the Hamas leadership. Despite a visit to Gaza then and a two-hour discussion between Prof. Migdad and Dr. Ahmed Yousef, a senior advisor to Hamas Prime Minister Ismail Haniyeh, that took place in the prime minister's office in Gaza, during which Dr. Yousef said that he would join our dialogue, the meetings never took place. The senior leadership of Hamas vetoed the talks, stating that no direct contact would take place between Hamas members and Israelis.

In September 2005, my wife's first cousin, Sasson Nuriel was abducted and murdered by Hamas in the West Bank. When he first disappeared, I tried to use my enormous web of contacts in the West Bank to attempt to locate him or at least gather information about his whereabouts. Shortly after, Hamas published a video of Sasson in captivity.[1] Soon after that, he was murdered. His body was found by Israeli security forces.

My wife, an Iraqi Jew, has a huge family—thirty-six first cousins—compared with me, an Ashkenazi Jew, who has only two. Sasson was my wife's age. He had been at my wedding years before. We had met at other family celebrations and occasions. Shortly before his murder, we had met at a condolence visit for a common cousin who passed away in Netanya, north of Tel Aviv, and Sasson traveled back to Jerusalem with us. On the way home, we talked politics. He spoke about his close relationship with his Palestinian workers in his candy factory, which was located in the settlement industrial zone of Mishor Adumin, the place where he was abducted by one of those same Palestinian workers with whom he had thought he was so close. At Sasson's funeral, standing over his body, I swore to myself that, if ever again I could prevent what happened to Sasson, I would do everything possible to save that life.

On June 25, 2006, early in the morning, eight Palestinian armed fighters exited from an attack tunnel inside the Kerem Shalom Israeli Army base next to the Gaza Strip. They launched a rocket-propelled grenade at a tank on the edge of the base. From the tank, which was engulfed by flames, emerged two Israeli soldiers, Hanan Barak and Pavel Slutzker—both were immediately shot and killed. One of the Palestinians climbed onto the tank and dropped a grenade inside. A shell-shocked and wounded soldier was pulled out of the tank and carried off to Gaza. It took the army about one hour to discover that Corporal Gilad Schalit was missing. The Israeli Army immediately began a hot pursuit into Gaza, but it was already too late. The Israeli cabinet authorized a military operation in Gaza—dubbed "Summer Rains"—to bring back the soldier and to capture the perpetrators of the attack. The Israeli Army bombed Gaza. A lot of infrastructure was damaged, including roads, bridges, water networks, and Gaza's main electricity plant.

Six days later, Prof. Mohammed Migdad called me and said, "Gershon—we have to do something. We are being bombed. We have no water and no electricity. The situation is bad, and it is going to get worse." I asked him, "What can we do?" Migdad suggested that we try to open a line of communication between the opposing sides. He got into his car and went to the Hamas prime minister's office. About thirty minutes later, I received a phone call from Dr. Mohammed Madhoun, the director general of the Prime Minister's Office. He told me that someone else would contact me shortly. A few minutes later, Dr. Ghazi Hamad, the spokesperson of the Hamas government and close advisor to Prime Minister Haniyeh, called. Later that day, based on a proposal by Ghazi Hamad, I organized a phone call between Noam Schalit, Gilad's father, and Ghazi Hamad. That was the beginning of a five-year-and-four-month-long story of trying and eventually succeeding in getting the government of Israel to listen to me and carry on a secret direct back channel negotiation to bring Gilad Schalit home.[2] Two and a half months into my attempts, I succeeded in getting Hamas to release a handwritten letter from the soldier to his family that was delivered to the Egyptian representative's office in Gaza. Even after that, it took five years to convince the Israeli government to listen to me. Finally, the Prime Minister of Israel appointed a senior Mossad officer, David Meidan to take charge of the case. Meidan had the good sense and complete understanding of the task at hand to agree to break long-held taboos and facilitate a direct secret back channel to Hamas. In May 2011, I conducted negotiations under David Meidan with Netanyahu's approval, and five months later Schalit was freed.

My contacts with Hamas continue today and have been used to advance cease-fire understandings, prevent escalation of hostilities between Israel and Hamas, facilitate attempts to bring home the bodies of two Israeli soldiers killed in Gaza in the summer of 2014, and to release three Israeli civilians currently held captive by Hamas.

In Pursuit of Peace in Israel and Palestine

Is Israel-Arab Peace Even Possible?

Is Israeli-Arab peace even possible? There are many, perhaps even a majority of people, not only in Israel, but throughout the Middle East, and perhaps all around the world who contend that it is not. The Jews and the Arabs will never be able to live in peace, they claim. For some, they say it is a clash of civilizations—two opposing worldviews colliding endlessly, periodically erupting in acute violence and bloodshed, deepening the hatred and the fear—this is the eternal cycle they describe and foresee. For them, there is never a chance for reconciliation and understanding. Many of those who hold this belief couple it with the contention that the Israeli-Arab conflict is a conflict of religions—fundamental beliefs regarding God, the divine will, and the intentions of the Lord regarding the land of Israel/Palestine, the people living on it, and the ultimate truth. If one feels he is in possession of an absolute truth—such as, "God gave this Land to us," there is little that can be said, which is convincing and rational, that has the power to persuade someone that there is even the slightest bit of room for a different possibility or that they may be wrong. If the Israeli-Arab conflict is in fact a conflict between Judaism and Islam, then it cannot be resolved. But, it is not.

Some take the position that Islam and Muslims will never accommodate Western liberal values and will always be in constant conflict with the West until the entire planet becomes part of the *Dar al-Islam*—the domain of Islam. Those who hold fast to this belief play up the threat of Islam to Europe, whose open-door policies on immigration have enabled large Muslim minorities to populate urban centers and inner cities, often becoming the newest lower classes of the rich European societies, and thereby giving rise to social unrest, high unemployment, and vast alienation. The underclass status of many Muslims in Europe pivots them into positions of revolt, unrest, and sometimes violence and terrorism—especially amongst the second generation, who were born into that status. There are Americans who hold on to this belief, and they are often the same ones who claim that President Barack Hussein Obama is a Muslim, which is evidence, they claim, of his deeply rooted hatred of Israel and of Jews. He is not, and this is not true.

On the other side of the fence, there are those who say it is the Jews that have colonized a land that may have once been theirs, but for two thousand years, was not. They came with Western support, money, and sophistication, which enabled them to maneuver the conquest of an entire land where they just recently made up only a small portion of the population. With their massive enlistment of world Jewry, mainly in the United States, they legitimized their struggle and delegitimized the indigenous Arab Palestinian people's claim to their own land, forcing them to become a stateless people. The success of the Zionist movement was so enormous that it pushed the Palestinian people into not only a stateless status but also into a status of nonexistence as a people.

But Zionism was not the same as the classic colonialist enterprises of European states in Africa and Asia. There are many differences—mainly that Zionism really is the story of a people returning to their historic land. Those who call Zionism Western colonialization refuse to recognize the legitimacy of Zionism and reject the notion that Jews are a people, asserting that Judaism is solely a status of religion. Ironically, while they demand the right of self-determination for the Palestinian people, they reject the idea that Jews too have that very same right—to determine their identity and to fulfill a territorial expression of their identity in their ancient homeland.

Likewise, on the other side, there are many who believe that peace is not possible because they are opponents of Palestinian national rights and refuse to recognize that something called a Palestinian people exists—even until today. These people argue that the Palestinians are a constructed myth and that no such separate identity exists. They claim that Palestinian nationalism was devised and created only to fight the Jews and to prevent the Jews from having a homeland in the Middle East. They claim the right of self-determination for the Jewish people and, as previously mentioned, deny the same right to millions of people who have determined that they are Palestinians and who also have a right to a territorial expression of their identity in the land in which that identity came into being.

There are those who put the burden of there being no chance for peace on Israel and claim that Israel will never agree to integrate into the Arab and Muslim Middle East. It will always be the stranger in the neighborhood and will never drop its paternalistic and patronizing attitudes toward the Arabs. Israel will always be the front line of the United States with its aggressive tendencies and policies that seek to dominate rather than to integrate and be a part of the region.

One can naturally find some truth in all of these arguments, as well as many untruths. This is a complex conflict, as most of them are, and the unraveling of the issues is complicated by the urge to delve into the narratives of each side. Working and rationalizing narratives is one part of resolving any conflict, but there are many other aspects to conflict resolution that must also be confronted. The task of making peace between Israel and its neighbors is rather daunting. Even the existing two peace treaties between Israel and Egypt, and Israel and Jordan can hardly be called a state of peace. They are at best a state of nonwar with open borders, in one direction mostly (from Israel to them), although used with less and less frequency. There is no state of peace between the people of Israel and those of Egypt and Jordan. Israelis are largely unwelcome in Egypt and Jordan, and even business relationships need to be well hidden in order to protect those involved and their desire to make money together. The only real aspect of peace that seems lasting is the cooperation between the intelligence services facing the same threats from Islamic extremists, state and nonstate actors who have brought so much instability to the entire region since the beginning of the "Arab Spring."

Even after all of these years of living side by side in the region, very few Israelis speak Arabic, and even fewer Arabs speak Hebrew (except for Israel's Palestinian citizens, Palestinians who spent years in Israeli prisons, and Palestinians who worked in Israel or continue to work in Israel). Very few on both sides view the other's media, read their literature, watch their movies, or even know very much about their internal politics. There are two areas that have broken barriers at least in one direction (from the Arab world to Israel): food and music. Beyond the stomach and the ears, enormous barriers exist between the Israeli and the Arab worlds. Despite the closeness of the Arabic and Hebrew languages, which would make them so much easier for each to learn the language of the other, the psychological barrier of learning the language of the enemy has left this potentially very powerful tool for building bridges to understanding almost entirely in the hands of security services who learn the languages for very different purposes.

The Israeli-Palestinian conflict has been centered on mutual nonrecognition and denial of the rights of each side to have a territorial expression of their identity—a piece of land they can call their own, on which they are the masters of their destiny. So much effort has gone into developing the "factual" evidence that the other side does not really exist, and therefore, does not have the same rights in making territorial claims. Often the mutual nonrecognition takes on additional weighty claims, and arguments that focus on the horrific things each side has done to the other have enhanced hatred and fear and have ultimately prevented any chance of recognizing the possibilities for mutual recognition.

The Jews, riding on the moral imperative to provide for themselves a safe haven after the horrors of the Holocaust, for many years held the higher moral ground. The countries of the world felt pity for the Jewish people over the extermination of one third of their people—six million innocent victims—and for their own failures to prevent the Holocaust. Their guilt was a powerful driving force behind global support for Zionism after World War II. The Jewish people and the Zionist movement held onto a commanding mobilization of resources, moral support, and solidarity both within world Jewry, the Jewish community in Palestine before 1948, and the international community, which was undeniably more powerful than the voice of the fractured community of Palestinian Arabs whose nascent national movement lacked a unified voice of common identity, purpose, and vision. Although backed by the Arab world, the competing interests within the Arab world and the lack of centralized, dedicated Palestinian national leadership willing to even engage in the thought of accommodation with the Jews led to the *nakba* and the dispersion of most of the Palestinian population from Palestine. The Arab and Palestinian rejection of partition in 1947, which would have occurred on far better terms than those that are suggested today, left the Palestinians dispossessed, dispersed, and broken. It would take years before some Palestinian leaders could even recognize the possibility of mutual recognition as the key to salvation for the Palestinian people on part of the land of Palestine. That happened in 1988, but before then, clinging to the dream of all or nothing, Palestinians ended up with nothing.

From 1948 until 1988, the Palestinian national movement clung to the all or nothing dream, even though there were voices of change rising in the mid-1970s. In the mid-1960s when the Palestinian national movement finally organized itself on the international stage, it engaged in terrorism, not only against the State of Israel but against Israel's supporters, as well. Led by Yasser Arafat, the Palestinian national movement had great difficulty in capturing the hearts and minds of most people in the West. In those years, Israel was seen as the David that took on the mighty and powerful Goliath—struggling for its own survival, it emerged victorious against great odds. Israel's egalitarian values and socialist structures, such as the kibbutz, inspired admiration and support throughout the world. At least until 1973, Israel captured the imagination of much of the world and saw its struggle for existence as just. The June 1967 war, in which Israel emerged as a regional superpower, created a sense of awe about the small and struggling nation that amazed the world with its unsurpassed military victory against armies threatening to annihilate the nation of the Jews. Even after occupying the West Bank and Gaza, the 1967 war passed relatively quietly, both locally and internationally, mainly because the Israeli government continued its policies of at least speaking of the offer of an outstretched hand and a willingness to exchange territories for peace. The Arabs, on the other hand, continued to capture the position of no recognition, no negotiations, and no peace. The rejectionists will almost always be denied legitimacy.

Israel's position in the world regarding Palestine began to change mainly with the election of the Likud government of Menachem Begin in 1977. Although surprised and pleased with Begin's drive to find peace with Egypt, much of the world was dismayed by Begin's refusal to deal genuinely with the Palestinian issue and the insistence of his government to construct settlements in the heart of the West Bank, which was clearly seen as a move to block any possible accommodations with the Palestinians on the basis of two states for two peoples. As a result of that very settlement policy, most of the world today puzzles over the incongruence between Israel's occupation of Palestine and its insistence on calling itself a democracy.

It took many years, but today most of the world has begun to perceive Israel as the Goliath against the Palestinian David. For most of the past century, it was Israel that represented the underdog against the massive anti-Israel fervor throughout the Middle East. Today, it is clear that the game is over—without making serious and genuine moves in the direction of peace, Israel has become the pariah nation, and Palestine is a country under occupation. With the turmoil in the Middle East following the failed Arab Spring and the emergence of radical political Islamic terrorism such the Islamic State, some Middle East states no longer really exist (Syria, Lebanon, Libya, and Yemen). The convergence of common threats face Israel and its enemies, and those threats create new opportunities for engagement between them. The immediate impact of the chaos in the Middle East has led to a decreased interest in Palestine and Palestinians, but this situation will not go away. The potential alliances between Israel and some of its neighbors in confronting the Iran-Hezbollah axis and the common threat of the Islamic State can only be fully operationalized within the framework of also addressing the Palestinian issue and by Israel stating that it is prepared to see the Arab Peace Initiative of March 2002 as the basis for future negotiations.

The eruption of another round of violence in October 2015, with young Palestinians stabbing Israeli soldiers and civilians all over Israel and the occupied territories, led to another drop in the chances that any accommodation was possible. However, even with half of the Palestinian house controlled by Hamas, which rejects Israel's right to exist, I still believe that peace *is* possible. I believe that there are more commonalities between human beings, regardless of their place of origin, than differences. I believe that people can be taught to live in peace—I have seen it with my own eyes and have experienced it firsthand. The opposite is also true—people can be taught to hate and real-life circumstances can be the most powerful ammunition for despair, fear, and hatred. But it seems clear to me that everyone wants to be understood. Everyone wants to be respected. Everyone seeks to have their own narrative told and understood. The problems emerge when each side holds onto its own national collective narrative as the sole truth, denying the legitimacy of the other side's narrative and at times even denying the very existence of the other side.

It is almost impossible to imagine a time when Israelis and Palestinians will be willing to accept the legitimacy of the each other's narrative without denying the truth of their own—at least this is the claim that is often made. Perhaps the most that one can seek to achieve at this time, in the midst of conflict, is the willingness to listen to and perhaps understand, even a little, the opposing narrative—even without agreeing to it. I call this *opening the window to view the other side*. There are conflicts where historical narratives have been rewritten after years of peaceful coexistence. The possibility for this in the Israeli-Palestinian case is quite remote.

I myself came to the challenge when confronted with a recurring nightmare, one in which I found myself given the task by the Palestinian government of designing the Palestinian National History Museum. Naturally almost all of the exhibits that I had to design consisted of all of the terrible things the Zionist movement had done to the Palestinians or the results of Zionist successes in the dismemberment of the Palestinian national movement and its people. Almost all of the photos and texts in the museum were graphic depictions of the tragedies that befell the Palestinian people throughout their history because of their clash with the Jewish people and their national movement—Zionism. (The construction of the Palestinian National History Museum began in Ramallah in May 2016; its content has not yet been determined.)

One of my challenges in the nightmare, the one that usually caused me to wake up, was an argument I had with the Palestinian leadership in which I demanded that the museum also include some self-reflection and soul-searching introspection into some of the bad decisions the Palestinians made throughout their history that contributed greatly to the plight of the Palestinians. I wanted, in my dream, to bring to them the Palestinian version of "The Sermon" by the Zionist thinker Haim Hazaz, who in 1942 wrote a brilliant play in which he put Jewish history on trial. His poignant message was that the time had come for the Jews to cease being victims and to take their fate into their own hands. This, in my mind, is one of the fundamentals of Zionism. With that thought, I would wake up to the reality that both sides, it seems, have become competitors in the Olympic Competitions of Victimization—each seeking the ultimate gold medal for having suffered more at the hands of the other.

NORMALIZATION–ANTI-NORMALIZATION

Contact between people is not sufficient to bring about attitudinal and behavioral changes in conflict settings, but in Israel and Palestine today, there is almost no contact at all. Freedom of movement is denied to Palestinians who cannot enter Israel freely. The areas controlled by the Palestinian Authority are off limits to Israelis, who are warned by the Israeli Army with large signs that it is illegal to enter those areas and they risk their lives in doing so. The conflict has created not only physical barriers that separate Israelis and Palestinians; it has erected psychological barriers that are even more difficult to penetrate. People on both sides are afraid of each other. There is a myth in Israel that the Palestinians are not afraid to enter Israel, and it is only Israelis who are afraid because of Palestinian terrorism. The truth is that the fear exists on both sides. Israelis and Palestinians do not know each other anymore, they do not meet, they do not talk, and they have enormous misconceptions about one another based on very partial facts and little firsthand knowledge. This is particularly true of the younger generation of Israelis and Palestinians.

Adding to the noncontact of a whole generation of young Israelis and Palestinians is the so-called anti-normalization campaign in Palestine, which calls for boycotting Israelis and threatening Palestinian individuals and organizations that organize activities with Israelis. The basic claim is that engagement with Israelis creates a sense of normalized relations between the two sides while Palestine remains occupied. Israel then uses those contacts as part of its propaganda machine, which claims there is no conflict between the people—only that caused by the Palestinian leaders. They further claim that Israel will gain legitimacy while it continues to occupy and to build illegal settlements on stolen Palestinian land.

I cross borders. I travel and meet people throughout Israel and throughout Palestine. With the exception of Gaza, which has been off-limits to Israelis since June 2007, I visit cities, towns, villages, and refugee camps throughout Palestine on a regular basis. Yes, I break the law in doing so. I am not afraid. I go and I listen and I talk, challenge, learn, and teach. I hear the same things from both sides: we want peace, but we have no partner on the other side.

In 1937, the Zionist leader Nahum Goldmann said: "The Arab problem can only be solved . . . by entering into direct contact with the population. . . . As long as we do not initiate such a policy . . . a bold effort to talk directly to the Arabs, to discuss the principles of neighborly friendly relations and co-existence, to thresh out these problems directly, people to people . . . the Arab question will remain a dark spot in the Palestine problem and the problem will remain unsolved."[1] From Goldmann's own direct contacts with Palestinian Arabs, he foresaw the grave errors the Zionist movement was making, and he warned about the consequences:

One of the great oversights in the history of Zionism is that when the Jewish homeland in Palestine was founded, sufficient attention was not paid to relations with the Arabs. Of course, there were always a few Zionist speakers and thinkers who stressed them. . . . And the ideological and political leaders of the Zionist movement always emphasized—sincerely and earnestly, it seems to me—that the Jewish national home must be established in peace and harmony with the Arabs. Unfortunately these convictions remained in the realm of theory and were not carried over, to any great extent, into actual Zionist practice. Even Theodor Herzl's brilliant simple formulation of the Jewish question as basically a transportation problem of "moving people without a home into a land with a people" is tinged with disquieting blindness to the Arab claim to Palestine. Palestine was not a land without people even in Herzl's time; it was inhabited by hundreds of thousands of Arabs who in the course of events would sooner or later have achieved independent statehood, either alone or as a unit with a larger Arab context.[2]

At least one Zionist leader and thinker understood the importance of reaching out directly to Israel's Arab neighbors, with respect and dignity and not with a patronizing attitude. Many of the Zionist movement's leaders were convinced that the Zionist movement would bring modernity, economic development, and jobs, which would be appreciated by the local Arab population. They were not wrong, and there were many Arab leaders in the area that understood this and sought to profit from it. The economic success of early Zionism brought with it a wave of Arab immigration to Palestine in search of a better life and more economic opportunities. This too, even with what may have been some good intentions, created class disparities and fostered a classic colonialist economic situation on the ground. But the economic growth in Palestine during the early years was not solely and perhaps not even mainly the result of Zionist settlement, but more so the impact of massive economic development and infrastructure construction by the British Mandate.

When I was growing up in the Zionist movement in the 1970s as a youth leader, we were taught with pride the importance of Jewish labor. We read with passion the texts of Aaron David Gordan and Ber Borochov, who both believed in socialism as the best way of creating equality for Jews in their new homeland. They preached the principles of Jewish labor in order to create "the new Jew"—a person connected to their land, farmers, and "normal people"—as Ber Borochov referred to them. We loved the inverted pyramid that taught us that Jews needed to do physical labor and not be moneylenders, bankers, and stockbrokers, but a people capable of building a state. As we embraced the ideology of the second and third *aliyot* (1905–1914; waves of Jewish immigration to the Land of Israel) with the kibbutz at its center and their noble values which shaped our own identities, we did not stop for a moment to think about the impact of "Jewish labor" on the local Palestinian population, which was being pushed out of economic development and opportunities in the name of these noble Zionist values. The socialist response to the exploitive labor policies of the first *aliya*, which employed cheap Arab labor to increase profits, was to remove Arab labor from the Jewish farms and to only employ Jews who would be working their own land and would not be exploiting cheap labor from Arab communities nearby. This led to Arab demonstrations and violence that only served to strengthen the resolve not to hire Arab laborers as the first walls of fear and alienation were erected between Jews and Arabs throughout the land. When I see Jewish companies in Israel today that boast that they employ only Jewish labor, I look at them with contempt, as fostering racist discrimination in what is supposed to be a democratic country.

During the early Zionist years, with the growing separation between the communities and resulting fear, there were at least two Zionist groups that fought against these trends—*Poalei Zion* and *Hashomer Hatzair*—both of which pushed to create joint Jewish-Arab workers unions in order to protect and to equalize the rights of all workers. "They believed Arab opposition to Zionism to be motivated solely by class interests of Arab feudal landowners and clergy—while the interests of the Arab worker lay in the economic and social development, the driving force of which was free Jewish immigration and settlement."[3] But these forces were minority voices both then and now, and because of their inability to become the majority, models of separation were built into the development of the State of Israel.

In 1948, Israel fought a war for its birth and survival. It was a justified war that was truly existential. But on May 14, 1948, when David Ben-Gurion read out Israel's Declaration of Independence, he put down his case very clearly:

> On the 29th November, 1947, the United Nations General Assembly passed a resolution calling for the establishment of a Jewish State in Eretz-Israel; the General Assembly required the inhabitants of Eretz-Israel to take such steps as were necessary on their part for the implementation of that resolution. This recognition by the United Nations of the right of the Jewish people to establish their State is irrevocable. This right is the natural right of the Jewish people to be masters of their own fate, like all other nations, in their own sovereign State.

Nowhere did Ben-Gurion make mention of the fact that UN Resolution 181 called for the establishment of two states in Palestine: a Jewish State (Israel) and an Arab State (Palestine). The second part of the resolution was ignored by Ben-Gurion and not only because it was rejected by the Palestinians and the Arab states alike. This, it seems, was part of a plan.

I believe that there is enough historical evidence to prove that both Ben-Gurion and the Zionist leadership conspired with King Abdallah of Transjordan to prevent the birth of the Palestinian state back in 1948. On September 22, 1948, the Palestinian leadership, together with the Arab League, declared the establishment of a Palestinian state in Gaza with what was called the All-Palestine Government. The government of Palestine was soon recognized by all Arab League members except Transjordan. The government's official jurisdiction covered the whole of the former Mandatory Palestine, though its effective jurisdiction was limited to the Gaza Strip. The prime minister of the Gaza-seated administration was Ahmed Hilmi Pasha, and the president was Hajj Amin al-Husseini, former chairman of the Arab Higher Committee and Nazi co-conspirator.

The All-Palestine Government is thought to be the first attempt to establish an independent Palestinian state. It was under official Egyptian protection, but it had no executive role. The government had mostly political and symbolic implications. Though the Gaza Strip remained under Egyptian control throughout the war, the All-Palestine Government remained in exile in Cairo, managing Gazan affairs from afar.

In response, and in order to prevent the emergence of an independent Palestinian state, on December 1, 1948, a conference sponsored by the Jordanian king—strategically held in Jericho, in the West Bank but adjacent to the Jordan River—called for the annexation of what was left of Palestine under the Hashemite crown. The conference was attended by numerous delegations including the mayors of Hebron, Bethlehem, Ramallah, the Arab Legion Military Governor General, military governors of all the districts, and other notables. The audience was estimated at several thousand.

These are the main resolutions adopted at the conference. They contained the following provisions:

> Palestine Arabs desire unity between Transjordan and Arab Palestine and therefore make known their wish that Arab Palestine be annexed immediately to Transjordan. They also recognized Abdullah as their King and requested him to proclaim himself King of the new territory. Expression of thanks to Arab states was also expressed for their generous assistance and support to Palestine Arab refugees.

Immediately afterward, the West Bank and East Jerusalem were annexed by the Hashemite Kingdom. This was rejected by the Arab League and the world, and only recognized by Britain and Pakistan. This illegal annexation prevented the establishment of a Palestinian state. It was not accepted in the newly emerging regime of international law. The granting of citizenship to Palestinians in the West Bank by the Hashemite Kingdom decreased criticism of the step, though hundreds of thousands of Palestinian refugees dwelled in refugee camps around the region. The Jordanian regime took aggressive steps to repress any expression of Palestinian nationalism on both sides of the Jordan River.

Judging from recent research and the outcome of the 1948 war, it appears that the newborn State of Israel had an understanding with Jordan on borders that would be established between them. This understanding was to prevent the establishment of the Palestinian state, which was perceived as a threat both by Israel and by Jordan. There were, it seems, three primary areas of nonagreement on the delineation of borders between Israel and Jordan: the Old City of Jerusalem, Gush Etzion in the southern half of the West Bank, and the Latrun corridor. The fiercest battles of the 1948 war, with the highest number of casualties to Israel, were in these areas, and Israel lost all three. There are reports that Jordanian forces launched attacks against advancing Iraqi forces in the north of Israel because they went beyond the agreed upon lines. After the war, as a result of the armistice agreements of Rhodes in 1949, Jordan transferred the area of Wadi Ara to Israel with all of its Arab villages, which was held by Iraqi forces—as per the understandings prior to the war.

Palestinian nationalism was crushed by Jordan on both the East and West Banks and would not appear in full force until Israel conquered the West Bank in June 1967. King Abdallah was eventually assassinated by a Palestinian nationalist on July 20, 1951, at the al-Aqsa Mosque in Jerusalem. King Hussein took over as a young man (followed by a short reign of his mentally unstable father, Talal bin Abdallah) and continued discreet security cooperation with Israel against Palestinian nationalism. The height of this cooperation was in September 1970, known as Black September, which resulted in the death of ten thousand to twenty-five thousand Palestinians according to the Palestine Liberation Organization (PLO) sources (other sources suggest only about two thousand casualties) and the expulsion of the PLO leadership, which had based itself in the Jordan Valley in the East Bank to Lebanon.

King Hussein made the mistake of his life when on June 6, 1967, hearing of Egyptian military successes against Israel on Egyptian radio, he decided to join the fighting by bombing Jerusalem and Tel Aviv, which opened another front for Israel and led to Israel's conquest of the West Bank and East Jerusalem. Americans sent King Hussein messages from Israel guaranteeing that if he stayed out of the war, Israel would not attack on the West Bank. He decided not to listen to that advice. The Israeli occupation of the West Bank and Gaza in 1967 put the local Palestinian population into direct contact and confrontation with Israel. Shortly after the end of the war, Israel opened its borders, and Palestinians began to explore Israel, which had been part of their homeland. Many Palestinians in the West Bank and Gaza who were living in refugee camps after Israel's birth came back to search for their original homes, which no longer existed for most. Israel experienced a period of rapid economic growth. Contacts began to develop between Israelis and Palestinians. Thousands of Palestinians found jobs in Israel, mostly jobs that Israelis did not want to do any more, such as manual factory labor, farm work, and construction. Palestinians were greatly disheartened by the Arab losses of 1967, yet many were also appreciative to have the new economic opportunities and economic growth that for them was very rapid. Initially tensions were not high mainly because Israeli settlement activities did not displace many people, and settlements were not being built by the Labor governments in the heartland of Palestinian communities. Even though seventy square kilometers of villages around East Jerusalem were annexed and then much of it built up for Jews only, 1967 to 1987 was a period of abnormal normalcy. I have been told that for most of that twenty-year period less than one division of the Israeli Army was required to govern and control the entire Palestinian population and territory.

That all changed with a road accident on the morning of December 9, 1987. The intifada was born.

Why Write This Book?

APRIL 19, 1983
Press Bulletin
*Government Ministries Back New Institute
for Jewish-Arab Coexistence*

2

Israel's first state-associated comprehensive educational project
for Jewish-Arab relations was launched yesterday with the official
inauguration of the Institute for Education for Jewish Arab Coexistence
between Jews and Arabs. The Institute is associated with the Ministry
of Education and the Office of the Advisor on Arab Affairs in the
Prime Minister's Bureau. . . . Its guiding principle is the belief that
Israel should be a Jewish and democratic state, as embodied in the
Declaration of Independence. . . . Gershon Baskin, the Institute's
young director, asserts that its approach is "one of taking responsibility, in which every citizen can and must be convinced of their ability
to have influence. If you care about the State's future, you are required
to say, I, a citizen of the State of Israel, am ready and able to work for
democracy in the State. I am ready to contribute my part in bringing
about coexistence.[1]

I have spent the last thirty-eight years of my life working for peace between
the State of Israel and its neighbors. This has been a work of passion, a calling, a sense of duty. I have done it despite endless frustrations and disap-
pointments, and always with a continued sense of opportunity and possibility, even during the darkest times of violence and rage. I have been called
a naïve optimist, an accusation that I totally reject. There is nothing naïve
about my outlook. Rational strategic thinking has guided me in developing
my worldview and approach to peacemaking. Strategic thinking requires
the ability to design a course of events, policies, and decisions that create a
different reality. Most people get stuck in the present and latch onto the past,
limiting their ability to imagine a different future. The reality that we have all
known between Israel and the Arabs is debilitating; it stunts imagination
and diminishes the ability to design policies that can change the conflictual basis of relations. Those relations—based on justified fear, influenced
by lack of human contact, and reinforced by continued violence—solidify
patterns of thinking and behavior that negatively influence public policies
and so end with sustaining conflict rather than breaking away from the en-

trenched animosity and turning a new page. What the parties in conflict say and do are mutually influential and keep the parties in conflict.

Leaders, with few exceptions (like Yitzhak Rabin and Nelson Mandela, to mention two) tend to be responsive in their words and deeds in conflict situations. It is often difficult for them to step out and go beyond what they believe their constituents may accept because of their own political constraints. In conflict situations, leaders wish to be perceived by their constituents as strong, meaning that they must demonstrate hardline positions vis-à-vis the enemy. Any sign of reaching out or rejecting the normal patterns of response that are usually framed as threats, and use of force is perceived as weakness in the eyes of the public, especially in conflicts like in the Middle East where the overriding importance of "national honor" is a guide in the need to win, to beat the other side. Amongst the Israeli and the Arab public perception of the conflict is that the other side only understands the language of force. Weakness is perceived as an invitation to be attacked by one's enemy. Both sides are constantly seeking to create deterrence, ensuring the other side is afraid enough that it will not challenge one's power. This pattern of behavior reinforces the use of force and actually deters exploring the possibilities of building partnerships.

The common understanding held by both the Israeli and Palestinian side is that while "we" (both sides) want peace, "we" have no partner for peace on the other side. This assertion is completely logical and can easily be based on reality. Both sides continue to act and to speak in ways that strengthen the mutual perception that there is no corresponding peace partner on the other side.

Israel's greatest military hero and leader, the late Yitzhak Rabin, broke ranks and charged forward on a course to create a partnership for peace with his archenemy Yasser Arafat, the leader of the Palestinian national movement. On the White House lawn at the signing of the Declaration of Principles for Peace on September 13, 1993, he said:

> We have come from Jerusalem, the ancient and eternal capital of the Jewish people. We have come from an anguished and grieving land. We have come from a people, a home, a family that has not known a single year, not a single month in which mothers have not wept for their sons. We have come to try and put an end to the hostilities, so that our children, our children's children, will no longer experience the painful cost of war, violence, and terror. We have come to secure their lives and to ease the sorrow and the painful memories of the past to hope and pray for peace.
>
> Let me say to you, the Palestinians: We are destined to live together on the same soil, in the same land. We, the soldiers who have re-

turned from battle stained with blood, we who have seen our relatives and friends killed before our eyes, we who have attended their funerals and cannot look into the eyes of their parents, we who have come from a land where parents bury their children, we who have fought against you, the Palestinians—We say to you today in a loud and a clear voice: Enough of blood and tears. Enough. We have no desire for revenge. We harbor no hatred towards you. We, like you, are people who want to build a home, to plant a tree, to love, to live side by side with you in dignity, in empathy, as human beings, as free men. We are today giving peace a chance, and saying again to you: Enough. Let us pray that a day will come when we all will say: Farewell to the arms.[2]

Yasser Arafat responded in this speech on that occasion:

Now, as we stand on the threshold of this new historic era, let me address the people of Israel and their leaders, with whom we are meeting today for the first time. And let me assure them that the difficult decision we reached together was one that required great and exceptional courage.

We will need more courage and determination to continue the course of building coexistence and peace between us. This is possible. And it will happen with mutual determination and with the effort that will be made with all parties on all the tracks to establish the foundations of a just and comprehensive peace. Our people do not consider that exercising the right to self-determination could violate the rights of their neighbors or infringe on their security. Rather, putting an end to their feelings of being wronged and of having suffered an historic injustice is the strongest guarantee to achieve coexistence and openness between our two peoples and future generations. Our two peoples are awaiting today this historic hope, and they want to give peace a real chance. Such a shift will give us an opportunity to embark upon the process of economic, social, and cultural growth and development, and we hope that international participation in that process will be as extensive as it can be. This shift will also provide an opportunity for all forms of cooperation on a broad scale and in all fields.[3]

This was a moment of great hope. That moment was created by the courageous leadership demonstrated by two leaders who stepped out beyond their pasts and reached out to the future. Both Rabin and Arafat had the historical collateral as military leaders to change their course and transform the relations between the two peoples from war to peace. They had both experienced the pains of war, seeing their best friends and colleagues die by the sword of conflict, and they were willing to take the risk to try to build a partnership between them. Tragically, they were not successful in delivering the promise of peace to their people. Rabin was cut down by an Israeli-Jewish murderer who not only killed the Prime Minister, he terminated the life of the peace process. Arafat lost his partner in peace and was never able to develop the same partnership with any other Israeli leader. Furthermore, Arafat failed his people after he succeeded in raising the issue of Palestine on the world stage by never making the full transformation from warrior to statesman.

In the twenty plus years of failed peacemaking, most Israelis and most Palestinians have given up hope that peace can in fact become a reality. They have not, however, given up on the desire for peace, on the longing for normalcy, on their craving for acceptance. Israelis have managed to create an acceptable reality with significant achievements to be quite proud of. Israel is a formidable state with a secure economy and levels of excellence in fields such as technology, medicine, agriculture, and water conservation that are the envy of the world. Yet Israelis continue to live with a high level of anxiety that one day it could all come to an end. In truth, with the continued failure of subsequent peace efforts, Israel is beginning to face a new reality in the world in which its very own legitimacy is being questioned and challenged.

The Palestinians continue to live under Israeli occupation, which has become increasingly sophisticated in its means of control. Their significant achievements, mainly in the West Bank, in creating relative stability, developing institutions of statehood, building infrastructure and pockets of real economic activity are not only impressive, given their circumstances, but there has been more normalcy in day-to-day life for Palestinians (at least, those who do not live next to Israeli settlements) than ever before. Yet it is also quite clear that without political progress eventually there will most likely be a return to violence. Near the end of 2015, another round of violence did emerge, different from the previous rounds with a much smaller level of public participation, but with a high level of public support.

I continue to believe that peace is possible, and that it is in fact the only option that Israeli and Palestinian leaders really have. For the first time in the history of Israeli-Palestinian negotiations, it seems that neither side has a better alternative to a negotiated agreement, yet they still avoid plunging into the only option that will bring an end to the conflict. Negotiation for the sake of negotiation is passé, and it is seen only as a means of stalling while additional actions on the ground happen that make partition more difficult. They are not successful at getting back to the table with clear terms of reference that could actually lead to a comprehensive agreement.

Failure of negotiations is bad for both sides, and both sides know it. Each round of negotiations created unrealistically high expectations and usually ended up in a new round of violence. Caution is wise, but there are solutions. This conflict, I maintain, is resolvable.

I often quote a great man, the late Dr. Yehuda Paz, who commented on his own optimism, "It is a genetic defect, I simply cannot help it." Like Yehuda Paz, it is in my DNA. I see the positive, the hopeful, the opportunities, and the chances that greet me on my path of life. I believe that my optimism is guided primarily by my strategic outlook, which enables me to identify opportunities where many others simply see obstacles.

Never accept no for an answer. It is never too early to work for peace. These are two mottos that have accompanied me throughout my lifelong journey on the road to peace. From my childhood through my adult life, I have been actively seeking peace. I would like to tell you a bit of my story.

In the Beginning

3 By an accident of history, I was born in the United States. In fact there is even an error of history in my name, as well. My parents wanted to call me *Gershom* (Hebrew: גרשום) the son of Moses who, as the story goes, was born in Median, in the Sinai Desert, far away from the land of Israel. The name actually means stranger (GER) in a strange place (Sham)—over there. At my circumcision, the attending *mohel* inscribed my name in a certificate as *Gershon*, according to the Torah, Gershon (Hebrew: גרשון) was the eldest of the sons of Levi, and the patriarchal founder of the Gershonites, one of the four main divisions amongst the Levites in biblical times. The Gershonites had a ritual role to play in the Holy Temple. There is no doubt that the name GERSHOM is much more appropriate for me as my life has unfolded. I guess in retrospect, it is better to have made an error in the name than in the real job that the *mohel* had to do!

I was born in Brooklyn where my parents were also born, but from the age of four until fourteen, I grew up in Bellmore, Long Island, New York, in a very Jewish neighborhood (about 90 percent Jewish). In fact, I had one non-Jewish friend in my group of schoolmates, Vincent, a Roman Catholic of Italian descent who got to attend everyone's Bar Mitzvah because he was everyone's one non-Jewish friend. I had never experienced anti-Semitism nor any form of racism. As a youngster, my first political experience that motivated me to work for social change occurred during a family visit to the historic Williamsburg, Virginia, in early 1964, prior to the enactment of the Civil Rights Act by the US Congress in July that year. This legislation was a landmark and outlawed major forms of discrimination against racial, ethnic, national, and religious minorities, and women. It ended unequal application of voter registration requirements and racial segregation in schools, at the workplace, and by facilities that served the general public.

In Williamsburg, I encountered for the first time in my life a restaurant with a sign in the window that said "Whites Only." I was shocked and confused. I was all of eight years old. My mother was a teacher and had the practice of transforming every emotional encounter into an educational experience. My parents explained to me the history of slavery and discrimination in the United States. When I got back to New York I was inspired to read the book *Black Like Me*, by John Howard Griffin, a white man. The book was first published in 1961 and became a best seller. Griffin took some chemicals to darken his skin and then traveled across America as a black man documenting his experiences. The book had a huge impact on me in the development of my social and political conscience and consciousness.

Four years later, I contacted a politician who was running for Congress from my district. He began the "Dump President Johnson Campaign" and led marches for civil rights (with Martin Luther King Jr.) and against the war in Vietnam. That man, Allard Lowenstein, was elected to Congress in 1968.[1] I volunteered in the campaign to elect Lowenstein to Congress and Senator Eugene McCarthy for president in the primaries. I met Allard Lowenstein and spent two or three weekends with him campaigning in the district. At a fundraiser in my neighborhood, I met Senator McCarthy. I was twelve years old. After McCarthy withdrew from the race in the primaries, I supported Senator Robert Kennedy, who was assassinated in June 1968 after winning the California primary. So later I worked for Vice President Hubert Humphrey in the attempt to prevent Richard Nixon from being elected president.

Although I was young, I knew what the issues were. I demonstrated against the war in Vietnam and for civil rights across America. I wore political buttons on my shirt every day to school. I read the *New York Times* regularly since the sixth grade. At the age of twelve, I was given the key to the Democratic Party headquarters in my town, and during that election season, after school I would open the office and distribute flyers protesting the war in Vietnam to men coming home from work on the Long Island Rail Road. The day that Nixon won the election was one of my saddest during those years.

I don't know if I would have called myself a Zionist at the age of eight, but that is the age I began urging my family to travel to Israel. I first visited there in 1969 when I was thirteen, for my Bar Mitzvah. I don't know where the desire to go to Israel came from, but I had two mental associations with the country—distant memories that might have something to do with it, but I am not entirely sure about it. My mother's grandfather, Yehuda Rosenblatt, an ultra-Orthodox rabbi and anti-Zionist, moved to Palestine in the 1920s after bringing his family to America and marrying off all of his daughters. He wanted to die in the Holy Land. He lived until 1940 and is buried in one of the oldest cemeteries in Tel Aviv. My mother had a bracelet from the Land of Israel in her jewelry box that her grandfather had sent to her. It interested me as a child and I remember playing with it. The second memory is that as a young child the book that I asked to be read to me most often was my favorite, the *Golden Bible for Children*. We were not a religious family, although my parents always belonged to a synagogue and believed that we should have a Jewish education. I loved the Bible stories and the wonderful pictures in that book, and I spent many hours studying its pages.

When I was in elementary school in Bellmore, schools in New York State were not closed on the Jewish holidays, but mine was because not only were almost all of the students Jewish, so were the teachers. We all belonged to the local conservative synagogue, and Jewish holidays were social gatherings where we gathered together as a community in the synagogue.

After the typically extravagant Bar Mitzvah party of my late older brother Richard in 1967, (which was held one month after the Six-Day War of June 1967) I told my parents that I didn't want all of the fanfare and expense for my own Bar Mitzvah, but would rather have the family go to Israel. I may have been influenced also by the tremendous sense of pride that most American Jews felt toward Israel after the 1967 war. I remember feeling proud to be Jewish after the Six-Day War and walking around school with a chest puffed up with pride—see what we Jews can do when we are attacked! I remember that feeling, and it was then that Israel entered my consciousness. So in the summer of 1969, we went to Israel. (I ended up with the fancy party and the family trip to Israel.)

My most vivid memory from that trip in the summer of 1969 was standing on the balcony of the home of our cousins, Avrum and Aya Brand (Avrum was my mother's first cousin, who had survived the Holocaust after losing his parents and two sisters and managed to get to Israel after the war). Looking out at Givatayim, a Tel Aviv suburb, I remember this overwhelming feeling of being home. Even now, more than forty-seven years later, when I think about Israel, my first association is that feeling. When I travel abroad, which I do quite often, seeing the coastline of Israel from the plane on my way back, I feel that I am arriving home. It is a very comforting and warm feeling, filled with emotion.

When I was fourteen, we moved to another town on Long Island, Smithtown, where there were very few Jews, and did as ethnic groups tend to do, whether Jews, Italians, Chinese, Japanese, or Arabs, that is, look for common folk. In a very non-Jewish neighborhood, I searched out other Jews and was searched out, as well. A new friend, Don Schertzman, who had spent the summer in Israel and whose family was planning to immigrate to Israel (to make aliya—to go up—as it is called in Hebrew), approached me to join a newly established (in our town) Zionist Youth Movement, Young Judaea.[2]

I joined Young Judaea to be with other Jews, to meet Jewish girls, and also because Israel interested me. In 1970, I became very active in the movement and rapidly rose to leadership positions. In the tenth grade, I was elected to the Long Island Executive Board of Young Judaea as assistant programming coordinator. The following year, I became the senior programming coordinator, responsible for developing the weekly activities for all of the chapters in the Long Island region and for planning the two annual conventions for all of our members. In my last year in high school,

I was elected president of the movement's Long Island region. I spent my summers at the Young Judaea national summer camp, Tel Yehuda, which strengthened my Zionist identity and my Jewish pride. The movement had a great impact on my entire being.

The Long Island region of Young Judaea adopted a Hebrew name during the period I served on the executive board—we chose *Gesher Shalom*—the peace bridge. There is no doubt that the movement became the most important part of my life, far more important than school. Most of the days in my last two years of high school were spent in the movement, in the office or visiting Young Judaea clubs across Long Island. I also led a junior club of junior high school–aged kids and taught Israeli folk dancing. My summers at camp Tel Yehuda in upstate New York expanded my world of contacts, as I met Jewish kids from all over the United States.

Being active in a Zionist youth movement gave substance to my life. My parents encouraged my involvement because at the time, as part of the tail end of the 1960s generation, they were concerned that, like many others my age, I could get involved with the drug culture. Young Judaea was clean and safe, but I don't think they really considered that as a result of my Zionist movement engagement I could end up picking myself up and moving to far away Israel. Years later, when I was already living in Israel, my mother told me that often people would ask her if she was proud and happy that her children were living in Israel. She would respond, "I would be much happier if it were your children!"

From 1970 to 1974, my high school years, Young Judaea was the focus of my being and Israel already set as my final destination. The movement provided an extraordinary opportunity for young people to demonstrate commitment to an idea, take on an enormous amount of responsibility, develop intellectually, and translate principles into life decisions. We were a lot more mature than our age in those days. I learned three important lessons (and subsequently taught them to many others in my own age group and younger): lead by example, live by what you believe in (your values), and take initiative. These lessons have been with me my entire life. There is a common conventional wisdom amongst Young Judaea graduates of my generation: everything important in life I learned in Young Judaea!

Fully engulfed in the movement of Young Judaea, I came back to Israel in December 1973 for the dedication of the movement's kibbutz, Kibbutz Ketura. In 1974–1975, when I finished high school, I spent the year in Israel in the Young Judaea Year Course educational program. During the Year in Israel program, I spent half the year on Kibbutz Ein Harod Ihud and half the year in Jerusalem studying. The kibbutz program included learning Hebrew for half the day and working the other half. Most of our work was picking grapefruit and olives, stomping on freshly picked cotton, and working in the kitchen; when we were really lucky, we got to work in the fish-ponds or move beehives around the Jordan Valley. Throughout the year, we had many days of hiking and seeing Israel on foot. It was an amazing year. The main goal of the program was to orient us to the idea that Israel is our home. So many times during the year, our leaders or teachers, and especially Alan Hoffman, the Year Course director, would begin a sentence with "and when you make aliya. . . ."[3] When I was sixteen years old, I decided that I would make aliya. The movement had a kind of unspoken understanding that you didn't say that out loud until you had spent the year in Israel taking part in the Year Course program. When I was on my Year Course in 1974, I stated outright that I was making aliya. In fact, after a few months in Israel I wrote home to my parents that at the end of the year I would stay in Israel, join the army (hopefully as a paratrooper), and begin my life where I felt at home. My parents panicked when they received that letter. Their response was immediate, and I received an urgent phone call from them on the kibbutz telling me not to make any decision I couldn't reverse. A couple of months later, while visiting me in Israel, they convinced me to return to the States to complete my undergraduate university education and then move to Israel with a degree in my pocket. Their main concern, I think, was to delay as long as possible my military service.

I came back to the United States to work in Camp Tel Yehuda, Young Judaea's camp for high school–aged kids. The Year Course program in Israel was very intensive. I had worked in the kitchen that summer as the dairy cook and spent many hours wandering around the camp and in the Catskill Mountains trying to absorb and comprehend what I had experienced over the year. After the year in Israel, devoid of any real responsibility, having gone through an emotionally and intellectually packed experience, I needed a kind of personal debriefing, integration, and understanding. Above my bed in the camp, I had a large map of Greater Israel, which included all of the territories occupied by Israel in 1967. I had little pins on the map that marked places that I had visited during the year. My main centers of activity were Kibbutz Ein Harod Ihud in the Jezreal Valley and Jerusalem, and I traveled back and forth between the two many times during the year. The route that I traveled was through the Jordan Valley, crossing the green line, going through Jericho in the West Bank.[4] I never thought about the fact that I was crossing into occupied territory, and I never really gave much thought to the Palestinian people living across that green line.

One day during the summer, I came back to my room and discovered that my roommate, Barak Berkowitz, had used a green marker and drawn in the green line on my map. I looked at the map and pondered the existence of a border through the land I traveled so often. I wondered how I would travel from the kibbutz to Jerusalem if there were a border that placed the Jordan Valley and the West Bank outside of Israel. It then suddenly dawned on me as a kind of epiphany: over the course of the entire year in Israel, not once did I ever have a serious conversation with an Arab. Imagine that, I had lived in Israel, about a mile away from an Arab village near the kibbutz and then on Mount Scopus in Jerusalem, surrounded by Palestinian villages and neighborhoods, and not once did I have a real conversation with an Arab! Some members of the kibbutz warned me against hiking to the Arab village of Naoura because it was dangerous. While living in Jerusalem, we were frequently warned about the dangers of walking through the Arab villages between Mount Scopus and the Old City of Jerusalem. We were told not to change our money with Arab money changers because the money went to the PLO to buy weapons to kill Israelis. (Such a ridiculous statement—these were legal money changers monitored by the State of Israel. If they were transferring money to buy weapons to kill Jews, would they be allowed to operate? But I heard that claim so many times and, as did so many others, simply believed it without question.) I then started to recall all of the myths that we learned about Arabs and about the Israeli-Arab conflict. I realized that something was very wrong with my education. I had a huge gap, a void, and I knew that I had to study in order to determine for myself what was true and what was rumor only. I had so much more knowledge to gain and experiences to have before I could understand the place that I was planning to make my home. I was overwhelmed by my own ignorance.

I got back home from the summer camp and started university, and immediately commenced "swallowing up" books that were the alternative to the books I was reading during the days of my involvement in the Zionist movement, like, *What's Wrong with Zionism?*, and *Arabs and the State of Israel*, and the *Arab Israeli Conflict*. I also discovered the liberal Zionist discourse, as well. One book in particular had a significant influence on my new thinking: *Zionism and the Palestinians.*[5] I must have read a hundred books that first year. That year, 1975, I wrote a piece in a Jewish newspaper, the *Jewish Radical* out of Berkeley, California, calling for the end of the Israeli occupation and support for the two-state solution. It was my first published op-ed piece on peace. At that time, only the fringes of Israeli society supported the creation of a Palestinian state next to Israel, and amongst American Jews, it represented the fringe of the fringe.

One of the most important values that I learned in Young Judaea and taught to generations of Young Judaeans after me is that immigrating to Israel, making aliya, is not merely a change of address. In moving to Israel, we had to commit ourselves to making Israel a better place—what we now call in Judaism *Tikun Olam*, or repairing the world. (In the 1970s, we didn't call it *Tikun Olam*, but that is what we meant.) I believed that in the late 1970s Israel was facing three major problems. One was the Israeli-Palestinian conflict; the second was how Israel defines itself in its relationship with its non-Jewish citizens, meaning the Palestinian Arabs (who were called Israeli Arabs at that time); and the third pertained to the social gaps that existed in the country between the rich and poor, developed and undeveloped, Mizrahi Jews (meaning from Arab or Islamic countries) and the European Ashkenazi Jews. All were interesting issues and needed dedicated groups and individuals to address them. I was most drawn to the issue of the Israeli-Arab conflict and decided that I would dedicate my life to resolving it. The main question was where and how to begin.

In 1973, a small group of American Jews launched a new organization called Breira (Choice or Alternative), which was the first American-Jewish organization of its kind that began questioning the positions held within the Jewish establishment by American Jews regarding the Israeli-Arab conflict. In its first public statement, Breira called for Israel to make territorial concessions and recognize the legitimacy of the national aspirations of the Palestinian people in order to achieve lasting peace. In December 1976, they agreed to meet with the PLO. This was crossing a red line within the Jewish community, but the initiative was supported by Jewish intellectuals and some well-known American rabbis. That same month, the *Jerusalem Post* ran a story portraying the organization as supporting terrorists, which caused a number of its members to leave the group. On February 20, 1977, when Breira held its first national membership conference in Chevy Chase, Maryland, the convention was attacked by Jewish Defense League members led by Rabbi Meir Kahane.

In May 1977, the Rabbinical Assembly of Conservative Judaism blocked two members of Breira, Rabbi Arnold Jacob Wolf and Rabbi Everett Gendler, from membership in the organization's executive council because it felt that Breira was giving aid to Israel's enemies. At that time, Breira had 1,500 members. Isaiah Kenen, the former American Israel Public Affairs Committee (AIPAC) executive director, while still serving as the editor of its *Near East Report*, helped to label the group as "anti-Israel," "pro-PLO," and "self-hating Jews." Kenen charged that Breira "undermined U.S. support for Israel." Rabbi Alexander Schindler, president of the Union of American Hebrew Congregations (the Reform Movement), was the only major leader of a Jewish organization to defend Breira. He called the attack on Breira a "witch hunt."

This was the political environment I entered while living in New York City and studying at New York University. In 1976, together with a few other Jewish students, we went and met with the PLO representative in the UN, Labib Zudhi Terzi. I was very excited about the prospects of meeting with the representative of the Palestinian people. I had hopes that it would be a life-changing meeting. The meeting itself was quite "amusing." The PLO ambassador would not receive us during work hours, and we had to enter via a back door of their embassy. We spent about two hours with him, trying to convince him that if the PLO would support the two-state solution, the PLO would be recognized by Israel, and we could start a peace process. His response was "over my dead body."

Ambassador Terzi's response reflected the mainstream Palestinian position expressed within the PLO charter: that Israel had no right to exist, it was founded as an act of imperialism and colonialism, and the Jews living there must go back to where they originally came from. While this was the Palestinian mainstream position at that time, some people within the PLO, mainly leaders like Issam Sartawi and Saad Hamami, began to gradually shift the movement toward accepting Israel's existence and agreeing to a two-state solution. Although having the support of Yasser Arafat, both Sartawi and Hamami were murdered by radical Palestinian groups for their contact with Israelis and for their beliefs that Palestine could exist only on part of historic Palestine, and not on all of it. In the mid-1970s, it was reported that Arafat himself was changing his opinion, and as he had more contact with Israelis from the left, he gained more confidence in the need to move the Palestinians to a more realistic stand. But the process was very slow.

Following my meeting with the PLO ambassador in New York and my attempts to create opportunities for dialogue with Palestinians in the United States, I did not think there was anything that could be done on the Israeli-Palestinian issue until a fundamental change took place on one or both of the sides in their willingness to recognize the national political rights of the other. Until then, I thought there was no starting point for true dialogue. We were in a situation of mutual nonrecognition, and there was no place to actually begin doing something that could be meaningful. I thought the social gap issue, while it was interesting and important, was not something that compelled me to invest my life in it, and I was very interested in the Jewish-Arab question, so that's where I decided to devote myself.

In 1976, I met Lova Eliav, who had been the secretary general of the Labour Party in Israel. Eliav had resigned his position as secretary general in 1971 over the Labour Party's refusal to recognize the existence of the Palestinian people. Prime Minister Golda Meir's famous statement that there was no such thing as a Palestinian people was one of the driving forces that led Eliav to leave his position as secretary general of the party. After the Yom Kippur War in 1974, he left the Labour Party completely and later joined with Ratz (a left Zionist party) to form Ya'ad (target), a new civil rights political movement. I was inspired by Eliav, his background as a Zionist leader, a doer, a man of action and principle. After resigning from the position of secretary general, Eliav devoted his time to writing the book *Land of the Hart*, first published in 1972. This book became the new manifesto for many Israelis who supported giving up territory for peace and recognizing the Palestinian people. The book also became my own personal manifesto, replacing *The Zionist Idea*, a collection of essays on Zionism edited by Arthur Hertzberg, which had accompanied me as my "bible" for years before. The politics of my youth, the values that I absorbed in the struggle for civil rights in the United States and against the unjust war in Vietnam had finally merged with my Zionism and my love of Israel. This merger created many dilemmas for me, but I never questioned my love of Israel and my very strong sense that Israel was my home and the place where I saw my future.

My Jewish/Zionist/Israeli political identity was now shaped and came into direct confrontation with the reality of being on the margins of Israeli society. I became deeply immersed in what could be called leftist Jewish politics. In my several visits to Israel, trying to talk to my relatives there and Israeli friends in the United States, I was constantly ridiculed by many of them, who told me, "You're a stupid naive American, you don't understand anything." "You weren't in the army, you don't understand the situation." "They will never accept us." The sentence that got to me more than anything else, and I heard it hundreds of times, was, "You don't know them—," *them* of course being the Arabs. It didn't occur to me to ask at that time, "Well, do *you* know them? What kind of experiences have you had that enabled you to know them? When was the last time you actually spoke to a Palestinian?" I wasn't knowledgeable or aware enough about Israeli society to be able to challenge them with those questions. However, it became clear to me that, if I was going to do anything meaningful in Israel as an Israeli, I would have to gain the kind of credibility that could not be contested.

At first I thought I would go and do a graduate degree at the American University of Beirut. I applied and was accepted. They sent me registration forms where I had to sign all kinds of waivers saying that I understood that Beirut was under war and that sometimes classes were moved from one campus to another and that the campus had been blown up a few times. I said, "This is a little too much for me to handle. I might be crazy, but I am not that crazy!" A friend of mine from Young Judaea, Ann Abrams, who was living in Boston, had seen a poster in the Hebrew Teacher's College library about a Reform rabbi who was looking for Jewish graduates to go and live in Palestinian villages in Israel (they were then called Arab villages) and do community work. It was called "Interns for Peace."[6] They had an office at 150 Fifth Avenue in New York, so I walked up there one day during my lunch break from my studies at New York University, went into the office, picked up the necessary forms, and realized that I had found what I was looking for. The next day, I came back and said, "How do I sign up?" I was quickly accepted to the program and became the first Intern for Peace. After completing my Bachelor of Arts in Politics and History of the Middle East at New York University in September 1978, I immigrated to Israel within the framework of Interns for Peace. After a six-month training program at Kibbutz Barkai, I spent the next two years living and working in the Palestinian-Israeli village of Kufr Qara. I used to joke that I made aliya to a Palestinian village in Israel.

Making Aliya to an Arab Village

4 Today, about 1.5 million Palestinian Arabs are also citizens of Israel. Israel's first president, Chaim Weitzman, wrote in his diaries, "I am certain that the world will judge the Jewish state by what it will do with its Arab population."[1] Almost seven decades later, how should we judge Israel on this issue? Two things are quite clear: there is no apartheid inside Israel proper, and after almost seventy years, there remains significant degrees of discrimination between the Jewish and Arab citizens of Israel.

When Israel was born and had managed to survive after its war for independence, there remained about 156,000 Palestinian Arabs within the borders of the state after the armistice agreements were signed. They amounted to twelve percent of the total population concentrated in three main areas—the Galilee, the little triangle, and the Negev. All of them were granted Israeli citizenship, and all of them were placed under a military government that lasted until 1966. Those who remained were mainly peasants—uneducated, poor, devoid of leadership. They were in shell shock following the war that led to the exodus of 800,000 to 900,000 of their brothers and sisters. Ninety-two percent of those who remained were illiterate. There were almost no teachers and no functioning schools left.

Fearing that these new citizens would continue their fight against Israel's birth, the state expropriated large amounts of their land in order to create "security belts" around all of the Arab communities. Soon afterward, most of the expropriated land was given to Jewish kibbutzim, moshavim, and small towns nearby. Almost all of the Arab communities were without public services, such as electricity, piped water systems, sewage systems, and local government. Even though the newly born state was underdeveloped and poor, the gaps between the Jewish sector and the Arab sector were huge.

Almost seven decades later, it is quite apparent that the Palestinian community of Israel made enormous progress. Education has become a primary value and illiteracy is nonexistent. Palestinian-Israeli university students increase in numbers and level of achievement every year. Economic prosperity has come to many of the Palestinian-Israeli communities, as is quite visible by the impressive villas one sees while driving through the Arab areas of the country. Yet significant gaps between Jews and Arabs remain, and discrimination still exists in many areas of life in the country.

Through Interns for Peace, I had the opportunity to live and work in a Palestinian-Arab village in Israel—Kufr Qara—for two years.

In August 2013, thirty-two years and two months after leaving Kufr Qara following two very concentrated years of living there, I returned for a month together with my twenty-seven-year-old daughter Elisha. We went for an intensive one-month Arabic course at nearby Givat Haviva (which houses a Jewish-Arab center run by the Kibbutz Movement) and decided to include a full immersion experience in Arabic by living with an Arab family. For me, there was no other possible place than Kufr Qara. Life has gone by so quickly, it is hard for me to imagine how thirty-two years had passed. I always talked about going back to the village and spending some real quality time there, but it never happened. From time to time, I would make short visits there, but never managed to get back for an extended stay. So much has changed over the years. It is no longer a small village with about 8,500 people, where everyone knew everyone else. Now there are 18,000 people, and life has completely changed.

When I lived in Kufr Qara, there were four telephones in the entire village. One of them was in the local village council, one in the home of the former mayor, one in the high school, and one public phone in a store that was almost never open, and when it was open, they did not sell the telephone tokens needed to make a call. There was no Internet, email, or even faxes then. I went to the post office in Hadera, the nearest city, to apply for a telephone. They told me that if I was lucky I would get one in seven years! (Seven years later, the village was connected to the national telephone systems and people got telephones in the homes—welcome to the twentieth, now twenty-first, century!) When I wanted to call the States to speak to my parents back in New York, I would send a telegram from the local post office and set a time when they would call me. I had a Vespa motorcycle that I would ride at 2:00 a.m. on the set day and go to the gas station on the main Wadi Ara Road near the entrance to the village. The owner of the gas station would allow me to use the phone to receive a call any time between 2:00 a.m. and 6:00 a.m.

In the period from 1979 to 1981, there were no supermarkets, pharmacies, dry cleaners, or any real clothing stores in the village. There were a lot of family-owned grocery stores that all sold the same goods. Once a month, we would go to Hadera for a major shopping trip, which was about thirty minutes away by shared taxi. Once a month, we would also go to Tulkarem in the West Bank. In those days, there was no physical border between Israel and the West Bank. West Bank taxis with their blue license plates (Israeli cars had yellow plates) would wait in the village and travel as a shared taxi to the West Bank city of Tulkarem, where everything was cheaper. It also took about thirty minutes to get to Tulkarem, and once there, you were in a different world.

Most of my time in Kufr Qara, I lived in a house that was at the edge of the village. The rent was paid for by the local government. It was a brand-new house built by an employee of the village council whose family were Bedouin in the past. They were a rather poor family. He built the house for his teenage son. Like most people in the village, when they had some extra money they would buy some cement blocks, or steel rods, or floor tiles, and so on, and gradually they would build the house, brick by brick, mostly using their own labor. In those days, most families had a shared multigenerational family finance account, kept by the family elder. Everyone would contribute part of their income to the family account. On many weekends, I witnessed entire families and friends working together to pour the concrete for the roof of a new house. I saw and participated in the same type of group work during the harvest season of a given crop. There was a real sense of family and community, and it was inspiring to be a part of. My participation in these weekend, extended family and friends "work-outs" to build a house, or pick a crop, sped up my acceptance in the village as part of their life and part of the community. I felt welcomed and I was always warmly received.

Initially I lived with a married couple from the States and another single woman from our program, Michael and Andy, and Batia. After a couple of months, the married couple left, and my housemate Batia and I were placed in the unusual situation of having to constantly explain that we shared a house, but we were not married nor were we physically or emotionally involved. It was hard for a lot of people in the village to understand, and I decided not to bother to try to explain—let them think what they want. Our house was on the top of a hill. The driveway wasn't paved and everyday served as a challenge for my developing skills on my Vespa. When it rained, which it did quite a lot the two winters I was in Kufr Qara, my Vespa would fall over and often then slide down the hill. Eventually some village friends, teenagers, helped me to lay some concrete down so I would have a place to park the Vespa next to the house without it falling and rolling down the hill. Our very modest house had one long hallway with a bedroom on the right side, a salon on the left, further down the hall another bedroom on the left side, and the kitchen and bathroom on the right side. My room was at the end of the hall on the left. Batia had the room next to the entrance. She left the program after a year, and I was alone for several months. I was later joined by another intern, Rob Hutter, and then David LaFontaine and his wife Esther joined us, but they lived in their own house with their daughter Tamar, who was born in the Arab village of Tamra in the western part of Galilee. We bought cheap furniture in Tulkarem. We had only the very basics—no washing machine, a two-burner stove, a refrigerator of the type I had only seen in the movies that must have been thirty years old. We had an oven that worked by placing it on top of the gas stove. I did my laundry in buckets. We turned the long hallway into a traditional Eastern *diwan* with straw floor mats and mattresses and pillows on the ground for sitting. I bought an old black-and-white television and had "rabbit ears" antenna attached to it that just barely made it possible to get Israeli television (there was only one channel back then) and also in the evening we could get the Jordanian television, as well, if it wasn't raining.

In the winter, we heated the main common space with a *kanun* (or "cha-nun," as they pronounced it in the village). This was a small aluminum barbeque in which we would light charcoal with kerosene, and in order to get rid of the bad smell, we would put apple peals into the coals. Because the coals also gave off poisonous gas, we would have to leave the door of the house partially open (somewhat defeating the purpose of heating the house). But that's what most other people in the village did, and so did we.

Our house had two large, heavy, metal doors. The locks on the doors did not work. So, our doors were open 24/7. In the winter, when the wind blew strongly, we would place a large plant in front of the door so that it would remain closed.

I bought the Vespa to get around the village. More importantly, I needed to have a way to escape the village. I needed a way to go to the kibbutz and to just travel around on "down time," when I was not an Intern for Peace, on show in the community and a representative of the State of Israel and the Jewish people. In the village, I was watched all the time, or least that is how it felt. Sometimes I felt as if I was under a microscope. Who are these Jews living in our village? Why are they really here? In the first weeks that we were in the village, a small article appeared in the Communist Party's Ara-bic daily newspaper *Al-Ittihad* (*The Union*) in which someone wrote that a group of four CIA spies were living in Kufr Qara, and the local govern-ment was even paying our rent. When we heard about the article, we pretty much panicked. It was the most read Arabic daily newspaper at the time, and we were sure that we would face problems. We immediately went to the former mayor, who had invited us to the village, Attorney Mohammed Massarwi—he was still a member of the village council and very influen-tial in the village and beyond. He told us not to worry. He wrote a small response in the newspaper stating that it was true—the CIA sent young Americans to spy on us in Kufr Qara because they were interested to learn how we grow cucumbers! After that he wrote a few words about Interns for Peace and what we really came to do. Massarwi's response put a speedy end to that crisis. He also made arrangements for us to meet with some of the young "communists" in the village from the Rakah (Communist) Party. (Massarwi eventually became Israel's consul general to Atlanta and a district court judge.)

Even though life in the village was very intense, I loved being there. It was a totally new experience, and every day was an adventure—just the way that life should be. I took every opportunity possible to meet people, to visit people in their homes. I tasted every new food introduced to me, and I even learned to drink coffee. Until that time, I simply did not like coffee. I had gone through twenty-two years of life without drinking coffee. I knew it would not be possible to live in an Arab village for two years and not drink it. The first time I was faced with the *finjan* (small demitasse cup) of thick Arab coffee, I said to myself, "It's now or never." I took down that small cup as if it was a shot of whiskey. The problem wasn't so much the taste, but that it was hot! Eventually, I developed a taste for the coffee and managed to become a coffee drinker. I also learned and gained appreciation for the culture of drinking coffee with all of the words of blessing that go with the process. My favorite is *'amar*, which you say when you finish drinking the coffee. It means "building or house," and it is meant to say, "May this house always be here to welcome guests."

During my time in the village, from age twenty-three to twenty-five, I kept a journal. Until working on this book thirty-two years later, I did not open the journal. My journal from my days in Interns for Peace contains the insights of a young man in his twenties making his first steps as a new immigrant in the State of Israel, in a very different way than most new immigrants to Israel experience. Even after all of these years, those insights are quite interesting. The following are some excerpts:

MAY 12, 1978
[four months before immigrating to Israel, written in New York where I was completing my BA at New York University]
Why am I going? It seems like the thing to do. I've grown up in the movement [Young Judaea]. I've grown to be a real Zionist through the movement and lately I've also begun to question all that has had real meaning to me. I'm constantly going through the struggle of convincing myself that Israel truly is the only place in the world for me. Why am I constantly finding aspects of life there that deter my long heartfelt desires to return to the land of my ancestors? All my teachers, leaders—those who I respect and look towards for advice all tell me that I must go and try to change the things I don't like there. Well, I'm going and I hope I can do something.

I arrived in Israel on September 29, 1978, and went to Kibbutz Barkai, where Interns for Peace was based and where we would spend the first six months in a training program.

This is the first entry I am making since my arrival to Israel. The minute the plane landed I knew I would have no problem in adjustment even though the problem of "Klitah" assimilation into Israel is a bit more complex that I thought. There is also a certain amount of ambiguity in it as well. I want to assimilate into the world of Israel; however, there are very specific things about my identity as an American that I would like to retain. I want to be an Israeli and to feel that I am Israeli, but I will always have the twenty-two years of America as part of who I am. Israelis want to copy everything that comes from America. I want to be an Israeli.

I am looking forward to studying Hebrew and Arabic. I realized how anxious I am when I was in Jerusalem last week and went to the Old City. I really want to be able to sit down and talk to people in their native language. I felt uncomfortable speaking Hebrew to Palestinians in the Old City. I really don't want to do that. It felt obnoxious. It will be great when I will be able to converse with them in Arabic.

NOVEMBER 7, 1978
Today I began researching the Arab Pioneer Youth Movement. I found a small pamphlet about it at the Givat Haviva archives [Givat Haviva, near to Kibbutz Barkai, is the ideological seminar center of the Kibbutz Artzi–Hashomer Hatzair movement. It also has a Jewish-Arab center and a library archive about Arabs in Israel]. The pamphlet was edited by Latif Dori, an Iraqi Jew who, after emigrating from Iraq in the early 1950s, adopted the socialist political party Mapam as his own, and Mapam sent him to work in the Arab sector. One of his jobs was working with the Arab Pioneer Youth Movement. [In June 2009, I traveled with Latif Dori to a United Nations conference in Indonesia.] It was apparently a real youth movement set up in the same way that Jewish youth movements are organized. It was considered to be a sister movement of Hashomer Hatzair as well as having official recognition of HaNoar HaOved v'HaLomed. The APYM was established in 1954, "these youth aimed at leading the struggle of the Arab youth in Israel for the removal of the Military Administration,[2] the modernization of the Arab village and the lifting of the shackles of economic stagnation, the establishment of a progressive Arab society founded on relations of brotherhood and equality with its Jewish neighbors, the development

of the concept of cooperation and the introduction of the pioneering socialistic spirit in the new Arab generation." This quote comes from the pamphlet. By 1957 there were 700 members.

My job now is to make contact with some of these members and to try and discover what happened to this movement. . . . My perception, after reading the pamphlet is that the best chance for achieving my goals is to work through the framework of a youth movement structure. There is a great deal of familiarity with youth movements in Israel and it won't be like starting from scratch. Right now my fears and speculation regarding APYM [is that it] might have become too nationalistic and turned into a group like al-Ard which the government later outlawed.[3]

Years later I discovered that what primarily undid the APYM was that the Arab members were too successful in absorbing the values and principles of the socialist-Zionist Youth Movement, Hashomer Hatzair. When they completed high school and went on to university or to the working world, they wanted to become members of kibbutzim. In their mind, this was a fulfillment of the values they were being taught. The kibbutzim in question, the Kibbutz Artzi–Hashomer Hatzair movement—had no intention of having Arab members in their closed communities. Some other members of the movement decided to try and form a kibbutz of their own, for graduates and activists of the movement. But they soon learned that the Israeli government and the Jewish agency would not offer them land or any other support for this idea. The movement fell apart amidst its own hypocrisies.

JUNE 13, 1979

The whole idea of Jewish-Arab relations is in question in my thoughts. Is it possible for more than a small part of the population to be involved? What does it mean to "break down stereotypes"? Living in an Arab village is like living in a different country. I do believe that increased interaction would help things, but I think that the interaction would be forced. This is a homeland of two people and neither people want the other here. We have to find a way to make the best of this situation that no one wants. There are so many problems in these Arab communities it is incredible. The services that exist here don't begin to compare with the Jewish communities. . . . I think that if there was an equalization of government priorities that would be the first step towards reconciliation with regards to Arab Israelis. Of course the central issue is political. This is where the major problem lies. It will be a long, long time before Israeli Jews are going to recognize the need for an independent Palestinian state next to Israel. I believe that until this is done there will never be Shalom Bayit (peace at home—between Jews and Arabs in Israel). . . . The Palestinian state must come into being. I believe that it is a matter of life and death for Israel. The left in this country is so ineffective it is incredible. There must be more rational souls here. I don't understand why more people do not perceive the danger of building settlements in the West Bank. How can we constantly dig ourselves into someone else's land? The West Bank is part of the Land of Israel but it should not be part of the State of Israel. It is very frustrating going to a demonstration against settlements and there are less than one thousand people there. Where are the Israelis who care about their future? The Begin government can't be known for its timing—just as the autonomy negotiations are beginning they start out by breaking the good faith by establishing a new settlement. It is a slap in Sadat's face who is busy battling the other Arab states because of making peace with Israel.

OCTOBER 2, 1979

One day before the school year began I was approached by the high school principal, Ali A'lemi, who said that they were opening the school year and were short an English teacher—would I stand in until they can find and hire a teacher? Of course I said I would. I am not a teacher, I did not study education, I don't know how to teach English, I don't know what the curriculum is, but I guess I can do a better job than others and at least the students will hear proper English from me. Ali, the principal is a very interesting person. Obviously educated, he speaks beautiful Hebrew. In the village they call the A'lemi family "Bedouin." I asked someone how long they were living in Kufr Qara, they told me more than 100 years. I asked if they were still nomads. I was told that they are not. The term "Bedouin" is historic and as the village life goes, it will stick with them forever. The A'lemi family is also connected to the Likud. That is hard for me to understand—how can Arabs in Israel support the Likud party? Maybe that's how he got the job of principal? I don't know.

I was completely overwhelmed the first week. I had to teach all of the English classes. School here in Kufr Qara is very different from the schools I studied in. The classrooms are bare. The facilities are bad. Just the basics, desks, chairs, an old black board, a small desk for the teacher. No lockers, no gym. No cafeteria. No real library. Certainly not the school I went to and certainly not the schools that you find in the Jewish side of Israel. Reality hits hard in the face. This is what there is, and this is what I will have to deal with.

The teachers don't seem to be particularly motivated. I would think that they see their teaching as a mission, but I have not gotten that sense from anyone I have spoken to. All the teachers are men, mostly young men, in their 30s and 40s. What I gather is that teaching is a kind of fallback position. There are few other "white collar" jobs available. If you go to the university, you will probably end up being a teacher. They did not become teachers because they see the importance of education. They became teachers because they couldn't do anything else. That is not a particularly high point for motivation. I haven't yet met someone in the school from the teachers who was really happy to be at work. Kufr Qara, everyone here says, has the highest percentage of university graduates from the entire Arab sector. There is a sense of pride in that, but it does not seem to translate into a sense of pride in the profession they have found themselves in.

The girls are the better students. The students told me what they want to study. They said they want homework and they want tests. They cheat on the tests and really challenge the teacher. There was an incident the other day when I caught someone cheating. I wanted to immediately give a zero on the test, but it was the best student in the class and a girl. I knew I made a mistake the minute I backed down. The level of English is really bad. I think that from all of the 12th grade students only eight of them will pass the matriculation exam at the end of the year. In the lower-level vocational classes, there are kids who can't read and write at all (in English). I don't know what to do with all of the classes. They are quite large. The 11th-grade classes have about 30 students—that's a decent number. The 12th-graders are a little less, but the vocational classes with the lowest levels are over 45 students in a class. The teachers in the school call them "the rejects." They have been clumped together throughout the years. They are a collection of failures and that is how they are treated. Most of them are just hanging out in school because they have nothing else to do.

I find that teaching the 12th-graders is the hardest. They are facing an extreme amount of pressure because they have the matriculation exam at the end of the year. It makes teaching them very difficult. They are not interested in learning, only in passing the exam.

Ali, the high school principal, approached me and asked me to take a salary and just become the English teacher. I rejected the proposal. That is not what I came here to do. I also told him that I did not come here to take a job away from a young Arab professional. I was fine assisting as a volunteer until they could find a teacher, which I urged him to do as soon as possible.

The teacher-student relationship isn't quite clear to me. Teachers are without a doubt an authority figure, yet they are called by their first names. The kids all call the teachers Usthaz—meaning teacher or professor—but then they add their personal name—Usthaz Gershon for example. There is a careful separation between the teachers and the students. During the breaks you don't find teachers and students talking. In fact something that is interesting is that during the breaks they clear out the building—no students are allowed in the building during the breaks. They all go out to the sports field and the parking lot. Later I found out that this is one of the few opportunities that the boys and girls have to talk to each other—which is very limited. They use the breaks to pass notes to each other, often using a relative from the opposite sex to pass a note to someone who is not part of the family.

There are no female teachers and in fact the only female staff person is the school secretary. I'm sure that this must cause problems for the girl students. It also means that the boys do not get to see women in positions of authority and as educators. The girls are the best students and were also the first ones to invite me to visit in their homes. I went to visit one of them one evening last week with her family. I hoped it wasn't a scandal. I didn't hear anything negative and after that several other girls invited me to visit in their homes too.

I dread the thought of going to school every day. I can't wait for the whole thing to be over. I am so glad that it is something I can get out of. . . . In the long run it really is a good experience and will in fact help me in my work here. It has given me a first-hand view of Arab education which is far from being dynamic.

I had an interesting experience with one of the 12th-grade classes. They were reading "My Dungeon Shook" by James Baldwin. I asked the kids to write a letter to a relative who does not live in Israel describing what their life in Israel was like. I couldn't believe what they wrote. It was like reading propaganda from the Ministry of Information. The way they sold Israel would make you think that they were Begin supporters. I immediately understood that they are conditioned to think that every Jew they meet or who comes to their school is a government official. They were writing to that government official and gave him exactly what they assumed he would want to read. I was really quite upset and didn't understand why they still suspected me of working for the government. It was really a shock. I thought that I had begun to develop enough trust with them that they would not suspect me of working for the government. I asked them all to write once again. They did and quite a bit of them were much more honest writing about feeling discriminated against. Several of them wrote of their experiences in meetings with Jewish kids. They went to visit the Jewish schools and saw much more modern facilities with a lot more equipment. They were very impressed by the Jewish schools and angry that theirs was not more like that. They also wrote about hosting Jewish kids in their homes and giving them the royal treatment as Arabs know how to do. They wrote that the Jewish kids hosted them at school and did not bring them home. They were obviously insulted by the treatment they received. It was very interesting to begin to learn how sometimes more contact can create more problems rather than resolve them.

OCTOBER 5, 1979

The time has come for some general reflections. I have a lot of questions about the feasibility of bringing Jews and Arabs together. The answer is not so simple. I've noticed that there not only remains a political question to overcome which seems unbearable in itself, there are also cultural problems. The Arabs here are becoming more and more Westernized, however by Western standards (which are Israeli standards) they are still considered quite backwards. This will prove to be a barrier for at least another generation. Jews consider themselves more advanced and are not willing "to walk backwards" as someone told me. Arab culture is rich and has a lot to offer but the village life is traditional and seems primitive to most Jews who look inside.

I don't know which of the two problems (political and cultural) are more difficult to overcome. As for me, I am waiting for the day when Israelis will be willing to fight for equal rights for every citizen of the State of Israel. Relations between Jews and Arabs will not be significantly improved until there is more equality and until a political solution is met. The Arabs in Israel will always be suspect of identifying with Israel's enemy and that will continue to make it almost impossible for them to be treated as full citizens. Many Jews will also not think of Arabs as equals until the Arabs westernize more. That is what many people, including members of Kibbutz Barkai, who live a few miles away from Kufr Qara, tell me.

I sometimes feel that I am wasting my time. I am learning a lot and gaining from the experience. I used to say that the program [Interns for Peace] will give me the authority to speak my mind in the Israeli-Jewish community. I'm not sure this is true. People will listen to me because what I have to say is interesting, but I am not sure that they will heed my advice.

The problem of radicalization amongst the students is a serious one. They are also influenced by the Iranian revolution which has intensified Islamic pride since the Shah left Iran in January 1979. More girls are wearing head coverings now than before. That is what people in the village are telling me. The impact of Iran is felt thousands of miles away.

The problem of discrimination against Arabs has to be dealt with on the national level. The solution is to solve the problems of legal discrimination. . . . The government of the State of Israel is and has been making discriminatory policies since the existence of the State. What bothers me is that here in this point I personally have become hypocritical. I believe that what occurred with the expropriation of lands and the destruction of villages is wrong but it was perhaps necessary when it happened. I do not want to return to the previous situation and I am against any further expropriations. What was once done should not be done any more. It is fact now and where villages once were [there] are now cities, towns, villages, kibbutzim, and moshavim. But that policy should have been discontinued in the early days of the State. It is not a policy that a mature state in the modern world can have and feel free and good about and to continue to call itself democratic. It is for me a policy of embarrassment. It gives me the feeling of shame in my country. This is my home and I am not willing to have its name slandered by its own foolish policies.[4] Change is coming. The PLO is changing and Israel is going to be forced to talk. Political change has to come. But this will also take time.

One of my main goals for joining Interns for Peace and living in an Arab village for two years was to gain credibility in the eyes of Israeli Jews. Otherwise, my experience speaking with Israeli Jews about politics was to be completely pushed off as being naïve and not able to understand the Arabs or the conflict. Even on Kibbutz Barkai, which hosted Interns for Peace and included many people who were still quite ideological about Israel and peace with the Arabs, members of the kibbutz were quite cynical about Interns for Peace and our good intentions. After being on the kibbutz for six months, our group moved into three different Arab villages. I moved to Kufr Qara, which was a few kilometers from Barkai. Another group moved to Arara, not far from Kufr Qara, and the third group moved to Tamra in the western part of Galilee. Once a month, the three groups would gather at Barkai for a half a day of work meetings. In recognition of the kibbutz's support, we volunteered half a day of work each month before our meetings. After three months in the village, I was working my half day in the kibbutz's plastic factory. At 10:00 a.m., there was a coffee break that usually lasted fifteen minutes. During the break, one of the veteran members of the kibbutz turned to me and asked, "Nu, how are the *arabooshim* [a negative term for Arabs]?" Well, I began to tell him about his neighbors who he lived next to for thirty-two years. Before I knew it, the entire workforce of the factory was standing around me, listening. Someone said, "Let's sit down," and over the next forty-five minutes, I told the members of the kibbutz about their Arab neighbors. When we finished and went back to work, I had this amazing feeling of accomplishment. I had achieved my primary goal—I became a kind of new authority on the subject of Arabs in Israel.

Traveling around Israel in those times, I would always get the same reactions from people when I told them that I was living in an Arab village. "Aren't you afraid?" "Is it safe?" I would explain to people that I was living in a house that didn't even have a lock on my door—it was open 24/7, and I never felt unsafe. I always invited them to come to visit me in the village. Most people said that they would like to. Almost none actually came. It was clear, even then back in the late 1970s, that fear played a major role in the understanding (or lack thereof) between the Jewish and Arab citizens of Israel. There was so little contact, so many false perceptions, such a dearth of knowledge and experience.

In those days, it was quite common to walk through the village, and as you would pass each house, someone outside would say "*fdadel*"—meaning, please enter, you are welcome. Most of the time this was just courtesy, common of Arab hospitality. I was never really sure to what extent people really wanted me to come into their homes. But being a foreigner and a kind of local celebrity, everyone knew who I was, but I did not know who they all were, and if I had time, I would accept the invitation. By my count, I visited about five hundred homes during my two years in Kufr Qara. People were always curious to talk to me. That was great, but one problem I faced was that people did not have the patience for my broken Arabic. Hebrew was also a new language for me, but my Hebrew was much better than my Arabic, so people would say, "Speak Hebrew—we want to understand you." So ironically, in the two years that I lived with the Arabs, my Hebrew improved to become much better and much faster than my Arabic.

In July 2013, when I went to Givat Haviva to study Arabic, I spent the month of Ramadan there together with my daughter Elisha who was living in Boston, first completing her MA at Brandeis and then working. Elisha came to Israel to work on a documentary film on the roots of the Israeli-Palestinian conflict. After completing filming, she too had a month of vacation, which turned out to be the month of Ramadan, so we decided to study together. It was the most time I had spent with her in years. It was also the first formal study of Arabic I'd ever had. Classes were Sunday through Thursday, 9:00 a.m. to 2:30 p.m. Givat Haviva is very close to Kufr Qara, so it seemed natural to turn our Arabic study program into a full Arabic immersion program. I visited Kufr Qara to look for a place to rent for the month of Ramadan. I had no success. I called a lot of people and posted on Facebook that I was looking for some place to live. I took a trip to the village to search for a place to rent and asked friends there to keep their eyes open for me. There were homes to rent, but no one wanted to rent for only one month. Then I received a phone call from Hassan Abdel el Ghani. I did not know Hassan nor did I know his family, but he heard I was looking for a place, and he invited me and Elisha to come and live with his family. Not having another option, I thought that we would go and stay there a couple of days until we could find a place to rent.

The wonderful hospitality of the Abdel el Ghani family was impossible to reject. They also refused to allow us to leave. Elisha struggled to understand the remarkable generosity of their hospitality. It was Ramadan; most of the family was fasting. We were invited for the breakfast, the *Iftar* meal, with them every evening. They wanted us to take food from them to have lunch at Givat Haviva. We did not do that, but instead we would buy fruits and vegetables in a local market and make big amazing salads for lunch. After class, we would usually sit in a coffee shop or a restaurant and study for a couple of hours. We also spent afternoons sightseeing in the area.

Back to Arab hospitality. This was an issue that I also confronted when I lived in Kufr Qara from 1979 to 1981. Until you experience the generosity, it is difficult to even describe it. I often felt uncomfortable because there were certainly times when I knew that the family was not very well off, but that was never expressed when serving guests. They would quietly send one of the children out to the nearby grocery store to buy some sweet drinks and other things to put on the table. I always felt bad because I didn't want to drink those sweetened beverages, but knowing of their situation I would gulp it down anyway. It took me quite a long time to learn the tricks to avoid receiving too much hospitality. There are tricks that can be used and will not result with an insult.

It took me a while to understand the whole Arab hospitality thing. We find it difficult to grasp—why are they spending so much time, so much money, and demonstrating such generosity? It seems so disproportionate to be treated that way when we would probably not come close to showing the same kind of hospitality. Then it dawned on me—it all has to do with the notion of "honor," which is a key value in these traditional Middle Eastern cultures. In Western society, the honor is to be the guest. In Arab society, the honor is to be the host. You gain honor and you show off your honor by hosting in the best way possible. Not only is this a foreign concept in the West, the relationship to "honor" particularly "personal honor" in the West is completely different from the way that Arab society relates to it. Honor is the core of one's existence. The honor of the individual embodies the honor of the family, all of its members, especially the women and, even more so, the elders. The collective honor of the family is embodied in the honor of the tribe or the extended family. This goes from the local to the national, where the concept of national honor becomes a core element in the Israeli-Arab conflict. It all can be distilled down to something that Westerners and Easterners can easily understand: dignity. Arab dignity is expressed, amongst other things, by their hospitality. Even the Arabic word to extend hospitality is *yehtarem*, meaning to grant honor.

I have heard so many stories over the years of Israeli Palestinians who hosted Israeli Jews in their home and showed them the generosity of Arab hospitality. I heard from the Arab hosts how insulted they were when their Jewish guests invited them in return and took them to a restaurant instead of inviting them to their home. The Jewish side, of course, felt that they were showing respect and generosity by taking their guests to dine out, and it didn't even dawn on them that this would be seen as an insult. I heard many times from young Israeli Palestinians who participated in encounter meetings with Israeli Jews within the framework of school. The first visit usually takes place in the Arab town or village and almost always includes a home visit, often for lunch. When the reciprocal visit takes place, most often the kids have lunch together in the school, and the Arab kids end up being insulted; they say, "Why didn't they bring me to their home like we brought them to ours?"

Becoming a frequent visitor in Arab homes enabled me to also gain an understanding of how to express to my hosts that their hospitality was sufficient, to stop them from going overboard. The first Arab wedding I attended in Kufr Qara was my first learning experience in this. In my home, growing up in my society, I was always told to "clean up my plate," meaning if you want to express your appreciation for a good meal, eat all of your food. In Kufr Qara in the days when I lived there, most weddings took place at home. It was a neighborhood affair for which the entire extended family was enlisted to prepare, cook, and serve. The wedding ceremonies would take place over the course of days. One of the celebrations was a meal for everyone who came, and the whole village would be invited. The women of the family would cook and prepare for days, and half of the village, it seemed, would come to eat. There were many tables set up, army style, and plates of food were put out, eaten, cleaned, and served again. I sat down after greeting and congratulating the celebrating family. A plate of food with meat, rice, and vegetables was placed in front of me. There was fresh baked pita bread on the table. Everyone has only a table spoon with which to eat. Well, the food was quite good and I ate all of it. Before I could do anything, another full plate was immediately placed in front of me. I felt embarrassed, and I had to eat that as well. I then learned that you must always leave some food on the plate—don't finish it all or else you will simply have another full plate of food to confront. When offered more food, which happens even if you leave some on your plate, I learned that you look them straight in the eyes and say *"Alhamdulillah"* (Arabic: الحمد لله) meaning "Praise to God." Then they know you've had enough and don't want more.

As I got closer to some families, I felt less formal and could begin to cross some of the boundaries that existed, particularly when an Arab Israeli hosts a Jewish Israeli. In the old days, when I lived in the village, I developed a "key" to determine how sincerely welcomed I was in the family home. During those days, every Arab home in Israel had a Western-style living room with big heavy sofas and chairs. That is where I was always brought at the beginning. I called it the sitting room for the Jews. You could tell that it was a room not used very much in the house, but they all had one. The room was usually dark, and they would open the curtains and blinds and windows to let in fresh air. I would be served the sweet drink, and they would put other food down, such as nuts, cake, fruit, or more. And the visit would always end with coffee or sometimes tea, as well.

The houses, I discovered quickly, also had an Eastern-style diwan room with straw mats on the floor, mattresses along the walls, and pillows between sitting places. People would take off their shoes before entering the diwan. As families became more comfortable with me, I was taken directly to the diwan, not the Western salon. The diwan was also the place where men and women sat together, as did the children, as well. In the Western salon, I would usually only sit with men, and the women and girls would serve us.

As I became even more comfortable with some families, or they became more comfortable with me, I would be brought into the inner sanctum—the kitchen. That was the best place to be. It was also the place I could sit with the women and hear their stories. I would also offer to help with the food, which was always entertaining for them. I told them I actually cooked for a living as a student and being one of three sons and with no girls in my house growing up, my mother insisted that we all learn to cook and do household chores. My mother asserted, "I will not be the servant to the men in the house." She was right, and I always have appreciated her wisdom.

When I was living in Kufr Qara, one of my friends and colleagues in the village, a teacher named Wahiba Massarwi married her cousin who lived in the *Askar* refugee camp outside of the West Bank city of Nablus. Because she knew Hebrew, she got a job there in the Israeli Bank Leumi branch. She had that job until the bank was burned down at the beginning of 1988 in the first intifada. Her husband owned a small women's clothes boutique in the center of the city. I visited them and stayed with them one weekend in 1980. It was my first time in a refugee camp and an enlightening experience.

In the evening, we went to the movies at Nablus's only cinema. We took a taxi from their home in the refugee camp into the center of Nablus to the boutique. After dark, Nablus was under curfew. Nonetheless, there was a taxi service that ran even after the curfew. The drivers all seemed to know quite well the routes of the Israeli Army patrols and when it was safe to drive. They drove in the dark without lights. When we got into the center of Nablus, we had to hide in the boutique with the lights out, crouched on the floor below the front window until the Israeli Army patrols passed. Everyone there knew the exact times when the patrols came. We then ran quickly from his shop to the cinema. The cinema front was dark. There were no lights on in the lobby either. They sold tickets inside. I have no recollection of what movie was playing. I think I was in shock from the whole experience. The movie was the least important detail. After the movie, we did the same in reverse. I remember thinking how absurd and frightening their life was. If we had gotten caught by the patrol, we would have been arrested and spent the night in an Israeli prison in occupied Nablus. For me as an Israeli, it would have been trivial, but for my hosts as Palestinians, it could have been quite severe, especially if it was not their first time getting caught. I remember thinking: I hope they are not going through all of this danger just for me. Apparently it was not just for me, but something that they did from time to time.

When I returned to Kufr Qara with my daughter in the summer of 2013, I had the opportunity to visit more homes, especially those of the younger generation. Kufr Qara has developed enormously over the past thirty years. It is really a small city today and has lost the village atmosphere where everyone knows everyone. There is still much greater familiarity amongst friends and neighbors than in most Western towns, even in Israel. When you mention the name of someone to another Qarawi (as the residents of Kufr Qara are called), they can usually trace the name to an elder and figure out who they are. To find anyone is easy because everyone knows more or less where everyone else lives. I went to visit Ali A'lemi, who had long retired from being the headmaster of the high school where I taught. He had moved to a new house many years ago, and I only knew where his old house was. No problem. Everyone knew where he was, and one of my friends took me to visit him. No appointment necessary. He opened the door and greeted me with a wonderful smile and welcome. Just he and his wife were home. Immediately out came the coffee, some sweets, a bowl of fruit, and lots of wonderful conversation.

It is now almost seven decades since the State of Israel was born and had within its midst a sizable minority of Arabs who became citizens. It is beyond my ability to accept that after all of these years, discrimination still exists against Israel's Palestinian Arab citizens. One cannot explain the discrimination away as they did thirty years ago by elucidating the huge gaps that existed when the country was founded, suggesting that it takes a long time to close those gaps. Israel is no longer a developing country, a poor county. Israel is a world leader in technology, medicine, agriculture, communications, and more. Israel, at the macro level, is a rich country. There are no excuses for the discrimination against more than twenty percent of its citizens on the basis of ethnicity or religion. Discrimination should be passé, and in its place, we should be talking about "partnerships" or the equal sense of ownership, and belonging in the country and to the country.

Perhaps it is not possible to eliminate all forms of discrimination while the Palestinian citizens of Israel are always suspect of being more loyal to their own people—the Palestinians—than to their state. As long as Israel is not at peace with the Palestinians and the Palestinians remain a stateless people, the Palestinian citizens of Israel will always feel animosity toward the state and the state will always look at them as a potential fifth column. Nonetheless, there must be a governmental decision, supported by all, to remove all institutional and legal discrimination within no fewer than five years. This is achievable. Equality for all citizens has been part of the by-laws of practically every government of Israel since 1948, but the statement of principles has never been fully implemented into policies that would remove discrimination. It is not by chance that seventeen of the twenty poorest municipalities in Israel are Palestinian-Israeli communities. Most of the big revenues awarded to local governments come from taxable commercial and industrial properties. There is not one industrial zone located in a Palestinian-Israeli municipality. Many of the workers in Israel's many industrial zones are Palestinian-Israeli, but they have to travel to the nearby Jewish towns and cities to work, where those properties are taxed and the revenues benefit the Jewish residents.

Any quick analysis of the state budget will demonstrate the unequal allocation of funds between Jews and Arabs in Israel—in every sector. This is inexcusable and must be changed. There is even a need for some reverse discrimination in specific areas, such as in education. There are not enough social workers in the Arab sector, medical clinics, and other social services. The number of Israeli citizens in prison who are from the Arab sector is larger than their proportion of the population. The list of examples of discrimination goes on and on. The Palestinian-Israeli nongovernmental organization, Adala, has detailed the formal list of discriminations between Jews and Arabs in Israel. It should be the goal of every Israeli government to see that list shrink in size every year until it no longer exists.[5] In 2016, the Israeli government decided (once again) to allocate large amounts of money to the Arab sector to close the gaps. This is a great decision, but the true test is in the implementation. Time will tell.

The question of partnership, of sharing ownership over the country, is much more complex and much more important. The question is how Israel can remain the nation-state of the Jewish people and also be a fully democratic state. This has been a pressing question on Israel's agenda since the state's establishment. Since there are other nation-states in the world with large minorities that are successful liberal democratic states with full equality for all citizens, in principle, this should also be possible for Israel. There are, however, a number of complicating factors. Being Jewish is not only being part of a people, a nation, it is also a religion, and joining the religion is not simply a matter of adopting new citizenship. Therefore, the basic definition of what Israel is would have to change in order to accommodate all its citizens. It is not good enough to simply state that Israel is the democratic nation-state of the Jewish people. It will require changing that statement such that Israel is the nation-state of the Jewish people *and* all of its citizens. How can Israel be any less a part of the identity of Muhammad, who was born in Israel and can trace his roots to the same spot for hundreds of years, than it is my state after immigrating here in 1978? It cannot be, and it must not be if Israel is to be a truly democratic state. There must also be recognition of the special character of the State of Israel as the nation-state of the Jewish people, based on the principle of self-determination—the same principle that the Palestinian people assert in order to have a nation-state of their own.

This is very hard for many to grasp—particularly non-Jews because being Jewish is complex. The biggest difficulty is in coming to terms with the fact that it is more than a religion. I try to assist some people in understanding the complexities of Jewish identity by using myself as an example. I tell them that I am an atheist—a secular Jew—yet I am VERY JEWISH. That definitely confuses some people but also challenges their understanding of what it means to be Jewish and what is meant by the nation-state of the Jewish people. People often speak about Israel as a Jewish state. I do not. Herzl's famous book *Der Juden Staat* has been incorrectly translated as *The Jewish State* when in fact what Herzl wrote was *The State of the Jews*, and there is a big difference between the two ideas.

The second difficulty is in the fact that Israel denies the right of the Palestinian people to self-determination and continues to occupy their land (the West Bank, East Jerusalem, and Gaza are still under Israel's indirect control while Judea and Samaria are also part of the Land of Israel and part of the Jewish people's heritage). It could be that what I propose is not possible until there is a Palestinian state that can exist in peace next to Israel. Until that time, Israel's Palestinian citizens will remain suspect, and Israel's legitimacy will be challenged in the international diplomatic battle that is waged against them because of the occupation.

The trend in Israel, whose population is exhibiting more and more reactionary right-wing behaviors typical of a country facing battle, is to move away from democracy and equality for all of its citizens. Proposed legislation that includes the desire to strengthen the Jewish aspects of Israel's identity in direct contrast to its democratic character are moving the country further away from confronting the challenge that I have posed above. The growing anti-Arab sentiment in the country will likely continue as Israel is faced with more boycotts and threats of sanctions for continuing to build settlements in the occupied territories and for its failure to support international diplomatic efforts to resolve the Israeli-Palestinian conflict. The round of violence that began in October 2015 increased fear, animosity, and hatred between the Jewish and Palestinian-Arab citizens of Israel.

If it were possible for the Palestinian-Israeli citizens to be more directly and actively engaged in the peacemaking process with the Palestinian people, at the same time asserting their loyalty to their citizenship, it could prove to be very helpful in removing discrimination and in confronting the issue of partnership. This would fulfill the dream of many in the Palestinian-Israeli community who have spoken for years about being a "bridge of peace" between Israel and the Arab world. Until now this has not been possible, largely because they are suspect both by the Israeli leadership and by the Palestinian leadership. Instead of being a bridge of peace, the Palestinian-Israeli community has been left outside of negotiations, and the discourse of peace has not included them (with a few exceptions, such as Member of Knesset [the Israeli Parliament] Ahmad Tibi who served as an advisor to Palestinian President Arafat although not specifically as a "bridge builder"). The Palestinian Israelis are marginalized both inside Israel and inside Palestine, which makes it difficult, if not impossible, for them to assume a more active role in peacemaking.

The creation of the United Arab List in the March 2015 elections may be a step in the right direction. The head of the list, Member of Knesset Ayman Ouda, made a significantly positive impression on the Jewish public via the moderate and unassuming manner in which he presented himself in the television debates. If the Arab members had a more effective political role in the Knesset, then that could help them become more effective in the possibilities to build peace between Israel and Palestine. Not enough effort has been placed on this in the past twenty years of peacemaking, and as almost everything else has failed, perhaps it is time to also examine how the Palestinian-Israeli population could be more helpful in assisting both Israel and the Palestinians to come to terms with each other.

One major challenge to this may be the rejection of the two-state solution by a growing number of Palestinian Israelis, particularly amongst the younger generation. The new generation of Palestinian Israelis do not see how the two-state solution serves their direct interests. More and more young Palestinian Israelis are talking about either a one-state solution or a two-state solution whereby the occupied territories become a Palestinian state and Israel becomes a state for all of its citizens and not a Jewish nation-state. This stems from the failure of the State of Israel to become a state with which its Palestinian citizens can identify. At the same time, it is quite clear to a majority of Palestinian Israelis that Israel is one of the best places in the region to be an Arab. With all of the instability and dangers that surround Israel in the Arab world today, Israel is an island of stability and security, and although there is discrimination when compared to Israeli Jews, Palestinian Israelis enjoy many more of the privileges of living in a democratic state than many other Arabs in the rest of the Arab world. But that fact does little to alleviate their sense of alienation from their state and the overwhelming feeling that their state would prefer if they would all disappear, or at least sit down and shut up.

Israel's President Reuven "Rubi" Rivlin, who until becoming president was seen as an extreme right-winger regarding the Palestinian question, does not accept the two-state solution and rejected partition of the Land of Israel. In his support of a one-state option, he speaks about true democracy and equality within that one state. The main problem though is that he conceptualizes that one state as the nation-state of the Jewish people and demands that the Palestinians accept that definition. Recently he has been voicing some new ideas, and as a standing president, these ideas are being heard in the country and around the world. He is certainly challenging the discourse. At the Herzliya conference on June 7, 2015, President Rivlin presented his profound understanding of the rifts and deep schisms that have developed inside Israel's soul. I strongly recommend reading his full speech, it is quite challenging. The following are a few of the most important elements he raised:

> In Israel, there is a word which has long since turned into a weapon: "Demography." This word is generally used when someone wants to validate a particular claim. However, those with a good ear understand that this usage is generally nothing but an ostensibly polite way of describing one or other population group as a "threat," or a "danger.". . . I have developed a profound distaste for that concept. . . . In the 1990s, Israeli society comprised a clear and firm majority, with minority groups alongside it—a large secular Zionist majority, and beside it three minority groups: a national-religious minority, an Arab minority, and a Haredi [ultra-Orthodox Jews] minority. Although this pattern remains frozen in the minds of much of the Israeli public, in the press, in the political system, all the while, the reality has totally changed.
>
> Today, the first-grade classes are composed of about 38% secular

Jews, about 15% national religious, about one quarter Arabs, and close to a quarter Haredim. . . . There is a reality in which Israeli society is comprised of four population sectors, or, if you will, four principal "tribes," essentially different from each other, and growing closer in size. Whether we like it or not, the makeup of the "stakeholders" of Israeli society, and of the State of Israel, is changing before our eyes. . . . This serious division of Israeli society finds expression primarily in the distribution between the different and separate education systems. . . .

A child from Beth El [a religious Jewish settlement in the West Bank], a child from Rahat [a Bedouin township inside Israel], a child from Herzliya [an upper-class large secular coastal city] and a child from Beitar Ilit [an ultra-Orthodox settlement in the West Bank]—not only do they not meet each other, but they are educated toward a totally different outlook regarding the basic values and desired character of the State of Israel. Will this be a secular, liberal state, Jewish and democratic? Will it be a state based on Jewish religious law? Or a religious democratic state? Will it be a state of all its citizens, of all its national ethnic groups? Tribe, by tribe, by tribe, by tribe. . . .

From a political viewpoint, Israeli politics to a great extent is built as an inter-tribal zero-sum game. One tribe, the Arabs, whether or not by its own choice, is not really a partner in the game. The other three, it seems, are absorbed by a struggle for survival, a struggle over budgets and resources for education, housing, or infrastructure, each on behalf of their own sector. In the "new Israeli order" in which each sector experiences itself as a minority, this dynamic will be infinitely more destructive. . . . We must ask ourselves honestly, what is common to all these population sectors? Do we have a shared civil language, a shared ethos? Do we share a common denominator of values with the power to link all these sectors together in the Jewish and democratic State of Israel? . . .

The "new Israeli order" now requires us to abandon the accepted view of a majority and minorities, and move to a new concept of partnership between the various population sectors in our society. Clarification of the essence of that partnership is the task of all of Israeli society. . . . I believe that there are . . . pillars on which this partnership must stand. The first is a sense of security for each sector, that entry into this partnership does not require giving up basic elements of their identity. . . . The sense of security that my basic identity is not threatened is a fundamental prerequisite for the ability of each one of us to hold out a hand to the other. . . . The second pillar is shared responsibility. . . . No tribe is exempt from proposing solutions to deal with the challenge of defending the security of the State; from facing the economic challenges, or maintaining the international status of Israel as a member of the family of nations. Partnership demands responsibility. . . .

In order to ensure the partnership between us, we must ensure that no citizen is discriminated against, nor favored, simply because they belong to a specific sector. . . . In order to create a strong basis for the partnership between us, we will have to ensure an accessible "Israeli dream" that can be realized by each and every young person, judged only on the basis of their talents, and not according to their ethnic or social origins. . . .

Despite the challenges the "new Israeli order" poses, we must recognize that we are not condemned to be punished by the developing Israeli mosaic—but rather it offers a tremendous opportunity. It encompasses cultural richness, inspiration, humanity, and sensitivity. We must not allow the "new Israeli order" to cajole us into sectarianism and separation. We must not give up on the concept of "Israeliness"; we should rather open up its gates and expand its language.

Mohammed Bakri, a leader amongst Israel's Palestinian citizens, the former head of the Israeli Communist Party and a longtime member of Knesset, published a response to Rivlin in the *Haaretz* newspaper on June 11, 2015:

Dear Mr. Rubi Rivlin, President of Israel,
I read your speech and I was moved by your sincerity and your courage. I, Mohammed Bakri, a citizen from the "Arab-Palestinian tribe" am prepared to be your full partner in building the new Israeli dream—if my dream will materialize. I dream of a state of all its citizens, in which everyone is equal, even if their national and cultural identities are different. I dream of genuine peace with justice between our two peoples—the Israeli and the Palestinian. I believe that the peace that we all want and hope for will not emerge without compromises from both sides. I also believe that this peace cannot come from the outside, only from within us, here from Israelis and from Palestinians—if we really believe not that we are destined to live together, but that we want to live together.

I want to live with you[,] will also allow my brothers to live with you, my brothers for 67 years have been refugees in the world, without rights and without a home. If you allow my brothers a home then I will be your full partner. If you give my brothers the right of return, as you give to your brothers, then I will love you and protect you from all harm. If you end the occupation and remove checkpoints and recognize the rights of the Palestinian people to an independent state, free and democratic, I will love you and defend you from all harm. If you learn my language and write to me in Arabic, as I write to you in Hebrew, you will lose your fear of me and love me as I love you. If you dream like me, I will dream like you. If you abide by "love your neighbor as yourself," I will be your neighbor. If you think that you are like me and not better than me, I will live with you for eternity. If you acknowledge your part in my tragedy and request forgiveness, I will forgive you and extend my hand to you and embrace you. I recognize you. Recognize me. If that all happens, you will be my brother. Your blood will be my blood.

President Rivlin and Mohammed Bakri present one of the key challenges facing the State of Israel, one that any person, such as myself, who belongs to the tribe of liberal peace-seeking Zionists must embrace. It is in meeting that challenge and rising to it that the State of Israel will rise or fall, excel or diminish. It is within this challenge that I have found my life, and through my love for Israel and the determination to make it my home, I have dedicated my existence to the inevitability of marching forward in the pursuit of peace.

Working for the Israeli Government

5 After two years of living and working in Kufr Qara where I developed a leadership training program for high school youth and laid down the beginning of what later was transformed into a community center, I came to the conclusion that the work to improve Jewish-Arab relations in Israel had to be done at the governmental level, something for which the State of Israel had to take responsibility. From what I saw, there were numerous nongovernmental organizations working for peaceful coexistence between the Jewish and Arab citizens of Israel, but the state itself did very little to advance understanding between its citizens. In 1980, while I lived in the village, we had a visit from a delegation of employees of the County of Los Angeles. Someone in the delegation worked on improving ethnic group relations there. He told me that the County of Los Angeles, at that time, employed 167 people to work on different aspects of ethnic group relations. That prompted me to conduct a small survey of how many people were employed by the Israeli government to improve relations between Jewish and Arab Israelis. The results were astounding, but not really surprising: zero! There was not even one single civil servant in the entire civil service of Israel who was responsible for improving Jewish-Arab relations in Israel.

I then immediately wrote a proposal to create a new position for myself, one that would be in charge of advancing understanding between the Jewish and Arab citizens of Israel, and sent it off to Prime Minister Menachem Begin. I made sure to quote the Israeli Declaration of Independence:

> THE STATE OF ISRAEL will be open for Jewish immigration and
> for the Ingathering of the Exiles; it will foster the development of
> the country for the benefit of all its inhabitants; it will be based on
> freedom, justice, and peace as envisaged by the prophets of Israel;
> it will ensure complete equality of social and political rights to all
> its inhabitants irrespective of religion, race, or sex; it will guarantee
> freedom of religion, conscience, language, education, and culture; it
> will safeguard the Holy Places of all religions; and it will be faithful to
> the principles of the Charter of the United Nations.

I also quoted Begin's mentor, Zeev Jabotinsky, from his famous essay, "The Iron Wall":

I consider it utterly impossible to eject the Arabs from Palestine. There will always be two nations in Palestine—which is good enough for me, provided the Jews become the majority. And secondly, I belong to the group that once drew up the Helsingfors Program, the program of national rights for all nationalities living in the same State. In drawing up that program, we had in mind not only the Jews, but all nations everywhere, and its basis is equality of rights. I am prepared to take an oath binding ourselves and our descendants that we shall never do anything contrary to the principle of equal rights, and that we shall never try to eject anyone. This seems to me a fairly peaceful credo.

My proposal generated interest. I received positive feedback from various people in the government. I met with some Members of Knesset who also responded favorably, but no one would make any firm commitments to me regarding the position. It took me fourteen months of intensive lobbying to eventually convince the government of Israel to hire me. My proposal was quite convincing and compelling, yet the main problem I encountered was that, due to the economic situation in the country, the government had decided on a hiring freeze. No new government jobs could be created. The government wanted me and was interested in the position that I proposed, but they simply could not hire me. Relief came through Member of Knesset Mohammed Watad, a member of Mapam (a leftist socialist party coming from the Hashomer Hatzair movement). Watad had been one of the founding members of the Arab Pioneer Youth Movement. He lived in the village of Jatt not too far from Kufr Qara. I actually met him the first time with Mohammed Massarwi, the lawyer, judge, and former mayor of Kufr Qara. Massarwi took me to his home one evening to discuss him joining a public support committee for Interns for Peace. Watad was extremely articulate; he spoke beautiful Hebrew. He had a sarcastic sense of humor, which magnified his intelligence. I also remember very vividly that his eldest son's name was Castro and everyone in the Arab areas called him Abu Castro.

During my months of lobbying for my government job, I went to see Watad in the Knesset. I showed him my proposal, and we became better acquainted. I spoke to him about my youth movement experiences in Young Judaea. He told me about his experiences as a member of the Arab Pioneer Youth Movement in the early years of the State of Israel. We hit it off really well. I think he admired my spirit, and he liked my proposal. He said that he would try to help me.

Watad came through. In his research into the Israeli budget, he came across an unused budget line in the Ministry of Immigrant Absorption for a program called "Project 200." This was a government program to encourage aliya—immigration—from North America for young, educated Jewish professionals. The idea of the program was that the young, educated Western immigrant professionals would be hired by the government for two years. The first year would be paid for by the Ministry of Immigrant Absorption, and the second year would be paid for by the ministry where the person worked. It was a great scheme and until the Arab Member of Knesset, Mohammed Watad, had uncovered it, the plan had not been used. Years later he joked with me on the irony of it all—an Arab citizen of the State of Israel who worked to encourage the immigration of an American Jew to Israel. Unfortunately in September 1994, Watad's life was cut short by a tragic car accident, a great loss to his family, the Arab citizens of Israel, and to the State of Israel.

I became the first civil servant in the State of Israel whose responsibility it was to work on the improvement of Jewish-Arab relations. I got a position in the Ministry of Education. I was officially under the direction of Mr. David Por who was the director of the Educational Executive, the highest policy-making body within the Ministry of Education. Actually I reported to the director of the Arab department in the Ministry, Mr. Emanuel Kopolovitz. That's right—Kopolovitz! The Arab department was headed by an Ashkenazi Jew. He did have an Arab deputy, but most people knew that the Arab deputy was mostly window dressing. I quickly developed a high regard and respect for Emanuel Kopolovitz. He was too conservative in his approach; I was a young radical who wanted radical change. But Kopolovitz understood the system and knew that slow and sure change was better and more likely to succeed. Mainly he knew that each day that passed without a mention of Arab education in the news made it easier for him to push for change in the Arab educational sector. He also knew and worked to ensure that he would be the last Jewish director of Arab education in Israel. Today when I meet veteran Arab educators in Israel, they have only kind words to say about Emanuel Kopolovitz.

The problems of education for Arabs in Israel were overwhelming and bewildering. Kopolovitz took me with him on several occasions to see the reality of Arab education on the ground. He took me with him to Nazareth for a gathering of all of the Inspectors of Arab schools, most of them Arab men who had been school principals and were promoted within the Ministry. This was part of Kopolovitz's plan to eventually have the Arab educational sector run by the Arabs themselves. Kopolovitz presented me to everyone in the ministry. He had Director General of the Ministry Eliezer Shmueli write about me in the monthly bulletin that the ministry puts out detailed policies and priorities. Shmueli instructed every official in the ministry to open their doors to me and to cooperate in my efforts, which were supported by the Israeli government, to build links between the educational system for Jews and for Arabs. On my tours with Kopolovitz to see schools for Arabs all over the country, I could see that in most places the physical realities of underdeveloped and underfunded buildings were blatant. There were new schools as well, built in the recent past, but in most cases, they were not at the same level as nearby Jewish schools. The funding gaps were obvious. I remember that in Kufr Qara there was an entire elementary school that was held in many rented rooms spread out around the center of the village, none of them built as classrooms and none of them meeting a basic standard to which a classroom should be held. I was glad that Kopolovitz "adopted" me and supported what I aimed to do in the ministry. The task was daunting, and having someone like Kopolovitz behind me was very important. He fully supported my mission. Something that I could not say about Director General Eliezer Shmueli.

Shmueli published a policy statement in the monthly bulletin that I wrote and Kopolovitz approved calling on Jewish and Arab schools to arrange meetings between the students. Interested schools were directed to contact me. Very quickly I received tens of calls and discovered that there were no serious models for conducting encounters between students. I recalled vividly the encounters that I had organized in Interns for Peace, but had absolutely no idea what I should do and how those encounters should be organized because I understood that there were almost no trained professional facilitators available and there was also no budget available to even subsidize buses to move the students from one school to another.

At the same time, I learned of a facilitator's course being organized at the newly founded Jewish-Arab village Neve Shalom–Wahat al-Salam, halfway between Jerusalem and Tel Aviv.[1] I contacted Neve Shalom and inquired about joining the course. They had already begun and I had missed the first weekend, but I was invited to attend the next course meeting and subsequent meetings that were held one weekend a month. It turned out that not only was this a course for Jewish and Arab facilitators of joint encounter meetings for high school students, it was an experimental laboratory for developing the tools and techniques for running the encounters. It became quite evident that Neve Shalom–Wahat al-Salam was developing models that would lead the field for years to come. I got the Ministry of Education to recommend that Jewish and Arab schools conduct joint encounters in Neve Shalom–Wahat al-Salam. That was quite a radical achievement in those days.

As more schools became interested in conducting encounters, the budgetary issue became an obstacle. I spoke with Kopolovitz about it, and he agreed to raise the issue with Director General Eliezer Shmueli. Kopolovitz came back from that meeting as if he had been hit over the head with a steel bar. Shmueli simply told Kopolovitz that he should understand that the work of Baskin and the encounters is "cosmetic," as he called it. He said it was mainly aimed at creating good public relations for Israel. This was an answer I could not accept. I thought it was insulting and wrong. I decided I had to do something. I thought that I had to find a way to have Shmueli's "cosmetic" statement be published in the media. It was obvious proof that I could never be an "establishment man."

Thinking strategically, I called the education correspondent of the smallest, least significant, perhaps least read newspaper in Israel, *Al HaMishmar*, the newspaper of the Kibbutz Artzi–Hashomer Hatzair movement. I knew they would publish the item in a prominent spot in the newspaper, and yet it was so small and so insignificant that it would not create too much anger from Shmueli when it was published. Well, *Al HaMishmar* published it on the front page as the leading headline in the Friday weekend newspaper: "Director General of the Ministry of Education: Jewish-Arab meetings of schools is cosmetic." Shmueli, Kopolovitz, and I had the whole weekend (Friday and Saturday) to digest the item. I was of course quoted in the text and explained the importance of Jewish-Arab encounter meetings and the work I was trying to do in the ministry. I also complained about not having a budget to do the work.

On Sunday morning when I arrived to work, Kopolovitz was waiting for me, quite agitated and nervous. He told me to immediately go to the office of the director general, who was waiting for me. His office was across town. I was quite nervous myself thinking about what his reaction might be. Would he fire me, ending my very short career in the field of Jewish-Arab relations? When I entered his office, it was quite clear that he was very angry. How dare I accuse him of not taking Jewish-Arab relations seriously? That was surprisingly the bottom line. He yelled at me for about twenty minutes, but I left the meeting with a budget of $15,000 to subsidize buses for encounters between Jewish and Arab schools, and he approved my overtime pay—which I didn't even ask for.

I punched a time clock in the ministry, but I spent many days on the road visiting schools or offices of the ministry, and I clocked more than double the number of work hours for a government worker. I didn't care about the extra hours, I loved my job and everything I was doing. If I had the financial ability, I would have paid them to allow me to work. But Shmueli had approved overtime for me. I think I learned some valuable lessons from that experience regarding Israeli government bureaucracy, decision-making, using the media, and dealing with superiors at work. No one will really listen to you until you force them to. But when you make noise, make sure it only awakens your target audience and doesn't deafen them to your voice. Selecting a small not very important newspaper made the noise but didn't create the trouble. I was heard and was able to continue to work. In fact, Shmueli appointed me to a newly founded state education committee to assess what the Ministry of Education could do to foster education for democracy and coexistence. The committee was headed by Ministry of Education Deputy Director General Arieh Shuval. The bulk of the committee's work over the next nine months came from Aluf Hareven, one of the directors of the Jerusalem-based, social-policy think tank, the Van Leer Institute, and me.[2] The main operative recommendation of the committee was to establish a department in the Ministry for Education for democracy and coexistence. The recommendation was implemented one year later.

The department functioned for about ten years. When President Yitzhak Navon was the Minister of Education, the department was established under his direct supervision. He handpicked its first director, former Carmiel high school principal Yitzhak Shapira. The two of them gave a huge push forward in integrating democracy and coexistence education into schools, primarily in the nonreligious school sectors. Eventually, the National Religious Party (NRP) regained control of the Ministry of Education from the Labour Party. The NRP converted the Unit for Education for Democracy and Coexistence into the Department for Values Education, meaning primarily their narrowly defined "Jewish values" and thereby removed almost all of the content and intentions of the designers and planners (myself included). Ironically, when Meretz MK Yossi Sarid took over the Ministry of Education under Prime Minister Yitzhak Rabin, there was little that he could do with the department other than close it down.

The Institute for Education for Jewish Arab Coexistence

6 During my tenure at the Ministry of Education, I was requested by the Prime Minister's Office (Menachem Begin was prime minister) to develop a proposal for a German government foundation (Hanns Seidel Foundation) to support the work of advancing Jewish-Arab coexistence.[1] I developed a detailed proposal for the creation of the Institute for Education for Jewish Arab Coexistence. The institute would conduct the work I was already doing in the Ministry of Education; would also work in other government ministries, particularly those that provide services to the Arab sector; and would have a relatively large budget for implementation. The idea was that every government official or civil servant who provided services to the Arab sector would receive from the institute special, additional in-service training aimed at increasing sensitivity to the needs of the group of citizens they serve. The institute would also explore and professionalize Jewish-Arab encounters, create new models, train facilitators, and research results, including attitudinal and behavioral changes following Jewish-Arab encounters. Lastly, the institute would create public debate on issues concerning the relations between Jews and Arabs in Israel in terms of democracy and coexistence.

In 1982, the Institute for Education for Jewish Arab Coexistence was founded, and I was appointed its director. I was twenty-six years old. It functioned independently, but was linked to the Ministry of Education and the Prime Minister's Office. The two government ministries had two representatives each on the institute's board of directors. The idea was that in order to successfully work with government ministries and officials on a topic that is perceived as political and controversial, it was essential to have the official backing and participation of the government. This was definitely a breakthrough because until then there were no official government programs actively working for Jewish-Arab coexistence on a citizen-to-citizen basis. This trailblazing model of government and nongovernment collaboration in the midst of a difficult course through the mysteries of conflict resolution very much became my favorite *modus vivendi* throughout all of the years that I have been doing this work.

The first challenge in directing the semi-independent, nongovernmental, semigovernmental organization came very quickly. The two representatives of the Prime Minister's Office came from the Office of the Advisor on Arab Affairs. This was a position of high power during the years of the military government, which governed all of the Palestinian citizens of Israel from 1949 to 1966. The military government mentality of the office remained for years after the military government itself was disbanded. This office was all about control, and any Arab who voiced opinions that were critical of Israel's policy was considered a radical and dangerous. The Advisor on Arab Affairs at the time was Benyamin Gur Aryeh. He was an Iraqi Jew who spent years in military intelligence, during the early years when the intelligence services were filled with Jews who came from Arab countries. In general, those people, including Gur Aryeh, held rather negative views of Arabs in general and of Israeli Arabs in particular. Most of the staff in the advisor's office held similar views to those of Gur Aryeh. The two who were selected to represent the Prime Minister's Office on our board of directors were Yehezkel Shemesh and Yitzhak Reiter. Shemesh was definitely one of the followers of the worldview of Gur Aryeh, and I found it very difficult to work with him. Reiter was from the new generation of native-born Israelis and also from military intelligence, but he got there because of his appreciation for the Arabic language and culture. Nonetheless, he was a representative of the "establishment." (Some years later Reiter left public service, got his PhD in Middle East studies, and became an academic. Shemesh became the Custodian of Absentee Property—the bank of all Arab properties of those who became refugees taken over by the state after the nakba.)

In those years, the number one "enemy" or adversary of the Office of the Advisor on Arab Affairs was Rakach—the Arab Communist Party, a legally represented political party in the Knesset. Rakach was perceived by the establishment as radical at a time when a majority of the Arab citizens of Israel voted for Zionist political parties. While Rakach maintained that it was an Arab-Jewish party and had Jewish and Arab members and representatives in the Knesset, Rakach was a non-Zionist party and perceived within the establishment to be an anti-Zionist party. Personally, I believe that Rakach was actually one of the primary moderating forces, certainly against the rise of political Islam, making inroads in the wake of the Iranian revolution. Rakach also placed a significant emphasis on education and advancement for women, which I believe is a key to the advancement of the Arab sector in Israel. I had difficulty accepting the extreme negative view of the Prime Minister's Office of any Arabs who were active in Rakach. The Advisor on Arab Affairs instructed his men on our board of directors to ensure that no members of Rakach would participate in any of our activities.

The first person I hired to work with me in the institute was Samir Abu Shakra from Um el Fahem. Samir was young, intelligent, angry, and creative. We planned to develop programs that would bring Arab culture into Jewish Israel. Samir had great ideas and a lot of energy. Shortly after he was hired and began planning a conference on Arab culture, I was ordered by the Prime Minister's Office representatives on my board to fire him immediately. I protested the decision adamantly. How could an institute for the education for Jewish-Arab coexistence take its first steps by firing a newly employed Arab employee because the Prime Minister's Office ordered it? It was a horrendous situation, an impossible dilemma for me to confront. The institute was founded on the principle of being supported by the government and the institute was funded by the German government, which was predicated on the support of the government of Israel. If I went against the government of Israel's representative on my board of directors, I would lose the German government funding and the institute would be shut down before we even got started. How could I do something that was so against my principles and that I knew was wrong?

I met with Gur Aryeh. He was a pig-headed man who refused to discuss the issue and ordered me to fire Samir. I demanded to have just cause. Why were they so opposed to Samir, who had impressed me with his sincerity, honesty, intelligence, and belief in coexistence? I left his office without answers and even more angry.

I went to see Aluf Haeven, one of the directors of the Jerusalem Van Leer Institute who was the most important person on the Ministry of Education's Unit for Education for Democracy and Coexistence. Aluf had been an intelligence officer, and he was very well connected to the intelligence community. Aluf told me he would speak to some people and get back to me. A few days later, he arranged for me to meet a Shin Bet agent who had Samir's file. I met the agent alone in Aluf's office, and he showed me the file and all of the "horrible" things Samir had done in his past. He also had the file of someone else who Samir had invited to work with us on organizing a seminar on Arab culture in Israel.

What can I say? I was speechless after seeing the file. They had dates and exact times, people whom Samir spoke with, things that he said, or that they claimed he had said, word for word. It was amazing. Even after examining all of this "evidence" against Samir, I failed to see any serious offense that he had committed. The "worst" thing that Samir had done was when he was a member of the Arab Students Committee in University he invited a leader of Abna al-Balad (Sons of the Village) movement to speak to the students. Abna al-Balad was a very anti-Israeli Arab nationalist movement based in Samir's home town of Um el Fahem. Samir was opposed to the ideology of Abna al-Balad, but he believed in democracy and freedom of speech. Abna al-Balad was a radical movement, but it was a legal movement. Samir broke no laws.

The second case file was very similar. No laws were broken, but these young Israeli-Arab university graduates did not fit within the molds that the authorities wanted. They were not quiet and would not be quiet. They were prepared to fight, democratically, for their equal rights. This was the new generation, the one that the political-military establishment feared so much. These were the people that the political-military establishment planned to keep outside of the realm of power and influence. In those days, it was almost impossible to get a job without the clearance of the Shin Bet. This was certainly true in any institution controlled by the state, such as the Ministry of Education. All Arab teachers had to be cleared by the Shin Bet to get a job. I saw this with my own eyes when I was working in the Ministry of Education. There was a man in the office, a rather pleasant guy, who I would see there every day, but I never really knew who he was or what his job was. Officially he held the title of Deputy Director of Arab Education–Administration. One day I walked into the office of the Director Emanuel Kopolovitz, and there was a very emotional and loud discussion taking place. It was about a teacher who was fired from the school system. It turns out that the Shin Bet tried to get this teacher to enlist his brother to collaborate with the Shin Bet and he refused. As a result, he was fired. Kopolovitz was arguing with his "deputy" from the Shin Bet to have the teacher re-instated. Kopolovitz argued that the teacher could not be punished because of his refusal to put pressure on his brother to be a state collaborator with the Israeli security service. Guess who won the argument. The Shin Bet, of course. To the best of my understanding, that situation no longer exists, and the Shin Bet, now called the Israel Security Agency (ISA), does not intervene in the hiring and firing of teachers, unless they can prove that laws have been broken.

Back to Samir, the Prime Minister's Office, and my dilemma. My board would not support my proposal to back Samir and go against the prime minister's advisor. They felt that if they did that we would lose the support of the Prime Minister's Office, then the Ministry of Education would be forced to withdraw and then the Hanns Seidel Foundation would cancel its funding. I had to fire Samir, something I have been sorry about for years. I would run into him every so often and always feel ashamed of what we did to him. But I did get the board's guarantee that all future hiring would be done by me without board oversight. The board had the right to fire me, but my staff was my decision. That ended the intervention of the Prime Minister's Office in all future hiring. It was a high price to pay, but without that agreement I would have resigned from the institute and then done everything possible to make sure that no Arabs would work with it in the future.

The institute worked in three main fields: education focused on developing and testing models for Jewish-Arab encounters for high school students and on developing curriculum that would add content on coexistence and democracy into the school system; training civil servants who provide services to the Arab sector; and raising issues for public debate on coexistence and democracy. The first successful and professional models of Jewish-Arab student encounters were developed, designed, and tested in the joint Jewish-Arab community of Neve Shalom–Wahat al-Salam in the early 1980s. The first course of Jewish-Arab facilitators, which I had the privilege of being part of, developed models for encounters based on the principle of cofacilitation—a Jewish facilitator and an Arab facilitator working together in pairs with mixed groups of Jewish and Arab students. The three-day encounters brought the participants through a process of getting to know each other through outwardly moving concentric circles of identity. The most inner circle was the personal (the "I"), the next circle was the family, then the community, then circles of religion, ethnicity, and then national identity. As the participants went through this process of examining their own identity and confronting the identities being presented to them by participants from the other community, they touched directly on the raw nerves of the Israeli-Arab conflict. The Neve Shalom–Wahat al-Salam model did not believe in conflict avoidance, as many of the previous models prescribed. This model led the participants to confront the conflict directly, but only after the participants were able to attach a human face, even a friendly face, to the people with whom they were arguing.

I believed in this model from the very beginning. I thought that it had all the basic elements for a successful encounter, but needed more work. The Neve Shalom–Wahat al-Salam model was based on a self-selection of participants. This was a matter of principle—only those who really wanted to participate should be participants—and the result of limited financial resources. The idea of limited smaller groups usually ensured greater quality, and the most motivated participants are usually the ones who show up. In some cases, classes selected their "ambassadors," and there were many occasions when the selection was made according to whom in the class could best represent a hard-line position. So sometimes the participants represented positions that did not allow for very much compromise or understanding.

The model was based initially on this one-time, three-day, intensive encounter and had little preparation and even less follow-up. The experience, as intensive and life changing as any three-day experience can be, left many questions unanswered. We were already getting a sense, not documented through research, but based on impression, that sometimes contact and encounters don't break down stereotypes—in fact, they sometimes reinforce them. You can often leave an experience with more evidence to prove that your stereotypes and preconceptions were correct. This led us to understand in the Institute for Education for Jewish Arab Coexistence that there is a very strong need for proper preparation and for follow-up work that can provide clarification for the participants and their teachers. Furthermore, we thought that the three-day experience should be given more substance by including additional meetings between the students before and after the experience, and that those should take place in the communities, with the schools providing more input, time, and experiences to help develop a more complex understanding of the situation. This required that we ensure the support of the schools' leadership—mainly that the principal was fully supportive of the project. Without the complete support of the principal, individual teachers participating and supporting the project would not be able to stand above all of the criticism and controversy that these programs always engendered, either from within the school, namely from other teachers, or from without, from the students' parents or from the students themselves.

Preparation for the meetings with the other side clearly became a key issue in planning the encounters. I recall a story I used to tell to Jewish classes prior to the three-day encounter. One of the problems I saw coming out of the encounters was the general attitude of many, perhaps most, of the Jewish students, which was that Arab culture in Israel was "primitive." They came away with this conclusion mainly after discussions about relations between boys and girls, dating and fixed marriages, sex before marriage, and the role and place of women in society. In many cases, the Jewish students lost respect for their Arab counterparts as a result of these cultural gaps. It is difficult to explain that when one observes and tries to understand a different culture, there is a danger of viewing it solely from your own perspective. There is a need, in order to have a deeper understanding and in order to challenge your own perspective, to view that culture from within that culture itself. This is one of the first things that any anthropologist is taught, and yet it is very difficult to detach yourself from your own perspective, values, and worldview.

The story that I told was this (and I was told the story by someone who said it was true):

In a village in West Africa where education standards and opportunities were very low, an official from the British Council discovered an extremely bright and promising young man of about fifteen years old. After a lot of work and scrambling for resources, the British Council awarded this young boy a full scholarship to one of the best private schools in the UK. This was an enormous gift, and the entire village celebrated their success and the promise that this boy would bring back after completing his education. On the eve of his departure, the boy had a nervous breakdown, not able to stop crying and shaking. It was quite clear that in this state he could not leave the village and take advantage of the scholarship. Several weeks later, the official from the British Council returned to the remote village to find out what happened. The official met the boy, who had returned to his normal happy and bright self. Perplexed by the situation, the official sat with the boy's father and some of the village elders. They explained to the British official that the nervous breakdown occurred because the boy had been told that in the UK when he would go to the bathroom, he would have to clean himself with toilet paper. He could not cope with that thought. It sounded so disgusting and primitive to him, because in his village when he went to the bathroom he would clean himself with soap and water. He simply could not cope with the primitive and unclean way the British handle their own hygiene.

When I heard this story, I thought it was the perfect trigger to discuss the importance of understanding different and foreign cultures, and to dig into the kinds of things the Jewish students would observe when they met the Arab students and got to know them. It allowed the search for answers regarding how the Arab students view their own culture rather than an immediate derogatory judgment.

We learned that it was essential to balance expectations prior to encounters and came to understand that this preparation was of equal importance to the encounter itself. Likewise, we came to understand that the follow-up to the encounter—meeting the students in their classrooms following their intensive three-day experience—was essential so that the students could voice their opinions, conclusions, and get answers to questions. Most often, the questions were of a political nature on how coexistence could be possible when the gaps in opinions were so wide between the Jewish and Arab students.

The value of what we came to call "uni-national" discussions, as we observed in the pre- and post-encounter meetings, was so high that we integrated them into the three-day encounters themselves. These three days were intense and often raised very high levels of emotion, which required that we enable the participants to take a time out and to sit in a room with their "own side" so that they could voice their thoughts and emotions in a safe environment. Usually they talked about the surprising things they heard from the other side and raised questions about the value of the meeting. These uni-national meetings usually took place during crisis moments, which always happen, almost always according to plan. There were often attacks from within each uni-national group against some of their members for voicing opinions that were outside of the norm or the consensus—usually more moderate expressions than what the rest of the group wanted to hear. Sometimes the attacks were against people who were too rigidly against the other side, and the group members expressed that they were misrepresenting the opinions of the majority. These airing out sessions proved to be a very important part of the encounters, and the time spent apart was not at all wasted time.

Years later, toward the end of the 1990s, we adopted these same methods in the Israel/Palestine Center for Research and Information (IPCRI) as part of our Peace Education Project, which focused mainly on work with Israeli and Palestinian teachers. In those encounters, which included Jewish- and Palestinian-Israeli teachers and Palestinian teachers from the West Bank, there was always an interesting and challenging question during the uni-national meetings: Where should the Palestinian-Israeli teachers go, to the Israeli group or to the Palestinian group? There were hours of discussions and debates for years amongst IPCRI's staff. We tried every possibility, including opening a third group just for the Palestinian Israelis. My own preference was to leave the decision of where to go to the participants themselves. The Palestinian-Israeli teachers would have to decide where they wanted to go and where they felt more comfortable. Not surprising to me, the majority usually chose to go to the Israeli group. In that room, they felt both more comfortable, more accepted, and I think they felt that their additional mission was to try to explain to the Israeli Jews some of the disturbing things they would hear from the Palestinian teachers. But perhaps the best solution was to have a third "uni-national" group for the Palestinian Israelis, understanding that they do not have a split identity, but rather a unique and important identity within the Israeli and Palestinian communities.

One observation that was often brought up by Jewish students who were able to overcome a lot of the anger that they heard from Arab students was that when one evaluated the demands that the Arab students were making with regard to their status in the State of Israel, the bottom line was that they were essentially demanding to be equal citizens. In their angry remarks about the lack of equality, the Arab students were demanding to be fully integrated into the state. Those were the demands made in the 1980s, and they remain the demands of today. The decision of a majority of the Palestinian-Israeli teachers to go to the Israeli uni-national meeting and not the Palestinian uni-national one is a reflection of the desire of these Palestinian-Israeli teachers to be accepted as full Israelis, once again demonstrating the potential for successful integration and full partnership between Jewish and Palestinian Israelis, if the real opportunities are created and made available.

These lessons learned are all very important. When I think back to my first experience creating encounters between Jewish and Palestinian Israelis, I recall the damage that resulted from the lack of professionalism and know-how that I brought to the field. It was when I was an Intern for Peace, living in Kufr Qara. Focusing on my own experience in a youth movement and my years of leadership training, I came up with the idea to organize a course in leadership training for young potential leaders. The value I was bringing to the table was that it would be a joint course with participants from Kufr Qara and the nearby Jewish town of Karkur. It took months to identify the local trainer from both communities and then more time to bring them together to meet, discuss, and agree on a program. Then we had to find the funding and enlist the participants, teens from both sides ages fifteen to sixteen. We succeeded in all of these tasks. The leadership training course was wonderful, and both sides learned leadership skills that at least in Kufr Qara were put to use later when we created a framework for a youth center that eventually led to the development of a full-fledged community center in Kufr Qara. The damage that we caused resulted from our lack of experience and knowledge about the best ways to get the Jewish and Arab students to interact positively. We engaged, against my better judgment and belief, in what I would call "conflict avoidance." This was the trend then, and even still exists today. It usually comes from people of good will who say, "Let's bring them together and do something neutral and avoid talking about the conflict." It sounds good, but it doesn't work. The participants from Kufr Qara and Karkur who participated in our leadership training program left the program with more negative attitudes toward the participants on the other side than positive ones.

Conflict avoidance does not work and should be avoided when bringing people from different sides of a conflict to encounter each other. It is possible to get Israeli and Arab scientists to cooperate on a scientific project, but if they avoid confronting the conflict, the relationship usually ends when the project is completed. After the signing of the Israeli Egyptian peace treaty in March 1979, the US Congress legislated the creation of a new project funded by the United States Agency for International Development (USAID) called MERC—Middle East Regional Cooperation. It was a well-funded program designed to encourage scientific research between Israeli and Arab scientists. It was the MERC fund that gave the first major grant to IPCRI's Peace Education Project and MERC's first nonscientific funded program. Being a MERC recipient in 1995 enabled me to take part in a research project conducted internally in USAID, the product of fifteen years of MERC grants. The evaluation examined the relationships that developed between Israeli and Arab scientists who were recipients of MERC grants. I encouraged the researchers to add an additional variable to their evaluation: To what extent did the participants engage in discussions about the Israeli-Arab conflict? This was not one of the areas they were planning to investigate. I speculated that those participants who dealt solely with their scientific research and engaged in the prescribed conflict avoidance would prove that the relationships basically ended when the funded research ended, in contrast to those who dealt with the conflict and so would yield a significantly higher number of participants who continued to be in contact following the conclusion of their work together. The results of this research were never published. The results were indeed dramatic. The overwhelming number of participants in the MERC-funded research programs stated that they had not continued to have contact with their colleagues on the other side, even when the research they had conducted was positive and added important knowledge to the professional literature. These people engaged in conflict avoidance. On the other side, a significant majority of participants who engaged in conflict confrontation and discussion did continue their relationships.

The Israeli Army Drafts Me

7

In 1987, at the age of thirty, I was drafted into the Israeli Army. It didn't come as a surprise; in fact, I had planned it in advance and was well prepared to make sure that the army would make the best use of my time and abilities. Had I been drafted at a younger age, I probably would have been a combat soldier and would have had to serve at least two years. In that situation, there is little doubt that I would have been confronted with political and moral dilemmas that would have forced me to refuse orders, such as serving in the occupied territories or serving in the war in Lebanon in 1982, things I would have refused to do and, therefore, would have landed me in prison. But fortunately for me, the Israeli Army has a special program for new immigrants who get drafted at an older age. Normally, Israelis are drafted at the age of eighteen, and young men serve for three years while young women serve for two years. Immigrants at the age of thirty and above, during my time, were drafted into *Shlav Bet* (second phase), a special program for older draftees that lasted a period of four months, which included basic training for seven weeks and then the remaining time with a unit to which you were assigned for reserve duty until the age of forty-five. Most of the draftees are sent to semicombat positions as guards in settlements or checkpoints, or in the army corps of engineers, or as combat medics.

In 1986, as director of the Institute for Education for Jewish Arab Coexistence, I led a project that consisted of writing a curriculum for Israeli high schools on Jewish-Arab relations. One of the teachers working on the project was Leah Praver, who taught civics and history at the Hebrew University High School. Leah's husband, Udi Praver, was then the deputy chief education officer of the Israeli Army and had the rank of colonel. (Udi later became famous while working in the Prime Minister's Office. He was in charge of the plan for the resettlement of the Bedouin, known as the Praver plan, which was highly unpopular and harshly disputed by the Bedouin and the Israeli left.) When our team completed the first draft of the curriculum, we asked Udi to read it and review it. Well, Udi didn't like it. He tossed it in the trash and said we needed to start over. Udi took two weeks off from work in the army and spent the next fourteen days with our small team, almost 24/7—it was one of the most intensive work experiences that I have ever had.

Writing a curriculum for the Jewish secondary school system in Israel on the question of Jewish-Arab relations, democracy, and coexistence requires quite a lot of ideological challenges and clarification. How democratic can a state be that defines itself as a nation-state of the majority ethnic/national/religious group, when it also has a significant minority population that does not identify with the state's raison d'état? The Palestinian-Arab citizens of Israel cannot identify with their state's symbols, such as the Israeli flag designed and modeled on the Jewish prayer shawl, the *Talit*, and the national anthem, *Hatikva*, which speaks about Jewish longing for the Land of Israel. Additionally, this minority group—the Palestinian citizens of Israel—are directly identified with the main enemy of the state—the Palestinian people. Our team, which included Leah Praver, Udi Praver, Ori Geva, a teacher at the Hebrew University High School, and Mohammed Abu Nimer, who worked with me at the institute and later was to become a world-renown professor of conflict resolution at American University in Washington, DC, and me. We spent countless hours arguing, discussing, role-playing. We worked from early morning until late at night in order to fully utilize Udi's two weeks with us. During those two weeks, we wrote thirty-two lesson plans. Ori's brother, the famous (late) cartoonist Dudu Geva, sketched several political caricatures for the final product, which we called "At the Crossroads."[1]

One of my favorite of the curriculum activities was a role-playing game in which the students were given the task to develop and act out a situation where they were Arabs in an Arab high school in Israel before Israeli Independence Day, and they had to prepare the school ceremony for that day. The various roles included the students, the teachers, the principal of the school, the head of the parents' committee, the town's mayor, and a senior Israeli-Jewish official from the Ministry of Education. This activity prompted the Jewish students to directly address the complexities of being an Arab citizen in Israel. It confronted symbols of the state, which are clearly Jewish (the flag and the national anthem), as well as issues of identity—my people and my state. Those ceremonies are no longer done in Arab schools in Israel, but the schools are required to fly an Israeli flag, and the principal's office will always have the symbol of the state (a menorah) and pictures of the president and the prime minister.

The curriculum was an instant "hit," and the institute spent the next years conducting in-service teachers' training in high schools all over the country. The in-service training was conducted in schools that agreed to have all of their teachers participate and was held over three evenings—once a week for three weeks, providing about fifteen hours of training. The program was a mix of lectures, discussions, and demonstrations of the thirty-two lesson plans in the curriculum. It was a great success, and the requests from schools to participate was far higher than our ability to meet the demand. Udi Praver adopted many of the lesson plans and integrated them into a course at the College for the Education of Officers.

The following year, we devoted equal time and resources to develop a curriculum for the Arab high schools. The principal authors were Mohammed Abu Nimer and his then girlfriend and later wife Ilham Nasser. The curriculum for the Arab schools was called *Misuliati*, meaning "my responsibility." It focused on what it means to be an active participant in one's society and went from concentric identity circles of the individual, to the family, the extended family, the class, the school, the town or village, the Arab citizens of Israel, the Jews of the State of Israel, the State of Israel, the Palestinian people, the Arab world, Muslims or Christians, and finally, the rest of humanity. It put an emphasis on personal and collective responsibility in the various circles of identity. The curriculum was built on exercises that focused on clarification of values, role-playing activities, discussions, and lectures. It too was a big success in the Arab schools in Israel.

Lt. Colonel, Deputy Chief Education, Officer of the Israel Defense Forces (IDF) Udi Praver decided to introduce the subject of "Jewish-Arab coexistence" amongst Israel's citizens to the Israeli Army's College for the Education of Officers, which was responsible for running educational courses about Israeli society.

In 1984, Meir Kahane and his racist Kach party was elected to the Knesset. The Kach party's platform was to expel Israeli Arabs from the country. After he was elected, a survey of Jewish youth attitudes toward Arabs was conducted by Professor Sami Smooha from Haifa University, which found alarmingly high rates of racism amongst Israel's Jewish youth. I proposed to the chairman of the Education Committee of the Knesset, Mapam Member of Knesset Elazar Granot, to convene a special session of the committee dedicated to the phenomenon of Kahanism amongst the youth. I was privileged to have been given the right to be the first speaker in the discussion in which I said that a cancer of racism was growing within our society and it was being treated with aspirin. We needed much stronger measures. My speech made the headlines of the next day's leading newspapers.

Udi Praver agreed with that assessment and was committed to finding a way to introduce this subject even within the educational programs of the Israeli Army. Udi put together a team at the College for the Training Education of Officers at Har Gilo to work on developing a program. He asked me to join the team. I gladly took part, and for the next two years, I volunteered to work on developing the program and then to be a lecturer and facilitator for courses. The college was running a three-week course on Israeli society, which was an obligatory course to get the rank of major. The new course that we developed included one week on questions of identity that were mostly focused on the axis of Israeli-Jewish and religious-secular, one week on social gaps within Israeli society, and one week on Jewish-Arab relations and democracy in Israel. During the final week, the officers even spent a full day in Um el Fahem, an Arab city in the center of the country, where they spent a few hours in the city's high school, went home for lunch with teachers, and met with local leaders in the afternoon.

The army used many of the lesson plans we developed for "At the Crossroads," and the one week on Jewish-Arab relations usually included a lecture from me. This program continued from 1984 until the end of 1987 when the first intifada began. It was quite amazing that the army decided to take on the challenge of dealing with this issue, and I was honored to be part of it. When I had proposed the visit in Um el Fahem, I had initially insisted that the participating officers go in "civvies," not in their uniforms. The chief of staff of the army refused, he said that they are officers of the Israeli Army and they had to wear their uniforms. I then insisted that they could not walk around Um el Fahem with their guns; this would cause a riot and create the wrong impression—rather than coming to learn, they would be seen as coming to conquer. Here, the army agreed with me, and two soldiers were left outside of the city in the bus with all of the weapons while the other officers spent the day in Um el Fahem, unarmed.

By volunteering for two years with the College for the Training Education of Officers in the Israeli Army, I knew that once I was drafted, the college would request that I be stationed there after my basic training. In March 1987, I was inducted into the Israeli Army. I spent seven weeks in the most basic of basic training a soldier could receive. Everyone in my group was older than thirty. Our officers and trainers were all nineteen or twenty years old. Many of the group were religious. Almost all were professionals. All were new immigrants, including a small group of Ethiopians who barely spoke Hebrew, having just arrived in the country.

We were "gunnery 02"—almost the lowest level of military training. We had to learn to use three guns: the M16, Uzi, and Galil rifles. We had to know how to use hand grenades. We had one week of basic field training, which reminded me of summer camp. And we had to learn basic first aid. We had the feeling that the army didn't take too seriously the need to properly train us for combat. When we got to hand grenades, they didn't have enough "dummy" grenades for us to practice with, so some of us threw stones and made believe that they were grenades.

Most of the graduates of our basic training did not become combat soldiers, but some did. Most became guards in settlements and checkpoints, and were in situations where they were in positions of real security responsibility. The level of military training was certainly not sufficient for those positions. I would say that we could have completed all of the training easily in two weeks. Most of what we had to learn was patience. Hurry up and wait. We were ordered to do things in periods of thirty seconds. Thirty seconds to get dressed. Thirty seconds to put on your shoes. Thirty seconds to take apart your M16, and thirty seconds to put it together again. We were ordered to run from place to place. The physical part of the basic training was not at all challenging. For me, the most challenging parts were all of the hours that we waited around doing nothing.

I spoke with my platoon commander and complained about the wasted time. I told him that we had a lot of really interesting people in the platoon, and we could use the time by having everyone make a presentation about something that they did in their life outside of the army. Even without the formal permission of the army, that is what we did. I, of course, spoke about the issue of Jewish-Arab relations.

We were stationed in the Dotan Army Base in the West Bank in the Jenin district next to the Palestinian village of Arabe. The village was on one side of the base and the village school was on the other. In order for the school-children to get to school, they would have to walk in front of the base. On mornings or afternoons when I was on guard duty, I would try to greet the children with a few friendly words in Arabic. They must have thought I was from another planet. They looked at me with a strange look in their eyes and crossed to the other side of the street so that they wouldn't have to talk to me. Over time, they would cross to the other side as soon as they saw me so that they wouldn't even have to look at me. I was a soldier, the occupier—how could it be possible that I was greeting them with a friendly voice and not yelling at them or telling to the run home? It was too strange for them. It was pretty strange for me, too.

While I was in basic training, my wife and daughter went to America to visit family. My daughter was about one year old. When they returned, I got an afternoon and evening off from the army to pick them up at the airport. I had to get back to the base early the next morning, which was not easy. There was no good public transportation, and I thought once I got to Hadera by bus, I would rely on hitch hiking. I arrived in Hadera and walked from the bus station to the main road heading out of town. As I was walking, a taxi honked at me. It was a friend from Kufr Qara. Now I was a soldier carrying an M16 rifle, not a volunteer community organizer working for peace. The driver, surprised to see me asked me where I was going. I told him that I had to get to my base in Dotan. He said, "Hop in, I'll take you." This was great, but what would happen when I arrived at the base coming out of an Arab taxi. We had explicit orders not to take rides from Arabs, foreigners, or UN personnel. This was not just a passing Arab car that took me. I knew the driver well. I knew his family; I had been a guest in his home. It was strange for me to be in his car as a soldier in uniform carrying my M16 rifle. I used to ride with him from Kufr Qara to Hadera frequently when I lived there.

When I arrived at the base and got out of the car and parted from my friend from Kufr Qara, I got a lot of strange looks from the guards on duty that were well aware of the prohibition against traveling in Arab taxis. I immediately reported to my commanding officer that I had returned and how I arrived. I didn't want any rumors floating around the base. This little story of a soldier and an Arab taxi driver is just one small example of the complexities and contradictions of daily life in Israel, especially for someone like me who travels back and forth over the conflict lines.

The most interesting part of basic training was a week we spent on the Lebanese border, going inside to Lebanon every day where we were employed in repairing barbed wire fences at army bases and outposts in the so-called "security zone." I learned that week how penetrable barbed wire fencing is and how to cut it, bend it, and make it completely ineffective. I also learned how to put it together and surround a large area. I never fought in Lebanon (or in any other place) as a soldier, but I do get to say that I was in Lebanon!

After basic training, I was invited by the College for the Training Education of Officers to join their team. The college was located in Har Gilo, a settlement on the top of Beit Jala, the Palestinian city above Bethlehem, just beyond the Green Line. The college was commanded by Lieutenant Colonel Rabbi Naftali Rothenberg. Naftali was an officer, a gentleman, and a rabbi—in fact, the chief rabbi of the Jerusalem suburb of Har Adar. Naftali was excited about having me under his command for the next three months. He wanted me to work with the officers running the three-week mandatory course on Israeli society that was a requirement for the rank of major—the course that I helped to develop. He had a problem though. My rank was private and the course participants were captains and majors. I could not be their commanding officer even during the short period of the course. So Naftali told me: don't wear your uniform, and then you won't have any ranks on you. If you don't wear a uniform, you can't carry a gun. And if the officers ask you what your rank is—tell them Lieutenant Colonel! In order for our little charade to appear real, he also ordered me to sit with him at the commander's table for all meals. This was quite an amazing way to do my military service.

To top it off, I was living at the time on Derech Hebron in south Jerusalem, the main street in Talpiot. This was the thoroughfare on which Palestinian shared taxis traveled to and from Bethlehem. I would stop a taxi in front of my house and travel to Bethlehem, getting off at the bottom of the road that leads to Beit Jala (and Har Gilo). This was all before the first intifada and before Oslo. There was no Bethlehem bypass road. Israeli traffic going to the south of the West Bank or going to the south of Israel via Jerusalem went on this road. At the bottom of Beit Jala, I would either get into another Palestinian taxi that would take me up to the top of Beit Jala and then I would walk ten minutes to Har Gilo, or a soldier or military vehicle would pass and take me. I was not wearing a uniform or carrying a gun, so this was the fastest way of getting from my home to the base every morning. I forgot to mention that I was also allowed to go home every day. On most days, I got a ride from someone from Har Gilo going to Jerusalem.

I finished my army service in September 1987 and became a reserve officer-lecturer in the college for the next fifteen years. At the end of December 1987, the first intifada broke out (we didn't know at that time that we would call it "the first"). Shortly after that time, the army college ceased the program on coexistence and democracy. In March 1988, I left the Institute for Education for Jewish Arab Coexistence and founded IPCRI. The intifada created the opportunity to foresee the eventual creation of a real peace process based on mutual recognition and the two-state solution.

Most Israelis had no idea what the intifada was about. The public was taken by surprise. The army was just as surprised by the sudden burst of political energy coming from a population that had been calm for twenty years. Overnight everything that we knew about the Palestinians or thought that we knew was changed. There were very few Israeli experts who could explain what was happening. I had begun spending most of my time meeting Palestinians throughout the West Bank (and a little in Gaza). I was gaining insights into the events of the intifada, and I began writing and publishing my ideas.

I was then called in by the College for the Training Education of Officers to lecture about the intifada and the Palestinians. In 1988, the Education Corps of the IDF decided to send all of its lecturers to spend a week in the north of Israel. This was one of the more bizarre yet interesting weeks I have ever had. I was asked, of course, to lecture about the intifada. Most of the soldiers stationed in the north either just came out of the Palestinian territories or were about to be sent there. They were curious about the intifada and wanted to have a greater understanding of what was going on, what the Palestinians were fighting for, and where it all would. For a week, I was driven around in a jeep to bases and positions all along the northern border between Israel, Lebanon, and the Golan Heights. In between giving lectures in small outposts to ten soldiers at a time, I would drive along patrol roads. We would stop command cars on patrol, they would get out of the jeep, and on the dirt road I would give them a short lecture about the intifada. Definitely a scene out of a movie. Too surreal to believe. The weather was great, the air fresh and the skies clear. There was no real plan for where I was going and who I would speak to. I was required to give a certain number of talks each day, and the coordination took place by walkie-talkie. I was one of about thirty lecturers roaming around the north in search of military subjects to listen to us. Some of the soldiers I met had received three or four lectures a day.

During the years when I lectured about Israeli Arabs, mostly in the Israeli army, I was paired with Shmuel Toledano, who had been the Advisor on Arab Affairs to several prime ministers. Shmuel was a great lecturer, and his background and demeanor gave him a lot of credibility in the eyes of the soldiers. I, on the other hand, would say almost the same things that Shmuel would say, but my words drew fire from the soldiers. I talked about the history of the Israeli-Arab population in Israel. My focus was on their desire to be integrated into the country on an equal basis. The issue of discrimination came up, and I would provide them with many examples of how the state discriminated against its Arab citizens. It was a lively talk and challenging and definitely provoked a lot of argument.

Once a soldier approached me at the end of the lecture and told me, "The only reason I didn't take my gun and shoot you is because I was sitting on my hands to prevent myself." My lecture was probably the first time that these young Israelis encountered the issue of discrimination against Arabs in Israel. They had been told so many times that Israel is the only democracy in the Middle East. The reality that I painted for them was too difficult to handle. But two hours later, they would hear the same thing exactly from Shmuel Toledano, and they accepted his message much more easily. We found, after doing the "Baskin-Toledano" show many times, that the impact of the two lectures together was much stronger than when either of us did it alone. I think that the "Baskin-Toledano" show performed at least one hundred times.

The First Engagement—The Intifada

8 I continued directing the Institute for Education for Jewish Arab Coexistence until the beginning of the first intifada, actually until the fourth month of the first intifada. The first intifada broke out on December 9, 1987. I, like most Israelis, was struck that something very different and new was happening. It took the Palestinians twenty years—since the beginning of the Israeli occupation in June 1967—to rise up against Israel. One evening in early 1988, I was busy conducting a teacher training on Jewish Arab coexistence in a Jewish High School in Beersheba. The Jewish teachers were talking about the intifada, and I heard them complain, "How could they do this to us, we have been so good to them. Under our rule they opened universities, schools and hospitals, they have work in Israel, etc." They, like parrots, repeated the myth of the "benevolent occupation" as if Palestinians should be thankful to Israel for occupying them and denying them independence and liberation. They didn't have the experience of living under occupation and only the few soldiers who then served in the territories really knew about it. From 1967 until the outbreak of the intifada at the end of 1987, the Palestinian population of the West Bank and Gaza was a relatively quiet group of people. They experienced quite significant economic development there after the beginning of the Israeli occupation. There were no real borders between Israel and the West Bank and Gaza. People were free to move, even in their own cars. Palestinian taxis drove the roads of Israel. At the high point, it is estimated that some two hundred thousand Palestinians were working in Israel. Many Israelis ventured into the occupied territories for shopping, eating at restaurants, repairing their cars, and even using Palestinian dentists, who were much cheaper than Israeli dentists. All of that came to an abrupt end with the beginning of the first intifada.

The first intifada struck me as something monumental that was happening in the occupied territories, and I really wanted to understand it. Was this the moment I had been waiting for since my meeting with the PLO ambassador in New York in 1976? On December 9, 1987, an Israeli Army heavy truck crashed into a Palestinian van carrying Palestinian workers from the Jabalya refugee camp in Gaza. Four of the workers were killed. Upon hearing news of the death of the workers, massive demonstrations spontaneously erupted in Jabalya and across Gaza. Thousands of young men and women led marches toward Israeli camps and military positions.

In twenty years of occupation, the Israeli Army had never seen such a show of resistance. Within days, demonstrations spread across the occupied territories into Gaza and the West Bank, as well. Yitzhak Rabin, the defense minister, was in Washington at the time the demonstrations broke out. On the second day of the revolt, speaking on Israeli radio, Rabin was asked, "Don't you think you should come back?" He responded that the demonstrations would end in a day or two. How wrong he was. They did not—in fact, they intensified. The intifada was born. Intifada was a new word in both the Palestinian and the Israeli vocabulary. In Arabic, the word means to shake off, intending to symbolize the Palestinian demands to shake off the Israeli occupation, but also to shake off the old, tired leadership and ideology of the Palestinian national movement.

I began reading the political leaflets that were being distributed by what was called the United Command of the intifada, which represented the four main political movements of the PLO: Fatah, the Palestinian Communist Party, the Popular Front for the Liberation of Palestine, and the Democratic Front for the Liberation of Palestine. The language used was quite new and very different from the PLO political platform. I searched for the words of the PLO ambassador in New York who in 1976 told me that the Palestinians would never recognize Israel and that the Jews should go back to where they came from. Gone were the calls for the destruction of Israel. Instead, they were demanding an end to Israel's occupation of the territories conquered in 1967. Instead, they wanted to establish an independent state next to Israel, not in place of Israel.

The first leaflet contained the normally bombastic rhetoric of the Palestinian struggle, but it did not include the demands of the Palestinian National Covenant, which called for Israel's destruction.

Excerpt from Comminiqué No. 1 of the Intifada (January 8, 1988)
In the name of God, the merciful, the compassionate.
Our people's glorious uprising continues. We affirm the need to express solidarity with our people wherever they are. We continue to be loyal to the pure blood of our martyrs and to our detained brothers. We also reiterate our rejection of the occupation and its policy of repression, represented in the policy of deportation, mass arrests, curfews, and the demolition of houses. . . . Down with occupation; long live Palestine as a free and Arab country.

On January 14, 1988, the United Command issued a document with its main political demands. The document was authored primarily by Dr. Sari Nuseibeh and Ziad Abu Zayyad, both of whom were in Jerusalem, and not from the PLO leadership in Tunis. This document is especially significant because it was issued by the local Palestinian leaders in the occupied territories and because it strayed significantly from the original PLO covenant in support of "one secular democratic state in all of Palestine." The emphasis of the document was life in the occupied territories:

> We call upon the Israeli authorities to comply with the following list of demands as a means to prepare the atmosphere for the convening of the suggested international peace conference, which will ensure a just and lasting settlement of the Palestinian problem in all its aspects, bringing about the realization of the inalienable national rights of the Palestinian people, peace and stability for the peoples of the region, and an end to violence and bloodshed:
>
> To abide by the 4th Geneva Convention and all other international agreements pertaining to the protection of civilians, their properties and rights under a state of military occupation. . . . The immediate compliance with the Security Council Resolutions 605 and 607, which call upon Israel to abide by the Geneva Convention of 1949 and the Declaration of Human Rights; and which further call for the achievement of a just and lasting settlement of the Arab-Israeli conflict.
>
> The release of all prisoners who were arrested during the recent uprising, and foremost amongst them our children. Also the rescinding of all proceedings and indictments against them. . . . The cancellation of the policy of expulsion, allowing all exiled Palestinians, including the four sent yesterday into exile, to return to their homes and families; also the release of all administrative detainees and the cancellation of the hundreds of house arrest orders. . . . The immediate lifting of the siege of all Palestinian refugee camps in the West Bank and Gaza and the withdrawal of the Israeli Army from all population centers. . . . A cessation of all settlement activity and land confiscation, and the release of lands already confiscated. . . . Refraining from any act which might impinge on the Muslim and Christian holy sites or which might introduce change to the status quo in the city of Jerusalem. . . . The cancellation of all restrictions on political freedoms, including the restrictions on meetings and conventions; also making provisions for free municipal elections under the supervision of a neutral authority. . . . The removal of the restrictions on political contacts between inhabitants of the Occupied Territories and the PLO, in such a way as to allow for the participation of Palestinians from the Occupied Territories in the proceedings of the Palestinian National Council, in order to ensure a direct input into the decision-

making processes of the Palestinian Nation by the Palestinians under occupation

I had to find out if these positions reflected what the population in the occupied territories was really demanding. I had to know if the Palestinians were developing a new agenda that would lead to the recognition of Israel and the support of the two-state solution. The reference in the beginning of the document to *"peace and stability for the peoples of the region"* was coded language referring to the Jewish people. Later in similar texts, the Palestinian leadership would use the term "peace and security for all of the States of the region," referring to Israel without mentioning Israel explicitly. I understood this to be the first official steps of the Palestinians on the road to the explicit recognition of Israel, which would lead to a peace process.

On Saturday morning March 5, 1988, I decided that I was going to go and meet Palestinians and find out firsthand what was going on. I knew that it was risky and perhaps outright dangerous, but I got on my little 1963 multicolored Vespa mini-motorcycle and drove into the Dheisha refugee camp. Dheisha is the largest refugee camp in the West Bank, situated on the main road that in the past was the main thoroughfare leading from Jerusalem to Hebron. There were no bypass roads in those days that enabled Israelis to avoid entering Palestinian areas. I knew the road to Bethlehem quite well because almost every Friday I would do my weekly fruit and vegetable shopping there. Also during 1986 and 1987, prior to the outbreak of the intifada, I often held staff meetings of the Institute for Education for Jewish Arab Coexistence at one of two restaurants in Bethlehem, not far from Manger Square.

During those days, there was a small Israeli command post on the road directly across from the refugee camp. The camp was surrounded with a metal fence about twelve yards high to prevent the "shabab," the young people, from throwing stones at Israeli cars passing by, which were, more often than not, either settlers or army vehicles. From the beginning of the intifada, most Israelis stopped traveling on this road that also connected Jerusalem and Beersheba. Going there that Saturday morning was not the safest thing to do, but nonetheless, my need to listen to Palestinians and to try to understand what they really wanted compelled me to go.

I drove into the UN school at the entrance to the camp, took off my helmet, and was immediately approached by a group of young people. With my less than fluent Arabic I told them that I was an Israeli and that I wanted to learn about the intifada from their eyes, from their perspective. I said I wanted to know what they were fighting for. We stood there talking for about twenty minutes and then one of the people invited us to go to his home and talk. About thirty other people came along. The "home" was little more than a one-room space that served as a kitchen, living room, and bedroom for a family of seven people. Mattresses for sleeping were piled high in one corner. There was a straw carpet mat on the floor. I took off my shoes, as is the custom, and we sat on mattresses spread around the room. I spent about six hours in Dheisha that day. Upon leaving, I was buzzing with energy and excitement (and not just from all of the strong Arab coffee I drank!) because I heard things there that I had never heard from Palestinians before then.

What I heard from these young people, mostly young men, in Dheisha in March 1988 was, "End the occupation, let us create the Palestinian state, and let's live side by side in peace." No one told me, "You should go back to where you came from." This was very different from everything I had heard from Palestinians before who said, "No two-state solution, only the secular democratic state." This was the official platform of the Palestinian National Movement until then. While I was aware that there were changes going on in the PLO since the 1970s, it was also true that those people who were leading the changes were subsequently executed, and Palestinian moderates within the PLO were not known to survive very long. Two prominent examples of PLO leaders who reached out to engage Israelis with the support of PLO leader Yasser Arafat were Said Hamami and Dr. Isam Sartawi.[1] Said Hamami was a Palestinian politician and diplomat who was murdered on January 4, 1978, in London, where he was serving as the PLO representative. In that position, he began advocating coexistence between a future Palestinian state and the State of Israel. He was murdered by the Abu Nidal terror group. Sartawi advocated positions supporting the proposed peace plan of US President Ronald Reagan and held public meetings with prominent Israeli leftists supporting Israeli-Palestinian peace. He was the PLO representative to the Socialist International and was murdered in April 1983 in Portugal at a meeting of the Socialist International. The Abu Nidal group claimed responsibility for his assassination, as well.

Now beginning in December 1978, here was an uprising that was based on the Palestinian population in Palestine, emerging from the refugee camps—the very symbol of Palestinian collective national memory—that was essentially calling to recognize Israel and establish a Palestinian state next to Israel and not in its place. Instructions weren't coming from the PLO leadership in Tunisia; they were coming from the West Bank and Gaza, from the refugee camps and from the leading Palestinian intellectuals living under Israeli occupation. I believed and hoped that the moment had come when Israeli-Palestinian engagement could occur.

Many of the political leaflets distributed throughout the occupied territories even made specific calls to the Israeli public, such as this one:

LEAFLET NUMBER 29, NOVEMBER 11, 1988
An active international conference under UN supervision with the participation of the five permanent members of the Security Council and all parties to the conflict [including] the PLO, our sole legitimate representative, as an equal party, and on the basis of UN Resolutions 242 and 338 with the right of self-determination for our Palestinian people. This emphasis demonstrates our people's devotion and sincerity and its aspirations to establish a just and comprehensive peace in light of the détente in the international arena and the tendency to resolve regional conflicts on the basis of international legitimatization.

What is particularly noteworthy here is that until the first intifada the Palestinian leadership rejected UN Resolutions 242 and 338 because they explicitly referred to the legitimacy of Israel's existence and make no mention of the Palestinian issue other than as a problem of refugees. Israel and the United States had demanded that the PLO accept these resolutions and renounce violence—the armed struggle—as a precondition for the PLO to be accepted as a representative party to the conflict. This was not yet the position of the PLO leadership in exile, but it seemed clear to me that change was coming. Resolution 242 established the principle of land for peace and would later become the international basis for the Israeli-Palestinian peace process.

On November 15, 1988, Yasser Arafat convened the Palestinian National Council, the body representing all Palestinians all over the world and declared the independence of the State of Palestine. Arafat had asked Mahmoud Darwish, the Palestinian national poet, to draft the Palestinian Declaration of Independence. Mahmoud Darwish was born in the village of al-Birwa in the Western Galilee in August 1942. In 1948, his family fled to Lebanon, but returned to the newborn State of Israel one year later. His village had been destroyed, and so his family relocated in Acco. He attended school in the village of Kafr Yassif where he finished high school. Darwish's formative years were already during the existence of Israel. He was an Israeli citizen until he left the country and denounced his citizenship in 1973 when he joined the PLO and moved to Lebanon. As a young Israeli attending a state school, Darwish was required to study Israel's Declaration of Independence. When Arafat tasked him with the drafting of the Palestinian Declaration, Darwish first referred to the Israeli document to see what was written there.

The primary drafter of the Israeli Declaration of Independence was Israel's founding father, its first prime minister, David Ben-Gurion. Ben-Gurion was conscious of the mounting pressure on the Jewish leadership to postpone its declaration of independence after the fighting emerged, following the UN decision on partition on November 29, 1947. Ben-Gurion knew that he would have to legitimize, without any question or doubt, the rights of the Jewish people to establish a state of their own in the Land of Israel. Israel's Declaration of Independence is a brilliant document that, paragraph by paragraph, justifies the existence of Israel and explains why the Jewish people have a right and an obligation to establish their state. The declaration begins: "ERETZ-ISRAEL [(Hebrew), the Land of Israel] was the birthplace of the Jewish people. Here their spiritual, religious, and political identity was shaped. Here they first attained to statehood, created cultural values of national and universal significance and gave to the world the eternal Book of Books."

Mahmoud Darwish, in reading the Israeli Declaration saw the brilliance of the document and decided that the Palestinians needed their own document justifying their existence as a people and their right to establish their state. The Palestinian declaration begins: "In the name of God, the Compassionate, the Merciful, Palestine, the land of the three monotheistic faiths, is where the Palestinian Arab people was born, on which it grew, developed and excelled. Thus the Palestinian Arab people ensured for itself an everlasting union between itself, its land, and its history."

I strongly recommend reading both documents in their entirety, but I would like to point out one very significant difference between the two declarations. The ultimate justification for the establishment of both Israel and Palestine is what is called "international legitimacy." This refers to the United Nations decision (UNGA Resolution 181) to partition Palestine into two states. Both declarations refer to this resolution. At the time of the UN decision, the Palestinians rejected the right of the international community to partition Palestine, yet forty years later, they use that very resolution to justify the creation of their state. In the Israeli Declaration, there is no mention of the decision to partition Palestine, only the decision to create the Jewish state. "On the 29th November, 1947, the United Nations General Assembly passed a resolution calling for the establishment of a Jewish State in Eretz-Israel." The Palestinian Declaration refers to the decision in this way: "Despite the historical injustice inflicted on the Palestinian Arab people resulting in their dispersion and depriving them of their right to self-determination, following upon UN General Assembly Resolution 181 (1947), which partitioned Palestine into two states, one Arab, one Jewish, it is this Resolution that still provides those conditions of international legiti-

macy that ensure the right of the Palestinian Arab people to sovereignty."
What I find particularly noteworthy is the mention of the "Jewish State" in
the Palestinian Declaration of Independence.

When I read the Palestinian Declaration and the political statement of
the Palestine National Council that was accepted with it, I was convinced
that the Palestinian national movement had turned the page of history and
was prepared to enter into what would become a peace process with Israel
on the basis of two states for two peoples. That moment that I had been
waiting for since my meeting with the PLO ambassador in New York City
in 1976 had finally arrived.

Inventing IPCRI

9 When I got home from my day in Dheisha on March 5, 1988, I wrote a letter of resignation to the board of the Institute for Education for Jewish Arab Coexistence, which I founded and had directed since 1983. I then drafted a small advertisement to publish in Palestinian daily newspapers. Remember that we are in the pre-email, pre-Internet, pre-Facebook era (sometimes hard to recall). I went down to East Jerusalem to the offices of the three leading Palestinian daily newspapers (*Al-Quds, Al-Fajr,* and *Al-Shaab*) and I published the ad. That in itself was not an easy task because I did not know the people who ran the newspapers and they did not know me, and suspicion was the name of the game. I wrote the ads in English and asked them to translate them to Arabic—they ultimately appeared in both Arabic and English. I asked that it go in on a Friday morning. Selecting Friday was part of my cultural ignorance at that time. I thought, like in Israel, the weekend newspaper is the one that is sold the most. In Palestine, Friday is the day off for many people, and it is the day when the least amount of newspapers is sold. I did not know that then.

The ad said, "If you believe in the two-state solution, if you believe that Palestinians and Israelis can work together to develop peace, if you are a university graduate, if you're curious about this, give me a call," and I put my home phone number. By Saturday night, I had received forty-three phone calls. I had some very interesting conversations throughout the weekend. I scheduled appointments with anyone who was willing to meet me. I took a table in the courtyard of the American Colony Hotel in East Jerusalem, and for five days I sat there and I met twenty-three people. At those meetings, the idea of creating IPCRI was born.

In preparation for those meetings, I wrote a one-and-a-half-page paper in which I suggested that the Israeli-Palestinian conflict was no longer an existential conflict. It was no longer "us *or* them." The political developments of the intifada had transformed the conflict to be about specific issues, from the existential into "us *and* them," and the question had become "how?" I proposed that the issues in conflict consisted of the following: (1) the creation of the Palestinian state next to Israel and the nature of its sovereignty; (2) the delineation of borders between the two states; (3) the physical link between the two Palestinian territories of the West Bank and Gaza with Israel in the middle; (4) Palestinian refugees and their rights; (5) the future of Jerusalem—the city central to both peoples identity, holy to three monotheistic religions; (6) the question of economic relations between the two states with a huge socioeconomic development gap between them; and (7) the issue of water and natural resources that are shared by both. I would now add as a specific issue (8) the challenges of security.

Amazingly, every single Palestinian of the twenty-three with whom I met during those days in March 1988 agreed with what I had written. There was no dispute. Intuitively I knew that the first step toward achieving conflict resolution is agreeing on what you are fighting about. It now seemed apparent to me that we had reached that point. There were so many questions without answers, but the starting point for working together was clear to me: the end game, or agreeing on the solution to the conflict, had to be stated at the beginning and then the details of how to implement it would become the focus of the work that needed to be undertaken. If we began bringing experts together from both sides to come up with proposals for how to resolve the issues in conflict, the starting point would be, I proposed, the two-state solution—ending the Israeli occupation over the West Bank and Gaza, creating the Palestinian state next to Israel, and developing relations and mechanisms for real, mutually beneficial, cross-boundary cooperation in every field possible. This idea was quite revolutionary at the time. Less than five percent of Israeli Jews supported the idea of a Palestinian state next to Israel. This was perceived as an existential threat to the State of Israel, and people who supported it were often thought of as traitors. It was also a quite radical approach because I said that, in order to make real progress toward resolving the conflict, we would not argue about the solution. The solution is the two states, existing side by side in peace. Now, the question is how to get there. Or put alternatively, the suggestion was that we engage in "reverse engineering"—if we want to get to the two-state solution, let's work backward from there and see what needs to be done.

I began to lay the groundwork by speaking to experts in the field, people who had more knowledge and experience than me. Almost everyone I spoke to was inspired and excited about the idea. Initially there was no problem finding Israelis who were willing to give their name and support, to be on the board of directors of this joint institute, and to participate in joint Israeli-Palestinian working groups. The people contacted were the "usual suspects," those who already supported the two-state solution, even though at that time they represented a small minority. The most important meeting I held was with Member of Knesset General (reserves) Dr. Matty Peled. Peled was a member of the left-wing party Progressive List of Peace, and although a general who served in the command of the IDF during the 1967 Six-Day War, he had come to realize that there was no military solution to the Israeli-Arab conflict, and as an expert in Arabic and Arabic literature, he sought out political solutions. Peled's advice to me was worth gold! He said, "Gershon, we don't need another leftist peace group that is going to organize demonstrations on dark street corners that no one ever sees. If you are going to succeed you must bring to the table the people who are in the center of Israeli decision-making. You must bring the Israeli establishment to talk to the Palestinians." He further said, "Don't tell anyone you spoke to me. If you need me, my door is always open to you." I listened to him carefully and then acted on what he said. Unfortunately, Peled passed away in 1995 at the age of seventy-two. In 1997, Peled's granddaughter Smadar was killed by a Palestinian suicide bomber in the center of Jerusalem. She was thirteen years old and laid to rest next to her grandfather.

On the Palestinian side, the challenge was much more difficult. I did not know people in the Palestinian leadership. My work for the previous ten years had been in the "Arab sector" in Israel. I knew all of the active players and important Palestinians leaders who were citizens of Israel. I now had to reach out to people who did not know me at all. I spent many hours meeting people in East Jerusalem, which at that time was the political capital of the Palestinian people. I had always explored East Jerusalem out of curiosity and interest, frequently in search of the best humus. East Jerusalem was not strange to me, but although I knew my way around and knew the geography, I did not know people there. I also had to go to Ramallah, including the main bastion of Palestinian politics at the time, Birzeit University. I had been in Ramallah a few times, but I can't say that I felt comfortable there. During this time of the first intifada, there was danger for a Jewish Israeli to wander around Palestinian areas. Israeli cars were often stoned on the roads in the occupied territories. Since there were no bypass roads, they all went directly through the Palestinian cities, towns, and villages. My new Palestinian friends advised me to keep a kaffiyeh in the car and put it on the dashboard when I traveled through Palestinian areas. I would remove it when passing by Israeli Army checkpoints or settlement areas. I bought a second kaffiyeh for when I would walk around in Ramallah or East Jerusalem or other Palestinian areas. I would leave one on the dashboard so that my car would not be torched; and the other I would wear around my neck like a scarf. I also adorned a button with an Israeli and Palestinian flag on, letting it be known that I was a supporter of peace in which Israel and Palestine would live side by side.

Beginning in October 2015 with the return of violence to our streets, I have found myself resorting to old habits. Now when I cross into Palestinian areas, I hang "worry beads" colored in the green, red, black, and white colors of the Palestinian flag from my rearview mirror. The worry beads help me to worry less about being stoned while driving in towns and villages in Palestine.

My first Palestinian partner was the late Dr. Adel Yahya, a political activist teaching history at Birzeit University and a high-ranking member of the Palestinian Communist Party. Adel introduced me to many people, mainly his comrades in the Communist Party. I had quit my job with the Institute for Education for Jewish Arab Coexistence and had begun collecting unemployment insurance from the State of Israel. That kept me going for five months, but I had no money and no institution through which I could pay the salary of a Palestinian partner. We had to begin on a voluntary basis with no funds for expenses.

Soon after Adel and I began working together, I received a call from a friend of his as he was being dragged off to the Israeli police station in Ramallah. The police and army were rounding up leaders of the intifada and Adel was amongst them. I knew that they could hold him under administrative detention for six months without being charged with anything or without even being able to see a lawyer and defending himself. This was my first political challenge in my role as the codirector of IPCRI. My partner was arrested by the occupation forces, and I knew that one of the reasons they picked him up was because of his strong support for the two-state solution—as ironic as that sounds. These people were seen as a bigger threat to the Israeli occupation than Palestinians who rejected Israel's right to exist. I was hearing more and more cases of Palestinians being arrested who were getting involved in activities together with Israelis. One of the big targets was the Israeli Committee for Solidarity within Birzeit University. The university was shut down on a regular basis, and the Palestinians involved with the Israeli committee were regularly arrested. I knew I had to act quickly and decisively to get Adel out of prison before he was sentenced to the six months of administrative detention.

I called every politician I knew personally in Israel. Then I started calling foreign diplomats—ambassadors and others that I had recently met when looking for financial support for IPCRI. The most responsive person I contacted was Phil Wilcox, the US consul general in Jerusalem. I made tens of phone calls on Adel's behalf, and I made sure that the people I spoke with knew who to call. I was volunteering once a week in the Moked—the center for human rights that was newly established in Jerusalem to help Palestinians find their loved ones after they had been arrested by the police or the army. It was a big mess then because there were massive numbers of people being arrested and systems hadn't yet been established by the Israelis to deal with them. People simply went missing. So I knew who had to be called and how a person could find out what happened to their friends or family.

Adel was released after spending three days inside the prison. When he left, one of the Israeli officers said to him, "You have some very powerful friends!" That was my first lesson in dealing with this kind of situation, one that I would face hundreds of more times in the coming years. Adel passed away from cancer in 2015 after an illustrious career as a historian focusing on Palestinian oral histories.

In trying to expand our base of support on the Palestinian side, I reached out to other leaders from Fatah and the Democratic Front for the Liberation of Palestine (DFLP). People from the Popular Front for the Liberation of Palestine (PFLP) refused to meet me. Initially it was quite confusing and difficult to figure out who was who and what political movement they belonged to. All of the political factions of the PLO were considered illegal by Israel, so people did not readily admit that they were a member of an organization. I also discovered that it was not acceptable to directly ask someone what faction or organization they belonged to. I quickly discovered that the four main political factions served as civil society organizations, providing services to the public in ways that normal governments would. It was in fact a kind of pseudo-government of Palestine that was already functioning, but in each area of concern, there were four different organizations providing services, each according to their political affiliation. As such, there were four main health organizations, four main educational organizations, four main agricultural organizations, and so on. The names of the organizations gave away their political affiliation. "Popular" committees were affiliated with the PFLP. "Democratic" committees were affiliated with the DFLP. Anything called "the people's" was generally the Communist Party, which later changed its name to the Palestinian People's Party. Fatah often used the name "General Union." It took me time to learn the code names and understand the internal politics. The increasing importance of the United Command of the intifada also provided a platform for more cooperation between the Palestinian factions, and the differences between them narrowed.

Each person I met gave me additional names of people with whom I could speak. Of the tens of Palestinian leaders that I spoke to, I only met one who said it was a bad idea. All the others said it was a very good idea, but "it was too soon," they weren't ready for it. Every Palestinian I spoke to wanted to know who else gave their names as supporters of the idea, and when I couldn't use any names, people said, "When you get someone's name, come back to me." One of the people who was most interested was Radwan Abu Ayyash, who was thought to be number two in Fatah in the West Bank. He ran an office in Jerusalem of the Arab Press Association, which he had established and was eventually shut down by Israel for being a PLO front. Radwan was acting as Fatah's number one person in the territories because the real number one, Faisal al-Husseini, was in Israeli prison.

Mr. Hanna Siniora, then the editor and publisher of the Fatah-affiliated *Al-Fajr* daily newspaper, was very interested and supportive of the idea of a joint Israeli-Palestinian center based on advancing the two-state solution. Siniora had been appointed by Yasser Arafat to represent the Palestinian people in talks with US Secretary of State George Shultz during the Reagan Administration. Bethlehem Mayor Elias Freij was supportive, as well. He was a very kind, old style gentleman Palestinian mayor who was respected all around, in Israel as well, but beyond the Christian community in Bethlehem, he was not viewed by many young Palestinians in the new generation as the leadership they wanted. Almost all of the Palestinians I spoke to told me I should contact the PLO in Tunis and get their approval, and then it would be easier to gain local Palestinian support.

It was very difficult to make contact with the PLO at that time. For one, it was against the law in Israel to speak to the PLO. On the technical side, there were no direct telephone lines to call Tunis where the leadership in exile was based. There were no direct telephone lines to any Arab country. Israel (and Palestine) were a communications island. I found out that Palestinians would call the Arab world through a company based in Cyprus. You would call the number in Cyprus and then give them the number in the Arab world, and they would connect you. It wasn't much of a company or a sophisticated communications web. Some entrepreneurial Palestinians rented an apartment in Cyprus and put in a couple of telephone lines that they were able to link together through a very simple switchboard. It ended up costing about five dollars a minute and was not a very good way to try and reach out to PLO leaders to introduce them to the ideas that I was promoting. It was also difficult to just pick up the phone to call PLO leaders, introduce myself, and present the idea. There was no email then and fax was a new technology that was expensive and still not in every office.

I was doing all of this work in a tiny office that was once a storage room that a friend of mine, Zvika Dagan, who was the director of the Intercultural Center for Youth in the German Colony in Jerusalem, allowed me to use, rent free, while I was establishing IPCRI. He gave me a telephone and allowed me to use the fax machine in his office. There were still no cell phones at this time, or at least, I did not yet have one.

Faisal al-Husseini, the son of Abdul Qadr Husseini, the leader of the Palestinian forces that fought against the creation of Israel who was killed in a famous battle on The Castle outside of Jerusalem in 1948, was the number one Fatah leader in the occupied territories. Faisal headed the Arab Studies Society located in the Orient House, an old Husseini family property in the heart of East Jerusalem. Over the years, Israel would close the Arab Studies Society repeatedly. The Orient House was also a frequent target of Israeli policies against Palestinian nationalism. Faisal al-Husseini was quite familiar with the inside of Israeli prisons. After the beginning of the first intifada, Faisal was arrested again. When he was released from prison in January 1989, I went to see him on the very night that he was released. I had never met him before, but I knew that he was a real leader by his reputation. I was told that he lived in Sawarneh—a neighborhood in East Jerusalem that I had never heard of before. People told me more or less where it was. I had never been to his home, but I found it by all of the cars and people around it. When I arrived, there were two or three hundred people waiting on line to shake his hand and greet him. The line moved slowly, but there was no way I was going to leave before seeing Faisal. I knew that I wouldn't have a chance to talk to him, but I waited on line like everyone else. I was the only Israeli there. I introduced myself when it was my turn, and I gave him a letter. I said, "I think this is very important and I would like you to read it." The letter described the idea of IPCRI, the efforts I was making to get it established, the list of Palestinians with whom I had already met, and a request that he support the idea. In the end of the letter, I asked for some time to come back to his house so that I could properly tell him what I was trying to do.

Surprisingly, the next morning I received a phone call from him. He had read my letter, and he asked me to come back that day at 4:00 in the afternoon. I came back and once again there were hundreds of people waiting to greet him. This time I didn't wait on line. I found a young man, one of his assistants, and told him my name and that Faisal asked that I come to see him at 4:00. He took me into the inner salon of his house while all the other people waited outside. I was amazed. Faisal questioned me for about twenty minutes, what were my motives, where did I come from, what was my background, who supported me on the Israeli side. I explained to him the idea. I told him how important it was that this be a joint effort, Israelis and Palestinians working side by side in the same organization, sharing the same office. He then said, "I'll support you and you can tell others that I'm supporting you." After Faisal joined, there was no problem getting Palestinians anymore. Every Palestinian leader or public personality I then spoke to said, "Faisal joined, you can include me too!"

I applied to the Israeli Ministry of Interior to register a nongovernmental organization (Amuta). I wasn't sure how official Israel would respond to the idea of registering an organization whose goal was to advance the creation of a Palestinian state next to Israel. I was also not sure, although I had my suspicions, that they would not like the name of the organization that I proposed ISRAEL/PALESTINE Center for Research and Information. As expected, I did not receive a response. Every time I called the Amuta office, I was told that the file is being worked on. I made several visits to the office only to be told the same thing. In fact, it took several years before I could actually register IPCRI in Israel. The registration of IPCRI in Palestine took even longer. During this time, I was working on a letter that stated that I had submitted documents to register a nongovernmental organization. That was not sufficient to open a bank account or to sign any document in the name of the organization. IPCRI had to be registered legally in some way, somewhere in the world.

A Day in the Life of an Israeli Peace Activist

10

WRITTEN IN DECEMBER 1988:
In Israel, Saturday is family day. All stores, public transportation, most restaurants, and other places of entertainment are closed for the Sabbath. Most religious families spend the morning at home, using the one day of the week when there is no work to catch up with family affairs, read the weekend newspapers, visit friends, and take a leisurely walk. For many of us in the Israeli peace movement, Saturday has become Palestinian solidarity day. The Israeli government rarely provides us with a reason not to protest. Every week, since the beginning of the intifada, Palestinians are killed or wounded, villages are put under curfew, homes are destroyed, individuals are placed under military detention without due process, or even expelled from the country. For those of us who are committed to peace with the Palestinians and believe that the Israeli military occupation must come to a rapid termination, there is always a reason to protest or voice our solidarity with the Palestinians. Often, our conscience aches and gives us no rest. We hear an inner voice that tells us that the Israeli soldiers and riot police are also acting in our names. We see the bloody results on television at night, we have tears in our eyes and anger in our hearts when we read the daily newspaper and listen to the radio news. I know that the news is bad, but like a magnet, I am drawn every hour to the radio to hear the latest developments. I wake up in the morning and grab the newspaper even before my eyes have begun to focus. It could be described as an illness, perhaps just a necessary hope that today things might change, today the peace process might begin. But it rarely does, and I weep in my impotence as the society that I have chosen to live in becomes more and more foreign to me.

As the Palestinians moderate their positions and as the uprising continues, the average Israeli's hatred and fear become more ingrained and the chance for peace fades further away. We in the peace movement see this process soberly, and yet we are unable to affect any real change. Many of us have radicalized our positions and our tactics during this past year. We are no longer afraid of confrontations with the army or the police. This is a dramatic change. Small groups of Israelis are beginning to take part in acts of civil disobedience as they stand firmly against the army and the police.

During this past year of protests and solidarity, Saturday has taken on a new meaning. Saturday is a day to cross the Green Line, to leave Israel and enter occupied Palestine. Saturday is the day when we hear the stories of death, prison, destruction, violence, pain, and most all— hope. On the seventh day, God rested. On the seventh day, Palestinian suffering is shared with Israelis who are willing to listen. On the seventh day, December 3, 1988, a group of thirty Israelis, most in their thirties, all experienced protesters, answered a call for help and support from a village in the Ramallah area, Kufr Malik.

On November 15, 1988, the day that Arafat declared the establishment of the State of Palestine, the villagers of Kufr Malik celebrated their victory. In doing so, they broke the law. They marched in the streets; they threw sugarcoated candies in the air for joyous children who had known little joy the past year. They flew their flag proudly from the minaret of the local mosque, and they sang their national anthem, *Biladi, Biladi* (My land, my land, oh how I love thee). But most of all, they angered the Israeli Army. In these times of uprising and oppression, Palestinians are not allowed to celebrate. Until November 15, 1988, the army also issued orders to prevent public joy. The orders were given by the defense minister himself. Israeli oppression had begun a new phase. First bullets, plastic bullets, house destructions, expulsion, school closings, store closings, and now oppressing public joy! In Kufr Malik, the joy expressed by its one thousand residents could not be put down. For the first time in almost a year, there was a reason to be happy, there was a reason for pride, and there was a reason for hope.

Hearing of the joy of the residents of Kufr Malik, the army decided that this was too much to take lightly. Something must be done. The residents of Kufr Malik must pay the price for their happiness. Curfew! A jeep with loud speakers travels through the small village on its narrow unpaved roads: "To the residents of Kufr Malik, you are now under curfew. Do not leave your homes. Those who leave their homes will be arrested. To the residents of Kufr Malik . . ." over and over again. It was not new to them. They have already experienced curfews on more than one occasion since the beginning of the intifada. In the past, the residents had been allowed out of their homes during the afternoon to buy food. However, this time it was different. No afternoon break. Supply trucks delivering milk and bread and other perishables were turned away by the army. Kufr Malik is under curfew; no one can enter and no one can leave.

On the second day, the army disconnected the electricity. At dark, candles were lit in most houses. Soon come knocks on the villagers' doors. Soldiers entered, candles were extinguished, furniture was broken, children were frightened, and men were taken to the school for interrogation, women cried, and soldiers screamed. This was no ordinary curfew. By the tenth day, the word was out. Nearly ninety percent of the homes in Kufr Malik had been vandalized by the army. There was a food shortage. The United Nations refugee relief organization, UNRWA, and the international Red Cross both tried to bring fresh milk and other supplies to the village. The Red Cross was allowed in; UNRWA was kept out. By day twelve, the word had reached the Israeli peace movement. "Come, help us! Come see what is happening to us."

On the bus ride to Kufr Malik, we were told that if the village was open we would visit with families and show our solidarity. If the village was still under curfew, we would hold a demonstration. After passing through the city of Ramallah, we turned off the main road and headed towards Kufr Malik. Stop! Road Block! Israeli soldiers! One of the organizers noticed a road sign that pointed in the direction of Jericho. "We're a group of Israeli hikers going for a day trip to Jericho," he told the soldier. The soldier looked in the bus, a group of young Israelis on a Saturday outing. Some people in the back of the bus starting singing patriotic Israeli songs, we all joined in "Eretz Yisrael yaffa, Eretz Yisrael porachat . . ." "Go on," said the middle-aged reservist, "Watch out for stone throwers."

About one kilometer up the road, a villager from Kufr Malik was waiting for us. He had sneaked out of the village in order to meet us. "Yes, the village is still under curfew. The army has closed all the roads from all sides, in and out. There is no way to enter." Soon we are alongside the village, but we drove by. We would turn around and surprise them. However, something went wrong. One of the soldiers must have noticed. Immediately, an army jeep was following us. We stopped. The jeep stopped fifty meters behind us. We continued.

The jeep followed right behind. We reached the next village, Tayba, and found a place to turn around. Now the jeep was in front of us. One of the soldiers was speaking on his walkie-talkie. We could no longer take them by surprise. Within two minutes, we were in front of the village. The soldiers physically pushed their bodies up against the doors. They could not be opened. The officer on duty, a major in the reserves, young, energetic, perhaps even understanding (he probably attends "Peace Now" demonstrations when he's not in the army) pulls out a written order, "Kufr Malik and all the roads leading to Kufr Malik are now a closed military area." From our windows, we could see some villagers on the rooftops and porches of their homes watching us. We pulled out our prepared signs in Arabic and Hebrew "Free Kufr Malik." "Remove the curfew from Kufr Malik." "Israel-Palestine—two states for two peoples." Several soldiers forced the windows open and tore our posters with passion. After several minutes of arguing, we drove on. Our Palestinian driver was sweating. His fear was showing; his face pale and his hands shaking. Palestinians are not accustomed to the kind of arguing that went on between the Jewish soldiers and the Jewish protesters. We knew that the soldiers would be slow to use violence against Jews. Had we been Palestinians, we would have been arrested within minutes and perhaps beaten.

We moved on and the army followed. Thirty protesters followed by more than forty soldiers in five jeeps and two command cars. Before reaching the road block and after leaving the access road to Kufr Malik, as the major's orders had specified, we jumped out of the bus, posters in hand. We climbed a small hill in front of a few Palestinian houses scattered behind us. Army jeeps drove by and within a brief moment we were surrounded. The soldiers approached us. They were confused. They aren't used to breaking up public disorder caused by Israelis. After my sign was torn brutally by a young soldier, I put my hands in my pockets and placed myself between other soldiers and my colleagues attempting to prevent them from tearing other signs. It was almost like a game of cat and mouse. The soldiers would reach over me, being careful not to push, but constantly trying to tear the signs that caused them so much grief and anguish. Suddenly the major arrived.

"Okay, you made your point, now get on the bus and get out of here," he said sternly. Several of us gathered around him. "The order you gave us told us to leave the village and all access roads to it. Surely this is not considered an access road. Maybe Jerusalem is also an access road?" we asked. Once again, the major pulled out the order and a pen, he added the words "all of Judea and Samaria." With the push of a pen, we were ordered to leave "our ancestral homeland" and the modern-day land of Palestine. The major pleaded, "I'm not completely unsympathetic, but you must leave. I have my orders and now you have yours."

"I have my orders," a very familiar sentence we yelled back. Shocked by that response, the not completely unsympathetic major granted us four minutes to stand on the hill and hold our signs.

After one minute, and out of nowhere, three more jeeps arrived. This time it was different. The green-bereted border police were known for their brutality, and their uncensored used of force would now take over where the army left off. They were less confused and less sympathetic. For them, we were worse than the Arabs, we were traitors, cancer, we must be shown who controls the country. Riot sticks and weapons in hand, they charged at us. The major's decision to let us protest for four minutes was no longer valid. Within seconds, our signs were torn. With no sign in hand, I stood firm and held my hand high, my two fingers proudly signaling "v," the peace sign. As a child in the 1960s, I flashed this sign for peace and withdrawal of American troops from Vietnam. Now on the hills of Samaria, I was facing my own people, now as an enemy to them, voicing my solidarity with the oppressed people of Palestine. "V" has come to mean Palestinian pride, steadfastness, peace, victory, and now, the solidarity of Israeli peaceniks with Palestinians. This act was too much for the young border policemen to accept, with burning hatred in their eyes, their riot sticks stretched out, I received a blow across my raised arm. My watch on my wrist went flying, my arm stinging from pain from the blow, and my mind confused from the initial shock, I was tumbled on the rocky ground by two other policemen. I quickly stood up, and in a rage I screamed, "I want your name and number. I demand that you give me your name and your number." The major now intervened, trying to prevent the situation from blowing up into more violence. It was clear that the border police's violence had the potential to escalate beyond control. The major knew that once the border police have struck the first blow the use of weapons with live ammunition could be the next step.

"Take my name and number," declared the major. I told him that his name didn't interest me and that by law the policeman who struck me had to give me his name. However, in occupied territories "law" has many interpretations, many enforcers, and little value for those who wish to preserve it and defend it.

We were ordered and physically forced onto the bus. When we were all inside, the police grabbed the last one of us and forced him into a waiting jeep. We declared that we would not move until he was released; however, we were trapped inside the bus on the side of a road that had been closed off to the public. Our Palestinian driver was frozen with fear. When we pleaded with him to open the bus doors, he was incapable of moving. He was not the Israeli peacenik who came for one afternoon to protest. For him, confrontation or the avoidance of confrontation is a way of life. If there was a price to pay, he would be the one to pay it. He could lose his license or even his bus. Until the major agreed that one of our people could leave the bus to escort the one who had been detained, the driver sat in his seat waiting without responding to our calls to open the doors. Eventually, the major had our person released, and we were ordered out of the territories. The major agreed that we would leave without escort. Upon making the agreement, the major said, "You give me your word that you are going directly back to Jerusalem without stopping and I'll give my word that there won't be an escort." We agreed, and we departed. In spite of our agreement, we had a military escort of two jeeps and a command car all the way back to the border of Jerusalem.

The story of the demonstration ends here; however, my confrontation with the occupier's law was only just unfolding as I departed from the bus at the Jerusalem border in order to go to Ramallah to meet with a Palestinian colleague who teaches history at Birzeit University in the West Bank. Arab taxis travel rapidly on the road between Jerusalem and Ramallah. Along the way, past new Jewish neighborhoods, army jeeps that patrol the roads periodically set up road blocks. They stop all Arab vehicles in order to check passengers and their belongings. Today the army was busy with Jewish protesters. There was no road block before Ramallah. All of the passengers, including myself, were relieved—we made it without encountering the army. The worst part of many road blocks one encounters throughout the West Bank is not the loss of time or even the fear, but the humiliation of standing outside of the vehicles while being searched or while having personal belongings checked. This is often done with the callousness that is expected from an eighteen-year-old, and although expected, it is rarely forgiven or forgotten. There can be no doubt that these experiences affect the way Palestinians view Israelis.

The taxi arrived at the central square in Ramallah, Manara Square. Except for a few vegetable vendors, their carts filled with their wares, the area was empty. Since the beginning of the intifada, Palestinians work 9:00–12:00 every morning, except during strikes when everyone stays at home. It was now 1:30 p.m. As I stepped out of the square, a border police jeep passed by. Suddenly I heard the screech of the brakes, and two green-bereted soldiers jumped out. I was wearing a button with a Palestinian and an Israeli flag on it that read, "End the occupation." I often wear this button, especially in the occupied territories. It lets people know that I'm one of the good guys. However, just last week, I was arrested with three other people at a demonstration in Jerusalem because of the same button on the charge of identifying with an anti-Israeli organization—a crime which carries a maximal prison term of eight years. We were all wearing the button and carrying a sign with the same insignia. Now I quickly removed the button and put it in my pocket before they could see it. They grabbed me and another young bearded Palestinian who by his misfortune was walking next to me. "What are you doing here?" asked the same young and vicious soldier who had just one hour before clubbed my right hand.

"Is it illegal to visit a friend in Ramallah?"

"Get in the jeep," he ordered. Here, alone, was not the place to make a scene. It is best to get into the jeep quietly and work out the matter at the police station. I don't want people to think that I am working with the police or the army. The fewer people who see me talk to them, the better. Unfortunately, they also took the Palestinian with us. This was too much to be quiet about. "I don't know him; I have never seen him before in my life. You must believe me. I swear on my mother." All this to no avail. I felt terrible. I felt scared for him. I didn't know his name. For myself, I felt no fear. I didn't break any law, and I didn't intend to break any law in Ramallah. However, a Palestinian can be stopped for no reason and sent to detention without trial. Now I, dedicated to fighting against the occupation, became the cause of a Palestinian's arrest.

At the police station in Ramallah, I was separated from my Palestinian "friend." He was left downstairs, and I was taken to a room upstairs. Two men in civilian dress were sitting down. I thought to myself, "These guys must be from the Shin Bet—the secret police." They spoke Arabic to themselves, unaware that I understand. They spoke Hebrew to me, "What are you doing in Ramallah?"

"I didn't break any law and I demand to be released. Is it a crime to visit a friend in Ramallah?"

"Don't get smart," he shouted at me.

"This is the guy who was in Kufr Malik—he called me a fascist," said the arresting officer. Now they started to curse me. They cursed me and my political ideas, they cursed my heritage, calling me an Ashkenazi bastard (indicating that my Jewish roots were in Eastern Europe rather than in the Middle East or North Africa), and they hoped I would return to the place I came from.

"You protest for the stinking Arabs and you call us fascists—you goddamned traitor. You should rot in hell." I remained quiet.

"If I am not being arrested I demand to be released and go about my business." They ordered me to wait outside on a hard wooden bench. After a fifteen-minute wait, I was called back and told that I was under arrest. The charge: insulting a police officer.

"What about the Palestinian you arrested with me?" I asked. "He's none of your business, you better worry about yourself." I once again insisted that I had never seen him before and didn't even know his name. Later I learned that he had been released without being charged. He was held for two hours.

Now it was time to interrogate me. This was the second time in one week. I was familiar with the process. I wouldn't answer any of the questions. I would only say that I've committed no crime.

"Were you at a demonstration by Kufr Malik?"

"I've committed no crime."

"Were you ordered to leave the area?"

"I've committed no crime."

"Didn't you call a policeman a fascist?"

"I've committed no crime."

By the fifth question, the interrogator asked me if I had a statement to make. I said, "Yes, I came to Ramallah today to visit a friend, something which the law still permits. I was accosted by two policemen together with an innocent bystander who had the unfortunate luck to be walking alongside me. I am being held against my will for no reason." I signed the interrogation report and waited to be released.

"Who can sign for your release?" I was asked.

"Don't be ridiculous, I'm not calling anyone from Jerusalem to come and sign for me." They asked me if I knew someone in Ramallah with an Israeli identity card who could sign for me. "Of course not, the only Israelis in Ramallah are soldiers." I pleaded with him to release me on my own recognizance. I was not a murderer or a thief.

"No, there are certain crimes that we can release the prisoner for with his own signature and then there are other crimes that we need someone to guarantee that you won't leave the country." This has to be out of a Kafka or Orwell novel. It was too bizarre to be real.

"How about someone with a foreign passport," I asked. I knew some Americans in Ramallah.

"Alright, tell them to come." I then called my friend Laura who works at Birzeit University. While waiting for her to arrive, the major showed up.

"What are you doing here? You were ordered to leave the area, the entire area!" I explained to him that after the demonstration, I left with the others as ordered. However, I returned to Ramallah not to protest, but to visit a friend. He accused me of being associated with the Palestinian uprising. He told the Shin Bet agent that I was to be escorted out of Ramallah and returned to Jerusalem. "You are a persona non grata—an unwanted person in all of Judea and Samaria."

"For how long?" I asked.

"Until further notice," he shouted back at me.

Even as I am writing these lines, I still have difficulty believing that this really happened. The story continues. Fingerprints. "Oh, come on, this is absurd," I said. The Shin Bet agent agreed that this was a little uncalled for, however, rules are rules. He then compromised and said, "Alright, just one finger!"

After fingerprinting, my friend Laura had arrived. Downstairs, Adel was waiting, the Palestinian friend I had come to visit. Just two months prior, Adel was arrested and held in the Ramallah prison for three days without reason. During those three days, I called everyone I knew who might help get his release. I spoke with four members of Knesset, six journalists, a military spokesperson, and the American consul general in Jerusalem, Phil Wilcox. Later when Adel was released, I learned that my phone calls had made the difference; as a result of all of this pressure, no charges were pressed against him. All of the other people who were arrested with him were sent to Ansar 3 prison camp for a six-month military administrative detention.

The Shin Bet agent now changed his mind—a foreign passport was unacceptable. "She could leave the country. Then how would we be sure that you will show up in court?" I then tried once again to get my release by signing for myself. "Out of the question. Don't you know anyone else in Ramallah?"

"Just Palestinians," I said. He agreed. The same Palestinian who I helped to get out of prison two months ago was now returning the favor.

With all of the papers signed, the question was how to get rid of me. The major ordered me out of the area. The Shin Bet agent suggested a taxi. I asked him who will pay for the taxi. I said that unless he was willing to pay for a special taxi from Ramallah to Jerusalem, it was out of the question. I would not get into the taxi. He then suggested that we call the service—a shared taxi with a set route, the same I had come in. I told him that they would have to take me to the service because no service would come to get me. Finally, they decided that I would be driven in a jeep to the service in the center of Ramallah.

When the jeep came to the police station, the reservist soldiers refused to allow me to ride with them. So, Adel, Laura, and I walked in the street as the jeep followed behind. What a scene, escorted out of town by sundown—right out of the movies. The jeep blocked the road in front of the taxi. We now had to wait until the taxi was full. "What's going on?" asked the driver. Adel explained that I was declared a dangerous person by the authorities and that my presence would endanger the continuance of the occupation. Before departing, the soldiers warned the driver that if he let me out before Jerusalem, he would lose his license.

On the ride back to Jerusalem, the other passengers looked at me in awe. What heroic act has this young man done in the name of peace and justice?

Becoming a Security Threat

11

In December 1988, I planned my first speaking/fundraising tour for IPCRI in the United States. I was planning also to meet a lawyer friend in Los Angeles and enlist his help to register a nonprofit organization in the United States to assist in fundraising and provide a legal status. My friend, attorney David Wapner, agreed immediately to work on the registration of the Friends of the Israel Palestine Center for Research and Information, Inc., US. But before arriving on the shores of the United States, something happened to me at Ben Gurion Airport in Israel that had a huge impact on me and my life.

I was traveling with my daughter Elisha, who was under four years old, and planned to leave her with my parents in New York. We arrived at Ben Gurion Airport and went through the security checks with no problem. When we arrived at passport control and handed our passports to the policewoman behind the glass window, she punched my passport number into the computer, picked up our passports, and told me to sit down. She said, "You are not allowed to leave the country!" My heart dropped. I could not comprehend what was happening. I was not allowed to leave the country! What did I do? I didn't break any laws. I paid my taxes. It must be some kind of mistake. I didn't immediately connect what was happening to the establishment of IPCRI. So I sat on the side with Elisha, quietly watching as hundreds of people went through passport control without any problems. No one spoke to us. Every twenty minutes or so I went back to the window and asked what was happening. "Sit down and wait," I was told. Half an hour before departure time, I insisted that the policewoman tell me what was going on. She said, "You are not getting on the flight, just sit down and wait." I think it was then that I broke out in tears. I was angry. I was scared. I was confused. I didn't know what to do. I didn't know who to speak to. What was going on and why? Ten minutes later someone called us to follow him. We went through the passport control, we were handed our passports and then driven out to the plane. No explanation, no apology, nothing. Sitting on the plane, I was bewildered, confused, upset, angry, and happy that I was on my way. I couldn't believe what had just happened.

I joined, without requesting it, the very exclusive club known as "the Israeli security list." For the next four years, until the beginning of 1994, every time I traveled via Ben Gurion Airport or on El Al Israel airlines from countries outside of Israel, I was held and told, "You are not allowed to leave the country," or "We have to wait for instructions to know if you are allowed to board the flight." I never missed a flight, but sometimes I was held until shortly before the flight was about to leave. Sometimes I was held when I returned from abroad. I was sometimes physically searched. On occasion, my luggage was removed from the plane and searched, and at times, just my carry-on luggage. I was removed from the plane several times after boarding to identify my luggage and have it gone through an additional search. Traveling from Cairo to Israel via bus, I was held with my family for more than two hours while the whole busload of Israelis and tourists were forced to wait for me. I was once held for three hours upon return from a United Nations conference on Palestine that was held in Vienna. Three Arab Members of Knesset kindly waited with me. I had collected nearly a full suitcase of papers, pamphlets, and books at the UN Conference. It was all taken from me, and for all I knew, they were photocopying it all. That would have been a lot of photocopies, and maybe that is why it took more than three hours.

I was never, absolutely never told why I was being held, even though I asked every time. I also always asked, "How can I get off this list?" The answer was always combined with a nonverbal shrug of the shoulders that said, "Don't ask me, I don't know." I was also never informed what their instructions were, in terms of what they are looking for and what scope of search they should implement.

The most nerve-racking experience I had at Ben Gurion Airport was in April 1990. I met my parents in Rome; they were there on a business trip. When I looked at the map of the Mediterranean and saw how close Tunis was to Rome, I decided that I would request from the PLO leadership permission to come and visit with them and inform them firsthand about the work of IPCRI. One of our supporters in the UK was Jaweed al-Ghussein, the chairman of the Palestinian National Fund. Jaweed divided his time between Abu Dhabi and London. He appointed his daughter Mona to serve on the board of IPCRI-UK. I established IPCRI-UK with the support of Rabbi Jeffrey Newman and Dr. Ahmed Khalidi, who served as cochairmen. IPCRI-UK was established to help with the fundraising but even more importantly to use as a platform for organizing meetings between Israelis and members of the PLO. We had held many Israeli-Palestinian meetings in Jaweed al Ghussein's mansion on the Bishop's Road in Hampstead in London. I called Jaweed and asked if he could arrange for me to visit with the leadership in Tunis. He received a positive answer from the office of Abu Mazen (nomenclature of Mahmoud Abbas). Abu Mazen was then one of Arafat's deputies and the person who was thought to be most knowledgeable about Israeli society and politics. Jaweed said that I should go and I shouldn't worry about the expenses. I was completely broke at the time, having quit my job directing the Institute for Education of Jewish

Arab Coexistence and starting IPCRI, which had no money to pay me a salary. The first five months after starting IPCRI I collected unemployment insurance from the government of Israel. I liked the idea that the start-up money for IPCRI came from the Israeli government. After that period, I still had no salary and barely enough money to keep me going. I had complete faith in the idea of IPCRI, and I was quite sure that I would eventually be able to find funding. I had to continue to struggle on until I could convince enough people that the idea was right and that I was the right person to do it. I believed that my meetings in Tunis with the PLO were crucial to my attempts to gain credibility and partners in the Palestinian territories. I arranged to travel from Rome to Tunis via Tunis Air and to return the same way and then to catch my El Al flight back to Israel.

In preparation for my trip to Tunis, I assumed that I would be traveling on my US passport because there were no diplomatic relations between Israel and Tunisia. I usually try to travel on my Israeli passport, whenever possible. The US passport I had was issued by the US consulate in Jerusalem, and I thought it might be a problem traveling to an Arab country. During my last visit to Cairo for a conference, I took the opportunity to meet Dr. Nabeel Shaath, one of Arafat's key advisors. I also used the opportunity to contact the US ambassador in Cairo, Robert H. Pelletreau, who I had met in the State Department in Washington during one of my previous speaking/fundraising tours. I called Ambassador Pelletreau and explained that I needed a second passport for the purpose of traveling to Tunisia. Prior to being the US ambassador in Cairo, Pelletreau had served as US ambassador in Tunisia and in 1989 was authorized to hold meetings with PLO representatives in Tunis. He was quite sympathetic to my mission, and he and his wife became early supporters of IPCRI and continued to be for years to come. I had to be in Cairo for a meeting, it was the weekend, and the US Embassy was closed, but the ambassador invited me for lunch and took care of issuing a new passport for me in the matter of a couple of hours. By the end of lunch, the passport was ready. It was a second US Passport, valid for two years only and issued in Cairo.

Traveling to Tunisia was a new experience for me; it was the first Arab country besides Palestine that I had visited. I didn't know what to expect, how I would be received. I was a bit nervous that they would discover that I was also an Israeli. When I arrived in Tunis, Hisham Mustafa, who I had met at a UN conference on Palestine in Vienna in August 1989 and who was an advisor to Abu Mazen, was waiting for me before passport control in the Tunis airport. We embraced, as is the custom amongst Palestinians, and I handed him my brand-new US passport. He looked at it and said, "Don't you have an Israeli passport?" I laughed to myself and handed him my Israeli passport. The PLO had a special arrangement with the Tunisian government, as a sort of state within a state. Foreign visitors to the PLO, especially Israelis, would not go through Tunisian passport control—they were not coming to Tunisia, they were coming to the PLO. The PLO would hold their visitors' passports during their stay in Tunisia and return the passports upon their exit. This was such a bizarre feeling, being the guest of the PLO in an Arab country, with my Israeli passport held by the PLO. This was not the last time that I would encounter some of the more bizarre aspects of crossing borders in the Israeli-Palestinian conflict.

I knew from friends that had visited Tunis before me that the PLO is a very complex organization with a lot of bureaucracy and mostly had people waiting around to see Yasser Arafat. I was told to try to see Arafat and that I should be patient. When I arrived in Tunis, Hisham Mustafa told me that Arafat was not in the country, and in fact, most of the leadership was away. It was Ramadan and most of the PLO leadership was out of Tunis and would be away for most of the month. I wondered why Jaweed al Ghussein didn't tell me this before I came. I could have found another time to come. I hoped that my time wouldn't be wasted and that I would accomplish my mission of getting full and official backing for IPCRI from the PLO leadership. It was becoming increasingly important back home on the Palestinian side to tell people that the leadership in Tunis supported the work. The intifada was launched in the occupied territories without the knowledge or direction of the PLO in Tunis. The intifada had changed the course of Palestinian politics, and it was essential for the PLO leadership outside not to become redundant and irrelevant. So, six months after the outbreak of the intifada, the PLO leadership was using its strong hand and its purse strings to take control. By the time I went to Tunis, the PLO leadership had taken control of the intifada.

Hisham took me to my hotel, the El Mechtel Hotel in the center of Tunis, not far from the old city bazaar. We had coffee in the lobby and he smoked a few cigarettes, even though it was Ramadan when most people are fasting and not smoking. He told me to wait in the hotel and he would call me. I checked in, went to my room, and waited. And then I waited some more. I didn't know exactly what I was waiting for, and I decided that I would venture out and see Tunis before dark. If Hisham wanted me, he could leave me a message in the hotel. Being Ramadan, the streets were not very crowded. I found my way to the old city, the Kasbah. I walked the French-style boulevards in the new city. I passed by the white synagogue building with a large fence surrounding it that was guarded by Tunisian police. I saw some people inside the courtyard of the synagogue, but I did not stop or try to talk to them. I was on business with the PLO, and I didn't know about the relationships and the sensitivities regarding the small Tunisian Jewish community. I really wanted to enter the synagogue and speak with the Jewish youngsters outside, but it seemed too risky and to be almost inviting trouble. So I kept my curiosity at bay and just passed by on the opposite side of the street.

I tried to speak Arabic and to understand their Arabic, but it was quite different from Palestinian Arabic. While speaking with my Palestinian dialect, I was overheard by someone who started to speak with me. It turned out that he was a PLO official who worked in Samed—the PLO economic department run by Abu Ala (Ahmed Qurie) who would later become very famous as the PLO head of negotiations in Oslo. We talked and he invited me to come to the Samed office with him. I wanted to get back to the hotel and wait for Hisham Mustafa, so I arranged to go back to Samed the following day. He told me that they had a great library, and I looked forward to using it and seeing what resources the PLO economic branch had at their disposal.

I did get to meet people from Samed. I did get to spend time with Hisham Mustafa, and I had the opportunity to explain to him what IPCRI was, what our intentions were, and why I needed the support of the PLO. I told him that it was essential that I send the message back to the Palestinian leadership in Jerusalem, the West Bank, and Gaza that the PLO accepted IPCRI and supported the idea. Unfortunately, I did not get to meet Arafat or Abu Mazen or any of the other significant leaders, but the word was out that I was there and I had come to meet with them and to get their support for IPCRI.

In 1991, after the Madrid Peace Conference, I was approached by one of the senior Palestinian participants of IPCRI's Economic Working Group, Samir Huleileh, who was working as deputy to Prof. Sari Nusseibeh, who had been appointed by Yasser Arafat to establish technical committees in Jerusalem so the Palestinians would be prepared for negotiations with Israel. Samir came to me and requested copies of all of the word-for-word transcripts of the meetings of our economic working group, which started in 1989. The request came directly from Abu Ala, from Samed. I could visually imagine people sitting around tables in the Samed library in Tunis working on the papers that I was photocopying for them.

On my last evening in Tunis, I treated myself to a meal in a Chinese restaurant that was near the American Embassy. This was certainly going to be a cultural experience. As I sat and waited for my food to come, the owners changed the music. Suddenly I heard something familiar. They were playing the new and popular album of Yemenite songs performed by the Israeli pop star Ofra Haza. This was too surreal to be true. Chinese food in Tunis, near the American Embassy, with Israeli Yemenite songs in the background.

After spending five days in Tunis, I boarded the Tunis Air flight to Rome.

Thinking about facing El Al security in Rome, before boarding I made sure to destroy any evidence of my visit to Tunisia. I landed in Rome and collected my suitcase. I removed the Tunisia Air baggage tag from the suitcase and tore it up into small pieces. I went through Italian passport control and then made my way to the El Al check-in counter. The only thing I had that could disclose my illegal travel was a camel skin bag I bought in the old market in Tunis, which I used as my carry-on. I checked in, handed over my suitcase, and got my boarding card. I made my way back through passport control and up to the El Al flight gate. There, as expected, my name was marked on the passengers list held by the El Al security personnel. When you fly El Al, the security is much tighter, and the Israeli security personnel are there doing all of the checking. I was told to wait on the side. My luggage was collected from the plane and my camel skin bag was taken. I was quite nervous. After about one hour, I was given back the bag and I had to go down to the area in front of the plane where I identified my suitcase. My luggage was sent back to the plane. No one asked me anything. I boarded and flew back to Israel with the feeling that I had managed to avoid being caught. I was quite sure that the Israeli Security Agency people (the Shin Bet) knew that I had been to Tunis; there was no way that they couldn't know. I was sure that they were monitoring my telephone.

In the years prior to being on the Israeli security list, I would enjoy my return flights home. When we would pass over the Israeli coastline before landing I would get that typical Zionist chill of excitement when coming home to Israel. Now, since being on the security list, I would dread seeing that coastline, and I would break out in a cold sweat wondering what I would face after handing over my passport. While everyone on the flight was elated to land in Israel, I would feel dread and apprehension. I hated the people who put me on that list, mainly for being responsible for giving me the feeling of dread about coming home to Israel.

While standing in line for passport control in Ben Gurion Airport, I did a last check to make sure I had no evidence that would disclose where I had been. In my back pocket, I pulled out a piece of paper and to my surprise saw my hotel receipt from the El Mechtel Hotel in Tunis. I tore up the paper into tiny pieces and saw in the back of the waiting hall a wastepaper basket. I looked around to make sure that no one was watching me, and I tossed the little pieces of torn up paper in the trash. I approached the passport control window and as expected, I was told to go to the side room for "interrogation." While waiting in the security control room, I noticed a barrage of closed-circuit television screens, one right over the trash basket with my condemning evidence. I was quite nervous, thinking that someone would now go out there and retrieve the little pieces of paper, and after putting the puzzle of torn papers back together, I would be in serious trouble. But apparently no one saw me throw the hotel receipt there, and as usual, after a waiting period of about thirty minutes I was released, no questions asked, nothing said.

I grew accustomed to the pattern of giving my passport, not hearing the rubber stamp on the open page, instead being told to sit down and wait. I almost always waited without being asked anything. Just sitting and waiting. Usually they left me no time to go to the duty-free shop, since I had to run to the plane in order not to miss the flight. I learned to arrive later to the airport so I wouldn't have to wait so long, but the disadvantage of that was I would often not get an aisle seat and would then have to sit in the middle in the back of the plane, or even worse, in the smoking section. There were no electronic tickets in those days, or booking online, or even getting your seat on the plane in advance of the flight. These were the kinds of dilemmas I faced every time I flew.

On one flight, after getting through passport control at Ben Gurion Airport, after waiting for the security people to do whatever it is that they do while I wait, I went upstairs to go through the security checks of personal and carry-on bags. Just after going through those checks, I saw a Palestinian friend who had also just gone through even more difficult security checks than I had. It was Nafez Aseili, who ran the "non-violent library on wheels" project in the West Bank. He was from Hebron and he worked in Jerusalem. He had worked with Mubarak Awad, who some people called the Palestinian Martin Luther King. Mubarak created the Palestinian Center for the Study of Non-violence and began a program during the first intifada of teaching non-violence as a strategy for defeating the occupation. He prepared a twelve-page handbook on passive civil resistance in the occupied territories. He translated books by King, Gandhi, Gene Sharp, and others. He ran workshops around the West Bank and Gaza. And then Israel discovered his activities and learned that he was living in Jerusalem on a tourist visa with a US passport. In May 1988, Israel arrested him, and after a court hearing, he was deported. Israel did not want this Palestinian troublemaker in the occupied territories. But his deputy, Nafez was a local and not an American Palestinian. I knew Nafez quite well. When I saw him in the airport, I greeted him with a hug and the traditional kisses on both cheeks. Well, some Israeli security personnel saw me embracing this Palestinian man and ordered me to follow them.

I was taken into a small booth, near the x-ray machines for carry-on bags. It was a booth with black curtains that did not reach the floor. There was a kind of podium inside. I was told to stand on the podium and strip. I took off all of my clothes, including my socks. I did not have to remove my underwear. For some twenty minutes, I stood there, almost totally naked, hearing people all around me, walking by without imagining that a naked Israeli man was standing there, feeling completely humiliated, almost in tears and filled with rage. After twenty minutes, I was given back my clothes. I got dressed and was released to board the flight. I was asked a few questions about the man I greeted and that was the end of the story.

Every time I went through one of these experiences, I wondered why I was on this security list and how I could get off it. No one had the answer, not even the Members of Knesset that I asked to inquire for me. I was trapped and had no way to escape.

IN DECEMBER 1993, MY FAMILY AND I joined seven other families for a Chanukah vacation in Sinai at our favorite place—Basata. Sinai was the ideal place in the world for rest and relaxation, sun, quiet, serenity. We met at the Taba crossing (the Israeli-Egyptian border). Eight cars with eight families, we disembarked and went in all together to the passport control on the Israeli side. There, as expected, I was told that I was not allowed to leave the country. By now, after four years, I was well acquainted with the process. I told the border policewoman to just call the "security people" and I would wait. She responded, "We have no security people here; we have to call them from Eilat. It may take some time, wait on the side." She of course held my passport and those of my family. I told all of my friends to go on without us, that we would catch up later. But they insisted on waiting. I told them that it could take a couple of hours. They decided to wait with us.

About thirty minutes later, two young men wearing shorts and colorful T-shirts showed up. They were the "security people." They escorted me to a caravan behind the Taba crossing. I sat down and they started by reading a computer printout, which I could not see but I imagined it gave them some instructions. They began by asking me why I was going to Sinai. I responded that I was going on holiday with seven other families for Chanukah vacation. They persisted, "Who are you meeting there?" This was actually the first interrogation that I had in all of the times I had been help up. I told them that I was not meeting anyone. I was planning to lie on the beach, listen to music, read, hike in the mountains, and play with the kids. They then looked at each other and said, "Why are you here?" meaning in this interrogation. I said to them that I thought it was a very good question and that I had no idea why I was on this security list. I told them about IPCRI and the work I was doing to bring Israelis and Palestinians together for discussions and research on how to implement peace based on two states for two peoples. They were interested in the work but understood that I was anxious to get on my way with my friends. Sensing their general openness and their friendly nature and appearance I asked them, "How do I get off this list?" They both shook their shoulders in the typical "I don't know" fashion that I had seen every other time I asked this question. Surprisingly, one of them suggested, "Try writing a letter to the legal advisor of the police, explain who you are and what you are doing and ask to meet with a security official to discuss removing you from the list." This was the first time in four years that someone actually gave me some advice on this matter.

During the entire Chanukah vacation in Basata near Nueiba in Sinai, I planned the letter in my mind. I wrote about my Zionist background, about immigrating to Israel. I poured out my guts about my connection to Israel and to the Jewish people. I wrote that I am an Israeli by choice and that I would never do anything to harm the State of Israel. I explained that my motivation behind my work was my deep belief that Israel had to arrive at peace with our neighbors and that I acted out of what I believed were the national security interests of Israel. I asked to meet with a security official to discuss my file in order to be removed from the security list.

About two weeks later, I received a phone call at home. "You asked to meet with a security official? I am the security official." We arranged to meet a few days later in the lobby of the Larome Hotel in Jerusalem. We sat together for about two hours. I told him my entire life story. I explained what I was doing and why. I told him about my military service in the College for the Training Education of Officers, where I lectured about the conflict and about Palestinians. I was an open book. I told him that I had contacts with PLO people, which was illegal, but obviously known to the security people. I hid nothing and thought that he would see and understand that keeping me on the security list had no reason or value. He listened carefully, asking me more questions. I answered everything. At the end of the two hours as he prepared himself to leave, I asked him, "Will you recommend removing me from the list?" He answered, "I cannot." I was totally shocked. I said, "Can you at least tell me why I am on the list?" He explained to me that they had no problem with my politics, that didn't even concern them. He said that I, as opposed to most "leftists," scared them because I knew the Arabs, lived with them, and behaved with them according to their cultural norms. He said that if someone in the Palestinian areas hears that I am traveling abroad and they ask Zakaria, my partner in IPCRI at the time, to ask me to carry a package for him that I would not be able to refuse to take it. He stressed "not that we suspect Zakaria." I hadn't even mentioned Zakaria's name during our two-hour session. I responded, "I don't take packages from anyone." He said that he could not accept that answer because if Zakaria asked me, I would not be able to refuse. I said to him, "If someone ever asks me, including Zakaria, to carry a package, I swear that as soon as I get to the airport I will search for the first security person I see and say, 'I received this package from someone, I don't know what is in it, please check it.'" He looked at me thoughtfully for about a minute, shook his head up and down as if in deep contemplation, and said, "With a heavy heart, I will recommend to remove you from the list."

Two weeks later, I traveled abroad. At passport control I handed over my passport and waited for the famous words, "You are not allowed to travel abroad." Instead, I heard the sound of the rubber stamp banging on the page of my passport. It was the sweetest sound I had heard in years, just like the ringing of the liberty bell.

The Magical Kingdom

After the Oslo Declaration of Principles was signed on the White House lawn on September 13, 1993, we made a decision in IPCRI that the time had come to enlist the business community in the area to advance cross-boundary cooperation. It was essential in our view that the Palestinian economy be jump-started in order to ensure that peace provide dividends every Palestinian and Israeli would enjoy. We thought that we had to help to create a situation whereby not having peace would be seen as losing something valuable. We devised the idea of an international business conference that would bring together Israelis, Palestinians, and internationals to propose joint ventures for investments in the region that would be mutually beneficial and create prosperity. We had hoped that we could encourage business people from all around the world to participate. Being that most of the countries of the region were still in a state of war with Israel, we realized that we should look for a sponsor and a venue in Europe. The Amsterdam Chamber of Commerce agreed to cosponsor the event, which we called "Opportunities 1994—Middle East." With our partners in Amsterdam, we would try to enlist the Jordanian business community to join in, despite the fact that there was no peace treaty yet between Israel and Jordan. I would go to Jordan together with a Dutch colleague from IPCRI, Dr. Peter Demant, to make our case. In order to travel to Jordan, I needed to get a visa in my US passport and receive permission from Israel to travel to what was still "an enemy state."

On my next trip to London for meetings of IPCRI-UK, I went to the Jordanian Embassy to apply for my visa, which I was granted after a couple of hours. Upon my return to Israel, I sent a letter to the Ministry of Interior and requested permission to travel to Jordan via the Allenby Bridge next to Jericho in the West Bank. The bridge was opened shortly after the June 1967 Six-Day War, based on the "open bridges" policy of Moshe Dayan, who understood the importance of not cutting the Palestinians off from the Arab world and having a pressure valve to avert tension and aggression from within the West Bank and Gaza. Tourists were also allowed to travel over the bridge, but Israelis were not, unless they held a second passport and received permission from the Israeli authorities in advance.

Two weeks went by without an answer from the Ministry of Interior. I called and was informed that my request was sent to the security service. A few days later, I received word that my request was approved. I would have to leave my Israeli passport and identity card at the Israeli side of the border. I went to pick up my Israeli passport and found it stamped "approved for travel to Jordan, leave passport at the bridge." I then began the process of organizing my meetings in Jordan. Over the four days that Peter Demant and I were in Jordan, we met with the entire "who's who" of Jordan's business community. It was fascinating and encouraging. The smell of peace was in the air, and the Jordanians didn't want to miss out on the opportunities that would come with it. In each meeting, people gave us more names and contacts to meet. One of those contacts was His Excellency Marwan al-Qassam, the Minister of the Royal Court and one of the most senior advisors to King Hussein and one of his confidants. On our last day of meetings in Jordan, Marwan al-Qassam was quite pleased to receive us in the Royal Palace. What a trip—I could hardly believe it. For me, Jordan had always been a kind of Magical Kingdom. I saw it so close, and yet so far, every time I traveled along the Jordan Valley route going north to Beit Shean or down to Eilat. I always wondered what was on the other side. I would see Jordanian television news from time to time, which was always quite humorous—in those days, it consisted of a daily report of the meetings and activities of the king and members of the royal family. Those reports never contained any substance, never any details of what the meetings and activities were about, just pictures of the king and the princes and princesses. I never lived in a monarchy, and it all seemed so foreign, strange, and comical to me. Nonetheless, here I was in the Royal Palace in Amman as the guest of the minister of the Royal Court. We also used the opportunity to visit the famous Red Stone of Petra down south.

We spent about three hours with Marwan al-Qassam. The discussion was fascinating. He wanted to know about the peace process and where it was heading. He had a million questions about Rabin and the Rabin government. He wanted to know about the business conference we were planning. He asked a lot of questions on how to resolve the main issues with the Palestinians, mainly Jerusalem and the refugee issue. He had his own opinions on all of the issues, which he shared with us. The most interesting was his position on the Palestinian right of return for Palestinian refugees. He suggested that they should go to Iraq. I was completely shocked by his proposal. He himself is originally from a family in Palestine, and yet his position on the key issue concerning the Palestinian people was to settle the refugees in faraway Iraq. I asked him if I could share his positions with people in Israel, including the media. He surprisingly said yes, but clarified that he was speaking on his own behalf and not on behalf of His Majesty King Hussein.

When I got back to Jerusalem I gave a short interview to *Haaretz* newspaper, and the next day a small piece appeared in the newspaper about my trip to Amman. The following week, I received a strange phone call from the Israeli Army. I was ordered to come for a security interrogation in the *Kiryiah*—the headquarters of the Ministry of Defense in the middle of Tel Aviv. I was told to come to the Sharona Gate at 11:00 a.m. on the given day. I had never heard of the Sharona Gate, which is one of the smaller gates of the compound. I wanted to make sure to arrive on time; the sternness of the voice on the other end of the phone had me quite concerned. I arrived early. My name was not on the list of people expected, and no one knew who I was or who was supposed to come for me. The soldier at the Sharona Gate suggested that I go to the main entryway, David's Gate. I did. No one there knew who I was either and my name was not on a list. I almost left, but I decided to return to the Sharona Gate once more to see if someone was there for me.

There was a soldier waiting for me. He was wearing a nondress uniform without any insignia of unit or rank; he was about forty years old, meaning he was probably in the reserves. He took me into the compound. I followed him without talking. He led me into an old British Mandate–era wooden shack, with no windows and a small, old wooden table and two wooden chairs. I sat across from him at the table. He took his little pad out of his shirt pocket and a pen and opened the pad, ready to write. Intelligence agents always have the same little note pad in their pockets. He asked me, "Do you know why you are here?" I responded that I had no idea. He said, "You went to Jordan." I said yes, but I had permission from the Israeli security, even a stamp in my Israeli passport from the Ministry of Interior. He said, "Yes, but you didn't inform your army unit that you were going to an Arab country." I started to laugh. I asked him, "Do you know what I do in the army?" I lecture on Palestinians and democracy in the Army College for the Training Education of Officers. He said it didn't matter what I did. I traveled to an Arab country, and I had to inform my unit. I said, ok, I didn't know and I was sorry. It would never happen again. He then asked me what I did in Jordan. I began to tell him about the "Opportunities 1994" conference and about IPCRI. After about ten minutes, he closed his little note book and returned it to his pocket. He said that he was finished. He asked me if I minded if we continued talking. He was interested in what I was doing and wanted to learn more. I told him what I always say, "I am willing to talk to anyone who is willing to talk to me!" We spent about the next two hours talking. At the end of our conversation, he asked me if I minded if he gave my name to some other people who might be interested in talking to me. I repeated, "I am willing to talk to anyone who is willing to talk to me!"

About two weeks later, I received a phone call from Koby Orgad.

From Security List to Advisor to the Prime Minister

13 Koby Orgad introduced himself as working in the research department of the Prime Minister's Office. He invited me to meet him at an office on the fifth floor of the Shalom Tower building in Tel Aviv the following week. He said the office had a sign on it, "Prime Minister's Office, Research Department." Well, I did my own little research only to discover that the Prime Minister's Office did not have a research department. Most strange! I showed up at the office at the set time and sure enough there was a bronze sign on the door with the insignia of the State of Israel: Prime Minister's Office—Research Department. I rang the bell and was buzzed in. Koby came out to greet me. There was a long corridor that appeared to lead to a series of doors next to each other—interrogation rooms. Koby began by explaining that Prime Minister Rabin created a secret team of five people from different branches of the intelligence community to advise him on the peace process. He had initially approached the army to advise him, but Chief of Staff Amnon Shahak told him with an unusual dose of candor that the army doesn't know how to do that. Shahak said that if Rabin wanted advice on how to launch the next war, the army knew how to do that very well, but they were not equipped to advise on issues of peace.

Rabin did not trust many politicians and nor did he have great appreciation for academics. The intelligence community spoke his language, and he felt comfortable with them. The team was top secret because he feared that enemies of peace from within the political system would object to him making use of intelligence resources for the purpose of advancing peace with the Palestinians. He did not want to open up another front with the likes of Geula Cohen (one of the most right-wing members of Knesset), Benyamin Netanyahu, and Ariel Sharon. Koby explained to me that they needed someone like me who had constant contact with Palestinians—leaders, academics, and professionals. He also said that they needed to hear fresh ideas on how to deal with the many issues that were on the agenda. They could not have direct contact with Palestinians, but people like me could have a major role in shaping Israeli policy on the peace process. I was thrilled to be enlisted. This was exactly the purpose of IPCRI and what I had strived to achieve. Now I had direct access to the prime minister on issues concerning peace. Just two months before, I was on Israel's security list, now I was advising the prime minister. Only in Israel!

Over the next two years, until after Netanyahu was elected following the assassination of Rabin, I spent about two hundred hours with Koby and other members of the team advising the prime minister on the peace process. The work was quite clandestine, and at times I felt like James Bond. We would schedule the day and the time of each meeting in advance. On the morning of the meeting, I would get a phone call with the name of a hotel and the room number. I was instructed to not knock on the room of the hotel if someone was in the hallway. I should walk pass the room and come back only when the hallway was empty. We would usually order coffee or something cold to drink from room service. When the order was delivered, I was instructed to wait in the hotel room bathroom until the room service person had gone. Secret meant secret. They tried to pay me for my time. Koby or one of his colleagues would take out cash from his pocket with a little printed note for me to sign as a receipt. I said that I did not want to receive any money from them. For one, I was doing my job, for which I was already paid by IPCRI. My job was to influence what they were doing. Secondly, I did not want to lose my total independence. If I take money from them, I work for them. I did not want to work for the Israeli government, nor for anyone else. I was my own boss, and I took orders from no one. Koby would plead with me, buy books with the money, he suggested. I insisted that I would not take any money from him. After two or three attempts, he ceased trying to convince me to take the money.

Koby was the main person I met with on a regular basis. He would come prepared with questions. Usually I would begin our meetings, generally lasting about two hours, with a description of what was going on in Palestine. I would enhance the picture by describing some of the meetings and discussions that I was having with various Palestinian leaders. I would bring transcripts of Israeli-Palestinian meetings that we conducted in IPCRI or from the various working groups we convened—the Jerusalem experts group, the water group, the economics and business group. I would try to fill in a picture of how reality looked from the Palestinian side and what were their concerns regarding the developing peace process and their thoughts leading up to negotiations.

I remember cautioning Koby and members of the team on many occasions regarding what appeared to me to be close relations developing between several former Israeli officials, from politics and the security forces, and people close to Arafat. This all smelled very badly of corruption, and the Palestinian people were angry with the apparent abuses of power committed by the newcomers from Tunis and some of the senior Palestinian security officials. Some of the people involved were very close to Prime Minister Rabin, and it appeared as if he had personally sanctioned this negative behavior. There were monopolistic economic deals being made between these Palestinian officials and past Israeli officials in the production of cement, fuel, cigarettes, and other very profitable products. Some people were accumulating great wealth overnight, and the appearance of sudden affluence, particularly on the Palestinian side, expressed itself in the construction of palace villas in Ramallah and Gaza by people who just a short time before had no known wealth. I warned Koby about the animosity developing in the face of this corruption and in particular of the negative perception of direct Israeli engagement in it.

The height of the corruption and the direct Israeli involvement in it was the Oasis Casino in Jericho. Everyone knew that Palestinian security officials close to Arafat and his own economic/business advisor, Mohammad Rachid, aka Khaled Salam, were directly involved in the casino. But people quite close to Rabin were also part owners in this enterprise, which resulted in thousands of Israelis gambling about $5 million there a week. It was impossible to detach the Israeli links to the Palestinian corruption, and I thought that Rabin, who seemed to be Mr. Clean, should know what was going on and the negative effects it would have on the peace process.

While standing on a street in Ramallah counting brand-new cars with the red license plates of Palestinian Authority officials, one was overwhelmed with this show of decadence, particularly when so many of the local residents held refugee cards and lived in refugee camps. It seemed quite apparent to me that this would lead to trouble.

I also suggested to Koby that the team should try to get Rabin to deliver a message to Arafat that he must begin to change his image and appear to be more a statesman than a guerrilla leader. The Palestinian revolution had run its course, and it was time for the Palestinians to engage in state building. The most prominent part of Arafat's image was his military uniform. I suggested that Koby propose the idea that Rabin would not meet with Arafat if he came in his military uniform. I said that if Arafat wants to be the general, then he should meet with IDF personal. If he wanted to meet with Rabin, he should wear a business suit. This message was delivered to Rabin, but ultimately he thought that it was improper to tell Arafat what to wear and that it was not his place to do it. I understand what Rabin meant; nonetheless, I disagreed with his decision. This issue had already been raised and discussed by Rabin in the White House with President Clinton prior to the ceremony for the signing of the Oslo Declaration of Principles on the White House lawn on September 13, 1993. The symbolism was quite important, and I believe that Arafat's own mindset could have changed if there was more pressure on him to behave like a statesman. The American president was not prepared to force Arafat to appear differently, nor was Rabin prepared to cease meeting with Arafat on this condition.

I shared all of the many policy papers I wrote during that period. They dealt directly with issues of the peace process, both relevant to the interim period and the permanent status negotiations. I remember that Palestinians were quite concerned about the size of the legislative council that they would establish under the interim agreement. This was being negotiated in the period between May 4, 1994 (the signing of the Jericho-Gaza agreement in Cairo), and the Interim Agreement, which was signed in September 1995. Arafat wanted to expand the council as much as possible. Israel's official position was to limit the authority of the Palestinians in legislation because they did not want to have the Palestinian self-governing authority appear too similar to a sovereign state. As the negotiations proceeded, Israel changed its position and did not really care about the size of the council, but they understood the importance of the issue to Arafat and decided to exploit it to gain concessions from Arafat on issues of greater importance to Israel—security coordination and cooperation. I was disturbed by the nature of relations demonstrated by this issue. It seemed to me to be dishonest, perhaps legitimate in negotiations, but to me it appeared to be a cynical use or abuse of power in very asymmetrical negotiations. I cautioned against this approach. I always preferred (and still do) a cooperative form of negotiations where the parties are much more open about sharing their positions, needs, and interests in order to maximize the possibilities for "win-win" scenarios. Over the years, with rare exceptions, the approach to negotiations between these two parties has been "the zero-sum game," where one party's concessions are the other party's gains, and vice versa. This is the classic Middle East bazaar negotiation. In my view, the focus should be much more on the outcome, which should be the future relations between the parties, rather than the short-term gains at the negotiating table.

On several occasions, Dan, the head of the team, joined Koby. I never learned Dan's full name. I am not even sure if Dan was his real name. For that matter, I am not even sure that Koby was Koby's real name. Koby described Dan to me as someone with the rank equal to general. I assumed that he came from the Mossad. When Dan came to meet me, the level of precaution and security was even higher. I would be asked several times if anyone saw me coming. Dan had lots of questions for me concerning certain Palestinian leaders and what their positions were. Dan's frequent participation in the meetings with Koby indicated the very high significance these meetings had for the team. I know that my insights and proposals were very useful to them, and for me, these meetings were the direct link to the negotiations and to Rabin that I had worked so hard to get. I finally felt that I could really have a direct impact on what was happening.

I remember putting a lot of effort into trying to convince the team that Rabin should open the permanent status negotiations as soon as possible. The Oslo agreement stated, "Permanent status negotiations will commence as soon as possible, but not later than May 4, 1996." It didn't seem to make sense to me to postpone those negotiations. The drafters of the agreement had hoped that the parties would develop more trust between them if the interim phase was implemented effectively, which thus could enable more successful negotiations on the core issues. Instead, I was witnessing the beginnings of negative relations on the ground, as bypass roads for settlements were being built. The civil administration of the IDF, which was responsible for the implementation of the agreements, did not seem to understand that we were supposed to be moving away from the Israeli occupation and its mentality of control to a new era when Palestinians should control their own lives and destiny.

There were several occasions when my contacts on the secret team proved the extent of their power and influence. Once while on a trip to visit Gaza, I witnessed an Israeli officer abusing his power with a show of physical force against a Palestinian laborer on line to leave Gaza at the Erez checkpoint. The officer was hitting this young Palestinian man with quite excessive force. I immediately picked up the phone and called the number where I would leave a message for Koby to call me back. It took less than two minutes for Koby to call me. I described the scene. His first response "amused" me. He said, "But this is against our policies." I responded that I guess the news about changed policies hadn't yet reached this officer. In less than two minutes, a more senior officer appeared and stopped the abuse instantly.

On November 4, 2005, at the demonstration of 250,000 people calling for "no violence and peace" where Yitzhak Rabin was murdered, I met Koby. He was there as an "observer"—working for the government, he was not allowed to participate in demonstrations. He, like I, was elated by the amazing turn out of support for Rabin and for peace. On the way home from the demonstration, after Rabin was shot and taken to the hospital, we already had a sense that he was dead. We had parked near Ichilov Hospital where Rabin was taken. When we arrived at our car, the police were cordoning off all of the streets around the hospital. A short while later, we heard the announcement of Eitan Haber, Rabin's chief of staff, "In shock the Government of Israel announces that Prime Minister Rabin was murdered." At that moment, I felt that not only was the prime minister murdered, but that the peace process was also dealt a fatal blow. It would never be the same.

Koby called me in shock, as we all were. We met a couple of days later. Rabin's coffin was placed in front of the Knesset and tens of thousands of citizens waited in line to pay their respects. From the Knesset, I went to see Koby in one of the hotels we frequented. I arrived and saw that he had been crying. His eyes were red. The whole country was in shock. People like Koby who worked closely with Rabin were most affected. Rabin knew who I was and he had heard my name many times from members of the "team." I had spoken face-to-face with him twice. I found the way that he imparted the feeling that he was sincerely interested in listening to whomever he was talking to truly remarkable. He asked me questions and listened carefully to my answers. I am sorry that I did not have the chance for more direct contact. I felt, through Koby, that my ideas and proposals did reach him, and I did have an impact on the peace process and how Rabin approached the difficult issues confronting him.

In March 1997, Israel broke ground on Har Homa, a new settlement in Jerusalem. Israel was afraid that riots would break out around East Jerusalem and the West Bank. On that day, I was invited by "the team" to undergo a prepolygraph investigation aimed at raising my security clearance level so that I could have even more direct contact with the team, now working under Netanyahu. Before going to the hotel room to meet Koby and someone from the ISA (formerly Shin Bet) who would conduct the interview, I took a ride around the area that would become Har Homa. The Jewish National Fund forest that used to decorate the mount had already been shaved off, leaving a bald spot on the mountain facing Tantur at the entrance to Bethlehem. My office in those days was in Bethlehem and I would see Har Homa every day. It was so sad to see the government of Israel launching another settlement that would negatively impact our chances of having peace with the Palestinians. If Rabin had lived, Har Homa would probably not have been built. I spent at least six hours with the ISA agent asking me questions that I would be asked once again during the polygraph, explaining that it was essential that I tell the truth and that my answers be the same when I am wired with the sensors. Koby spent the time driving around Har Homa while he waited for us to finish.

My invitation to come for the polygraph never came and my security clearance was never upgraded because Benyamin Netanyahu, Prime Minister of Israel, decided to break up the team. He didn't need advice on the peace process. He had already decided that he would freeze it.

While writing this book, I have made numerous attempts to locate Koby. I Googled him; no luck. I found someone with the same name in a death announcement of Rafael, the Israeli military weapons systems developer, and spoke to the chief of security who told me it was a different person. I spoke to people who worked with Rabin. No one had heard of the team or the name Koby Orgad. I spoke with Eitan Haber, the head of Rabin's office. Haber told me that he knew of Rabin's weekly meetings with a team, but he was not invited and understood that Rabin kept him out of the loop, so he did not inquire.

I spoke with Danny Yatom, who was Rabin's military attaché and later head of the Mossad. I spoke with Rabin's daughter, Dalia, and his son, Yuval. I spoke with Ami Ayalon who took over the ISA after Carmi Gillon, the head of the agency who served when Rabin was killed, resigned. I spoke with Yaacov Perry, a minister in Netanyahu's government until 2015 and a former head of the ISA. None of them knew the name Koby Orgad or had heard about Rabin's secret team.

I am still looking. When the team was disbanded by Netanyahu in 1997, I met with Koby one last time. He brought me a gift from the team—an album about Israel written by the Israeli journalist Nissim Mishal. Unfortunately, he did not sign it nor did the other people on the team.

Bringing Security to the Table

After the election of Yitzhak Rabin on June 23, 1992, it seemed that the chances of transforming the Palestinian political achievements sparked by the intifada into a peace process were becoming clear. Being completely cognizant of the major concerns both to the new prime minister and to Israeli society at large regarding Palestinian independence, the first issue on the agenda had to be security. There could be no Israeli withdrawal from any territory if matters of security were not the core element of political agreements. For this reason, I thought it was essential to initiate a discreet dialogue with security experts and officials from both sides. Due to the sensitive nature of these conversations and the need for decision makers to listen to their outcome, it was mandatory that the participants be people with impeccable records and be closely linked to decision makers.

On the Israeli side, I began with a conversation with Yossi Ginosar, a former senior Shin Bet agent who had been involved in a scandal several years before. Following an illegal cover-up, Ginosar was forced to resign from the service. Nonetheless, Ginosar remained very close to Prime Minister Rabin and served as an advisor to him on Palestinian issues. I met Yossi at a popular Tel Aviv café that was famous as the place where several of Israel's top leaders rendezvoused with their mistresses. Yossi liked the idea of the talks that I proposed. He agreed to participate and suggested several other participants. He also wanted to know, of course, who the Palestinian participants would be.

I had contacted Dr. Ahmad Khalidi in London, who was an associate professor at St. Antony's College at Oxford University. Ahmad was the chairman of IPCRI-UK, which I created to help organize and facilitate meetings between Israelis and PLO officials, though doing so was illegal under Israeli law. He had written several articles about strategic concerns facing the Palestinians. He was well connected with the PLO leadership in Tunis, particularly Abu Mazen and some of the PLO's top security people. Ahmad suggested that we also include Prof. Yazid Sayegh, another Palestinian academic from a prestigious family who had also written about Palestinian strategic issues. Ahmad connected me to Nizar Ammar in Tunis, who he said was the best person on the Palestinian side with whom to discuss military and security planning. Nizar was a member of the Fatah High Security committee. When the Palestinian Authority was established in 1994 in Gaza, Nizar was introduced to Israelis as Brigadier General Nizar Ammar, the director of planning of the Palestinian security apparatus.

So in October 1992, a year before the Oslo agreement was signed, we launched a series of "Track II" talks in London on security issues that would face both sides if and when they entered a peace process aimed at leading Israeli to withdrawal from territories that would be transferred to Palestinians. The Israeli group included General Shlomo Gazit, former head of military intelligence; Yossi Alpher, then acting head of the Jaffee Center for Strategic Studies, formerly a Mossad agent; and Aryeh Shalev another reserve army general working at the Jaffee Center. Yossi Ginosar was to have participated but was unable to do so due to illness.

The Israelis did not want the Palestinian delegation to consist only of Palestinians from abroad. They did not want it to appear that they were having direct talks with the PLO when it was still illegal for Israelis to speak to the PLO. I contacted Faisal al-Husseini, the most senior Fatah personality in the occupied territories and asked him to nominate someone. He responded that no one in the territories knew anything about security issues, which were all handled directly by the PLO. He said that there was someone who had just returned to the territories after completing a PhD in the United States at Columbia University in New York, Dr. Khalil Shikaki, "who studied something to do with strategic issues—try contacting him."

Despite having never met him, I contacted Khalil and asked him to join. He was the brother of Fathi Shikaki, the head of the Palestinian Islamic Jihad, living in exile in Syria. Israel assassinated Fathi Shikaki in October 1995 in Malta. Khalil agreed to participate on the condition that he received written assurances from Israel that he would be allowed to return to the territories following the meeting.

After making inquiries, the IDF informed me that they do not give such assurances in writing. I spoke to General Gazit, who decided to call Rabin. Gazit informed Rabin of the planned London meeting and about the problem involving Shikaki. Rabin phoned the military governor of Tulkarem, which is where Shikaki is from, and instructed him to issue the letter to Shikaki. Rabin asked Gazit to report back to him following the meeting so he could learn what the Palestinians had to say.

The meeting got off to a shaky start when the Israeli security at passport control in Ben Gurion Airport told me (as usual) that I was not allowed to leave the country. Here I was with a group of generals who heard that I was being detained on security grounds. I was of course released before the flight left, but once again, I was driven out to the plane just prior to take off.

During the four days of talks in London, funded by the newly established United States Institute of Peace, the subjects concerned security coordination, the size of the Palestinian force required to take control of the territories, combating terrorism, prisoner releases, and weapons. These discussions were unimaginable at that time. Who would believe that Israelis and Palestinians could discuss security coordination?

But they did, and what's more, they even found a number of things on which they could agree. The Palestinian team reported directly back to Arafat in Tunis on almost an hourly basis. Sitting in Arafat's office was Momduh Nofal, who had been a member of the Popular Front for the Liberation of Palestine (PFLP; the organization founded and lead by George Habbash), and later one of the founders of the Democratic Front for Liberation of Palestine (DFLP). In 1991, Momduh joined Yasser Abed Rabbo and founded the Palestinian Democratic Union Party (FIDA), splitting from the DFLP (Nayef Hawatmeh's organization). FIDA as opposed to the DFLP supported the Oslo process. Momduh was also member of the Higher Military Council of the Palestinian Revolution since its establishment. He served as the commander of the forces of the revolution in Lebanon from 1985 to 1988. Momduh, who later became personally involved in Israeli-Palestinian negotiations, told me that he was sitting with Arafat, receiving hourly reports from Nizar Ammar. They were all shocked by the talks in London and couldn't believe that senior Israelis were talking not only about the return of the PLO to Palestine but also that there would be Palestinian security forces that would cooperate with the Israelis in fighting against terrorism. Years later, the late Motta Gur, the former chief of staff of the IDF and then deputy defense minister, told me that what convinced Rabin to give the green light to the Oslo talks was the content of the agreements reached in the London talks.

Our project on internal security issues and security arrangements was unique for a number of reasons. It was the first time that Israeli and Palestinian security experts met together in order to confront the issues of internal security during an interim period in a peace process. The project was also unique because the Palestinian side included all three elements of the Palestinian community: the territories, the diaspora, and the PLO leadership.

The issue of arms control was already being dealt with in the ACRS (Arms Control and Regional Security) framework of the Madrid peace conference, which created multilateral talks. The Israeli-Palestinian bilateral security concerns were not yet being addressed in any framework. For Israel and the Palestinians, the need to discuss issues of security is less a strategic question than one dealing more directly with the ability of the Palestinians to enforce a peace treaty with Israel, and with the willingness of Israel to cease using its military forces in the territories. For Palestinians, security was interpreted as the ability to conduct their lives freely without the fear of Israeli military checkpoints, interrogations, arrest, house demolitions, expulsions, and so on—the ability to move about freely. For Israel, security vis-à-vis the Palestinians meant more than anything else an end to terrorism: knifings, kidnappings, bombs on buses and in market places, and so on.

As we saw it in 1992, the primary purpose of the interim period in an agreement between Israel and the Palestinians was to allow for both sides to disengage themselves from decades of conflict and to begin developing trust. The Israelis were saying that if the Palestinians were successful in taking control of their own affairs, and if, as a result of this, the level of violence decreased, then in a second stage of negotiations, it would be possible to discuss further separation, including the issue of turning over territory to full Palestinian control. The Palestinians, from Israel's point of view, would be engaged in a sort of a test of the Palestinians' ability and willingness to engage in peaceful coexistence. The security experts we involved stated that the only real test for Israel is within the realm of internal security. They did not care about the ability of the Palestinians to run their own civil affairs, or at least that was far less important. They said once the Palestinians can control their own population, preventing hostile acts against Israel and against their own regime, then it will be clear that they are ready to make peace with Israel.

During this period, bilateral negotiations between Israel and the Palestinians through a non-PLO led team (directed by the PLO but without official PLO participation) were taking place in Washington, but the issue of security was not on the agenda. Israel's position in those talks was that during the entire interim period Israel would retain full responsibility for all aspects of security. The Palestinians could be charged with crowd control, but they would not have any responsibility or ability to protect the Palestinian Independent Self-Governing Authority (PISGA, as it was then called) against enemies from within, or from the outside. Israel understood that there might be many enemies and opposition parties that would try to sabotage the peace process and the Palestinian regime, but those enemies of peace would be the sole responsibility of Israel. Israeli soldiers, border police, and Shin Bet agents would continue to maintain the same high profile that they had prior to the creation of PISGA.

The Israeli security experts said that Israel's problem included more than 110,000 settlers in some 150 settlements over which Israel must retain full security responsibility and authority. The Israeli experts explained to their counterparts that if there were no Israelis in the West Bank and Gaza, they could more easily withdraw and say to the Palestinian "sink or swim," but that was not the case and even then, when there were considerably fewer settlers in the territories than today, their presence was a major obstacle to turning territory over to full Palestinian control. The Palestinians rightfully said that if Israel maintains the same security profile in the territories during an interim period then essentially nothing changes.

Israel found itself, as stated by the security experts, in a catch-22 situation. Israel wanted to disengage from the Palestinian population, increase its level of security, and test the Palestinian's ability to run their own affairs, but Israel could not decrease its security presence because of the need to protect the settlers.

The Palestinians were also in a difficult position. They needed to show real changes on the ground. Autonomy without control over security issues, they said was a very half-empty glass. Continued Israeli control over security affairs meant that very little would change on the ground. But they also pointed out the difficulties they would face if they took over internal security issues—the divisions within their own population could threaten the existence of the Palestinian regime. They questioned whether they would have the ability to create a Palestinian Shin Bet. Could they interrogate political opponents? Could they institute administrative detention? Could they incarcerate political prisoners? Could they establish an effective and obedient chain of command?

At the London meeting, the Israeli and Palestinian security experts estimated that the Palestinians would need a security force of eighteen thousand to twenty thousand people. There would have to be an effective and well-trained intelligence apparatus. There would have to be a liaison mechanism between the Palestinian force and Israeli forces. The only way that Israel could agree, they said, to the existence of such a force would be if Israel still retained full control over the security of the settlers and settlements, and there was full security coordination and cooperation between Israeli and Palestinian forces. They said that over time, once the Palestinian forces prove their effectiveness, there could be a gradual draw down of Israeli security presence, but this could only happen if the Palestinians internalize the belief that their own security is directly linked to the security of Israel. A mutual understanding of security issues could pave the way for future agreement on wider Israeli security withdrawals.

What about the test? The security experts said that it was in Israel's interest (as well as the Palestinians) to see that aspects of internal security are transferred to the Palestinians as soon as possible. When the Palestinians themselves have to prevent attacks against Israel or Israelis, then it would be possible to judge to what extent coexistence would be likely. The experts suggested that the transference of security responsibilities to the Palestinians would be gradual and that the process would begin in certain geographical locations and not throughout the territories. The establishment of a Palestinian internal security police force, its training, and the creation of an effective chain of command would take three to five years.

Gradually it might be possible to turn over certain limited areas to Palestinian security control. If they succeeded in one locale, another area could be added. The experts suggested beginning in Gaza and then in the main cities in the West Bank.

The Palestinians claimed that there was a substantial gap in their approaches to the issue of security with the Israelis. The Palestinian experts expressed that security is their right and cannot be denied by Israel. The Palestinians, they said, aspire to achieve security for themselves. The primary lack of security is caused by the powers of the occupation. They said that there is a close linkage between an agreement on security and other political agreements. They said that there is a kind of ultra-sensitivity on the Palestinian side regarding security cooperation with Israel, but there is room for cooperation nonetheless.

The Palestinians stressed that the formation of an effective Palestinian security force is in Israel's interest. Retention of security control by Israel would result in a weak and incapable Palestinian political authority. Security responsibilities taken by the Palestinians would legitimize any agreement in the eyes of the people, which is necessary in order to maintain stability. Transferring security authority would help to create mutual trust and coexistence with Israel. Through the development of mutual security, the two sides would be able to allow for areas of cooperation and coordination, which could be established through specific mechanisms created for that purpose. The Palestinians said that if they were responsible for security affairs, they would be responsible politically, as well. The Palestinians accepted the idea of phasing as well as the idea of security coordination.

The Palestinian experts explained that they must find ways to address Israeli security fears because those fears create Israeli constraints, which would make it impossible for the Palestinians to function. The Palestinians proposed that first the parties should reach an agreement on the transference of security authority. The next thing is to agree to a time table. In the early period, they agreed that Israel would be responsible for security, but when the Palestinians finish building the foundation for their own security apparatus, security responsibility must be transferred to them. At that point, the Palestinians would be willing to exchange information and coordinate actions. The Palestinian experts emphasized that their political future would rest on their ability to maintain control of the territories and its people.

Both sides agreed that the most complex and contentious issue is the settlements. Israel's position was that no settlement could be removed during the interim period and that the responsibility for the settlers and the settlements must remain under Israeli control. The Israeli experts underlined the politically explosive nature of the settlement issue within Israel. The security of the settlements and the settlers would be problematic because they would continue to move around the territories taken over by the Palestinians, and this could cause problems. The Israelis, therefore, felt it was foolish for the Palestinians to demand security authority over the settlers and the settlements, it would only be a constant source of friction, and situations could easily get out of control.

The experts also confronted the issue of the roles of third parties. The Palestinians saw value in international presence and also voiced their interest in having security training provided to them by third parties. The Israelis objected to any form of international presence. This was an issue on which there was no agreement.

Lastly, the participants also dealt with the issue of prisoner release from Israel as a dynamic element of security. Prisoner release would provide great political legitimacy for the Palestinian regime, thereby lessening potential opposition. Furthermore, many of the released prisoners would be the first cadets in the newly formed Palestinian forces. They are already defined as soldiers in the Palestinian cause, and they are loyal to the leaders and understand a chain of command. This part of the discussion was quite new for the Israelis and provided a real challenge in expanding their consciousness and understanding the Palestinian mind-set.

After the talks concluded, General Shlomo Gazit contacted Prime Minister Rabin and arranged to meet him. Gazit reported to Rabin that the Palestinians were ready to assume security responsibilities with the understanding that they would be fighting against terrorism aimed at Israel. Furthermore, he said that the Palestinians were prepared to establish a mechanism for security coordination and cooperation with Israel. They discussed numbers of Palestinian troops necessary for the Palestinian security forces and all of the other issues raised in London. Rabin was impressed by the seriousness of the talks and by the Palestinian understanding of Israel's security threats and needs.

I really had a sense at the time that we were in the process of laying the foundation of an Israeli-Palestinian peace agreement. We were able to bridge the gaps on some of the most basic fundamentals of the Israeli-Palestinian relationship: control, occupation, and security as a two-way street—my security is your security. Even the issue of prisoner release was dealt with sensibly and without emotion. For the military/security people, there was a clear understanding of the important role that a prisoner release would have in changing the political dynamic surrounding an Israeli-Palestinian agreement amongst Palestinians. While Israel viewed most of the security prisoners as terrorists, to Palestinians, they were heroes and soldiers in the cause of Palestinian liberation. The release of prisoners for Palestinians was equivalent to enhancing security. For Israel, it was exactly the opposite. This dynamic of reverse perceptions is common in conflict situations, particularly when there is such an enormous difference in symmetry between the parties.

One thing that was quite unique in the London talks was that the Palestinians were not focused on their suffering. The sense of victimhood was not on the table. The Palestinians were focused on real issues and on coming up with solutions that would meet their needs and interests, and if possible also serve the needs and interests of Israel. They did not have the desire to score points by beating the Israelis or scheming ways that would give them the upper hand.

The Israelis were of equal seriousness and put politicking and scoring points outside of the room. The meeting was successful because it was based on the approach fostered by IPCRI's philosophy and purpose, which was that the end game solution of two states was on the table as the point of departure, not the point of contention. Focusing on this element in these most sensitive talks enabled the participants to focus on confronting the problems that they perceived would develop on the ground as the peace process took real shape and form.

The al-Aqsa Intifada, September 2000

Despite disclosures made by Suha Arafat, Yasser Arafat's widow, that her husband planned and prepared the second intifada, I don't believe it. Former minister of communication in Arafat's first government, former Hamas leader Imad Faluji also made a similar claim. I have not found substantial evidence that these claims are true. They seem to me to be assuming credit or blame after the fact for the horrific events that unfolded under the name the "al-Aqsa Intifada." I believe that the launching of the intifada was neither planned nor strategically imagined by the Palestinian leadership—be it the Palestinian Authority or the Fatah Tanzim (the "organization" meaning the Fatah leadership that rose to power during the first intifada). It was a series of events that developed rapidly, escalated, and got out of control. Decisions regarding its continuation and its course were made mostly following the events themselves. Arafat had a chance to control it and to rein it in, but he chose not to. This is how events unfolded, as I see it.

The Ariel Sharon visit to the Temple Mount with hundreds of security personnel on Thursday, September 28 ended almost without incident; however, in riots in the West Bank, five Palestinians were killed and more than three hundred were wounded. There were only about two thousand Muslim worshipers on the Mount at the time of the Sharon visit. There was some stone throwing, but only after Sharon had already left. On Friday, September 29, the Palestinian leadership called for demonstrations all over the territories and in particular on the Haram al-Sharif (the Temple Mount). At the end of Friday prayers, some fifty thousand worshippers faced battalions of Israeli police and border guards who came to maintain public order. Riots broke out immediately. One of the first stones thrown hit Jerusalem police commander Yair Yitzhaki directly on the head. He was removed from the Mount on a stretcher having suffered a bloody concussion. Several days later, I spoke to one of the officers who was there; he told me that when the police saw their commander removed from the Mount with what looked to be a serious head injury, they lost control. No one was in charge, and live ammunition was used to disperse the rioters. Four Palestinians were immediately killed on the Mount, another two in the Old City, and four more in Gaza with a total of more than seven hundred wounded. On Saturday, October 1, Israel was celebrating Rosh Hashana—the Jewish New Year. Another ten Palestinians were killed and more than five hundred wounded. Also on Saturday, Palestinian citizens of Israel joined in the rioting, and main thoroughfares throughout the country were cut off including most of the roads in the West Bank, in Wadi Ara, and in the Galilee. The country was under siege, and people on both sides were very angry. By Sunday, October 2, Palestinians had buried thirty-three dead compatriots. The situation was completely out of control. Well into the first day of riots, the Fatah Tanzim pulled out their arms and opened fire on Israeli targets in the West Bank and Gaza. Arafat's regular police were not directly participating in the fire, but they were also not stopping it. The Tanzim managed to get the masses out on the streets particularly as they came out to participate in the funerals all over the territories.

Inside Israel what started as demonstrations against what people perceived to be Israeli plans on the Haram al-Sharif swiftly turned into complete civil unrest in response to the brutal force used by the Israeli police against Palestinian citizens of the state.

On Sunday night, IPCRI organized a meeting in Ramallah with West Bank Preventive Security Chief Jabril Rajoub and two Members of Knesset from Meretz—Avshalom (Abu) Vilan and Mosi Raz. Abu Vilan had served as an officer under Ehud Barak in the elite unit he commanded and, despite his membership in the left-wing Meretz party, maintained a very close relationship and friendship with Barak. In preparation for the meeting, Vilan spoke with Barak, who conveyed a message for Arafat. Until that point, there had been no direct contact between Barak and Arafat since the beginning of the intifada. Rajoub called Arafat and delivered Barak's message: Netzarim and Joseph's Tomb are yours in negotiations, but if we are shot at we will defend those places and all others. In Barak's name, Vilan asked Rajoub to ask Arafat what were his terms for a complete cessation of all the violence. Arafat responded with six conditions, I wrote them down on a napkin that was on Rajoub's desk:

1. An end to the closures
2. A return of all forces to their positions of September 27, 2000
3. A removal of all the extra Israeli police forces from Jerusalem, the Old City, and around the Haram al-Sharif
4. A reopening of all of the crossing points—Allenby Bridge, Rafah crossing, and the Gaza airport
5. An end to the siege of the Palestinian cities
6. An international investigation of the events of the past four days

Vilan called Barak who was at his home in Cochav Yair. Barak responded that he was having the information cross-checked by another source. Fifteen minutes later, Barak's military attaché confirmed that they had received the same information from another source. Arafat, through Rajoub, suggested that he and Barak meet that evening to work out the details. Barak requested some more time. Jabril Rajoub instructed his people to prepare for a meeting in his office between Barak and Arafat. Arafat was in Ramallah. After half an hour, Barak's military attaché informed Vilan that another channel of communication had opened and that Barak preferred that channel. The other channel was Yossi Ginosar, former deputy director of the ISA, emissary of Rabin and Barak to Arafat, and business partner to Arafat's chief businessman, Mohammad Rachid.

About fifteen minutes later, Barak's military attaché informed Vilan that Barak would agree to conditions 1 through 5, but that condition 6 was out of the question. He further informed Vilan that he would not agree to see Arafat that evening. At around midnight, we were escorted out of Ramallah by Rajoub himself and his troops. Later that evening, a meeting took place between Ginosar and Arafat that was a catastrophe and ended up as a screaming match between the two.

The rest is known.

On October 17, 2000, an emergency summit of leaders was held in Sharm el Sheikh. President Clinton chaired the meeting. The following are excerpts from his remarks at the end of the summit:

> Even as we meet, the situation in the territories remains tense. Yesterday again was violent. This is a reminder of the urgency of breaking the cycle of violence. . . . Our primary objective has been to end the current violence so we can begin again to resume our efforts towards peace. . . . First, both sides have agreed to issue public statements unequivocally calling for an end of violence. They also agreed to take immediate, concrete measures to end the current confrontation, eliminate points of friction, ensure an end of violence and incitement, maintain calm and prevent recurrence of recent events. . . . Both sides will act immediately to return the situation to that which existed prior to the current crisis in areas such as restoring law and order, redeployment of forces, eliminating points of friction, enhancing security co-operation and ending the closure and opening the Gaza airport. . . . The United States will develop with the Israelis and Palestinians, as well as in consultation with the United Nations secretary-general, a committee of fact-finding on the events of the past several weeks and how to prevent their recurrence. . . . If we are to address the underlying roots of the Israeli-Palestinian conflict, there must be a pathway back to negotiations and the resumption of efforts to reach a permanent status agreement based on the UN Security Council Resolutions 242 and 338 and subsequent understandings.[1]

So fifteen days after our meeting in Rajoub's headquarters, with Barak on one phone and Arafat on the other, Barak agreed to all of Arafat's demands to end the second intifada while it could still be controlled. An international investigation (The Mitchell Committee) was launched. Senator Mitchell's report concluded the following:[2]

> We have no basis on which to conclude that there was a deliberate plan by the PA [Palestinian Authority] to initiate a campaign of violence at the first opportunity; or to conclude that there was a deliberate plan by the [Government of Israel] to respond with lethal force. However, there is also no evidence on which to conclude that the PA made a consistent effort to contain the demonstrations and control the violence once it began; or that the [Government of Israel] made a consistent effort to use non-lethal means to control demonstrations of unarmed Palestinians. Amid rising anger, fear, and mistrust, each side assumed the worst about the other and acted accordingly.

The Sharon visit did not cause the al-Aqsa Intifada, but it was poorly timed, and the provocative effect should have been foreseen; indeed, it was foreseen by those who urged that the visit be prohibited. More significant were the events that followed: the decision of the Israeli police on September 29, 2000, to use lethal means against the Palestinian demonstrators; and the subsequent failure, as noted above, of either party to exercise restraint.

The Mitchell committee issued a conclusive report on what caused the second intifada. Amongst its recommendations were the following:

- The GOI (Government of Israel) and the PA (Palestinian Authority) should reaffirm their commitment to existing agreements and undertakings and should immediately implement an unconditional cessation of violence.
- The GOI and PA should immediately resume security cooperation. . . . Effective bilateral cooperation aimed at preventing violence will encourage the resumption of negotiations.
- The PA and GOI should resume their efforts to identify, condemn, and discourage incitement in all its forms.
- The PA should make clear through concrete action to Palestinians and Israelis alike that terrorism is reprehensible and unacceptable, and that the PA will make a 100 percent effort to prevent terrorist operations and to punish perpetrators.
- The GOI should freeze all settlement activity, including the "natural growth" of existing settlements.

- The GOI should ensure that the IDF adopt and enforce policies and procedures encouraging non-lethal responses to unarmed demonstrators, with a view to minimizing casualties and friction between the two communities.
- The GOI should lift closures, transfer to the PA all tax revenues owed, and permit Palestinians who had been employed in Israel to return to their jobs.
- The PA and GOI should consider a joint undertaking to preserve and protect holy places sacred to the traditions of Muslims, Jews, and Christians.
- The GOI and PA should jointly endorse and support the work of Palestinian and Israeli non-governmental organizations (NGOs) involved in cross-community initiatives linking the two peoples.

Very little of the above happened. The violence continued and escalated significantly. Israelis were being blown up in shopping malls, and the room in which Rajoub tried to end the intifada was hit by tank shells ordered by IDF Chief of Staff Shaul Mofaz.

The violence of the second intifada was horrendous. The peace process was dead, replaced by the culture of hatred and fear. A new generation of Israelis and Palestinians would come of age in an era of terrorism, death, destruction, and violence beyond imagination. I knew that we in IPCRI had to continue our work. We had to continue to demonstrate that there were Israelis and Palestinians still committed to peace. The work became increasingly difficult. It was almost impossible to meet inside Israel or Palestine. The West Bank and Gaza were closed and dangerous for Israelis to be there. It was very difficult to get permits for Palestinians to enter Israel. We were constantly struggling with the Israeli Army to grant us permits. When we were able to secure permits, on so many occasions the planned meetings had to end early because of security concerns or because there was an attack in Israel and the Palestinians were afraid to stay or an attack in Palestine and the Palestinians were afraid that they may not be able to get home or that someone from their family had been hurt.

In the beginning of the intifada, two of the many teachers involved in IPCRI's peace education program were killed. The following is what I wrote about those two peace education teachers:

On July 17, 2001, a Palestinian teacher was killed by an Israeli Apache helicopter missile. He was not the target of the attack—only one of its victims. The teacher, Isaaq Saada, was a peace activist, not a very popular activity during these times in Palestine. Isaaq (51 years old) had for the previous five years been a teacher of Peace Education, one of about 300 Israeli and Palestinian high school teachers involved in the Peace Education Project of the Israel/Palestine Center for Research and Information. The day before he was killed, Isaaq phoned the office of IPCRI expressing his desire to increase his involvement and his commitment to peace education. At the very hour that he was buried on July 18, he was supposed to take part in a joint seminar with other Palestinian teachers and their Israeli colleagues.

Some of Isaaq's Israeli colleagues recalled that he had recently spoken about his personal difficulties in confronting his students and family with his own activities in peace education. Many people, he said, could not understand why he continued to meet with Israelis while they were so brutal against the Palestinian intifada and against Palestinian rights. Isaaq told them he had a brother who was an activist in Hamas. He said that he wanted his own children and his students to follow the path of peace and not to "fill their hearts with hatred"—that, he said, would only be bad for the Palestinian people.

Isaaq was assassinated by Israel in what is called "extra-judicial killings." Israel has justified these killings as legitimate acts against terrorists, or what they call "ticking bombs." These assassinations also kill completely innocent people—like Isaaq. The Israelis were after Isaaq's brother, Omar. Omar and two other people were sitting behind their small house in a poor section of Bethlehem when an Apache Helicopter suddenly shot two missiles at them. Isaaq was in his house when he heard the explosion. Isaaq ran out of the house followed by two of his ten children upon hearing the explosion and was immediately killed by a third missile.

The Israeli official media reported that "Four Hamas Terrorists" were killed by the IDF while planning a terrorist bombing to take place at a public event in Jerusalem. Much of the international media picked up the Israeli story and reported it in the same way. A senior Israeli security official admitted to a Member of Knesset whom I queried that Isaaq Saada was not a terrorist and that his death was an accident. No public statement of that kind was made.

Isaaq left behind ten children and a wife. Will his children learn and live the values and lessons of peace that Isaaq has wanted to pass onto them, or will they grow up in a world consumed with dreams of revenge? Isaaq didn't have life insurance, there's no such thing in Palestine. The Israelis will offer no assistance to his family. The Palestinian Authority will grant the family a few dollars every month—far short of what is required for minimal subsistence. IPCRI established a fund for the family of Isaaq Saada.

On October 22, 2002, another IPCRI peace education teacher was killed, Orna Eshel. Orna was from Kibbutz Maabarot in the center of Israel. She had moved with her husband and three children to a settlement just on the other side of the Green Line. She said that she didn't move there for ideological reasons, but for economic ones. It was the only place that she and her husband could have a home of their own with enough space to raise her family. This is what the Israeli Foreign Ministry's web page wrote about Orna:

October 29, 2002—Orna Eshel, 53, of Hermesh, was one of three people shot dead by a Palestinian terrorist who infiltrated the settlement north of Tulkarem. The terrorist first fired into the Eshel house, mortally wounding Orna and moderately wounding her husband, Yuval, before shooting Hadas Turgeman and her best friend, Linoy Saroussi, both 14, as they were chatting at the entrance to Linoy's house. The attacker was killed by soldiers and local residents. A soldier and a resident were wounded in the assault.

Orna Eshel had moved with her husband to Hermesh from Kibbutz Maabarot several years ago, but the couple returned to the kibbutz at the outbreak of the intifada. They moved back to Hermesh in August 2002, after the security situation had calmed down.

Orna wholeheartedly believed in peace and engaged in many educational activities promoting Israeli-Arab coexistence. Orna Eshel was buried in Kibbutz Maabarot. She was survived by her husband, Yuval, two sons, and a daughter.

This was the environment in which we were functioning. Each day coming to the office was a challenge. I knew that I had to continue to be optimistic and to look forward to better times. It was very difficult to continue to believe in peace with all of the hatred and death surrounding us.

Dilemmas of a Peacemaker

16

This is the text of an email I sent to IPCRI friends and supporters, written on Monday, April 8, 2002:

Two weeks after the beginning of "Defensive Shield," Israel's military operation to crush the second intifada.

Even before the latest Israeli invasion of the Palestinian territories following the Passover suicide bombing in Netanya two weeks ago, the work of peacemaking between Israelis and Palestinians has been a Sisyphus-type task. The frustrations far outweigh the feelings of success and every day is a new struggle to find hope to feed the motivation to continue. Many articles have been written over the past nineteen months in newspapers around the world about those of us who continue to work for peace in Israel and Palestine. Always these articles contain the question: Can they continue?

After a brief holiday abroad for Passover I came back to face the staff of IPCRI, our colleagues and friends, many of them living under curfew, in the midst of a brutal war, their families and themselves under risks of imprisonment or even more violent fates. I too followed the news by the hour from thousands of miles away, checking my email and the Internet at least four times a day, being glued to the 24-hours-a-day news programs on American television. One morning I woke at 7:00 a.m. to put a video movie on the television for one of my children. The TV was set to CNN. In the background I saw a picture from Israeli television—it was my supermarket, 100 meters from my home, that had been bombed. Two Israelis were killed, Chaim Sabar, a 55-year-old security guard, and Rahel Levy, 17, a young girl from my daughter's school class. It seemed that each morning we were greeted by more and more bad and worsening news from home. I spent additional hours each day phoning friends and colleagues in the West Bank to find out how they were. Many friends and family members suggested to my wife and to my children that maybe we should stay in America for a while—a year or two or more. No one apparently had the courage to offer me the same advice. I felt too far away and I was anxious to come home.

But coming home isn't easy. What should we do now? How can we be effective to change this awful reality? I spoke with some Palestinian leaders and asked them for advice—how can we help, what difference can we make? One senior Palestinian official told me that the most important thing to do is to find the way to get the Palestinian medical services functioning once again. People are dying because of lack of functioning hospitals, doctors are under curfew, ambulances are shot at, supplies are finished, blood is running out, no electricity, no water, etc. Thinking that perhaps the Israeli Minister of Health, MK [Member of Knesset] Nissim Dahan from Shas, might be willing to raise his voice, I phoned another MK from Shas, a deputy minister who had been involved in some of IPCRI's back-channel talks in the past. In the past, MK Yitzhak Cohen had even come to IPCRI's office in Bethlehem to meet Marwan Barghouthi and other senior Tanzim officials. I thought that if I use the Jewish term "pikuah nefesh"—for the sake of human lives, I might be able to convince him to speak with his fellow Shas MK, Minister of Health Dahan. I called Yitzhak at home on this past Friday morning. I was told by him that the only "pikuh nefesh" that he was concerned with were of Jewish origin. He said to me, "Do you want an IDF soldier to be killed by a terrorist hiding in an ambulance?" as ambulances have already been used for the purpose of transporting terrorists. I had little to say to him. I suggested that they should at least let the doctors get to the hospitals and allow medicine to enter the Palestinian territories. My requests fell on deaf ears. He told me to speak to the army. For the sake of "pikuh nefesh," I did call the IDF and spoke to several senior officers, but they too seemed less than interested in helping.

In our staff meeting yesterday in IPCRI with those members of the staff who could come to our office, located on the border between Jerusalem and Bethlehem, we held a discussion for several hours trying to figure out what we should/could be doing now. From our office, we can hear the shooting in Bethlehem just 100 meters away. The tanks are moving in and out along the road adjacent to the entrance to our place. We have two members of our staff under siege in Bethlehem, one in a refugee camp, visible from our office, and another one further inside the city—her house had been in the middle of the fighting the night before and seven bullets penetrating their windows into their living room. We began the meeting by having each person express what they felt and thought about their own personal situation and experiences and their more general view of the situation. Most people spoke about being attacked by friends and family for continuing to work with people from the other side and continuing to believe in peace with them. Everyone also spoke with an overwhelming sense of pessimism and despair, all of them looking at me with the hope that I would provide the message of hope and a bit of optimism. Not an easy task these days.

I said that perhaps the most important thing that we could/should do during these days is to keep our own personal contacts and lines of communication open and encourage all of our colleagues and friends to do the same. Our message must be one of solidarity with those people on both sides who still want peace. We know that there are still people on both sides who believe in peace. We must try to provide humanitarian aid wherever and however possible. Yesterday I helped a shipment of donated food supplies to get to a refugee camp. These small elements of help can provide some small relief from the suffering. We must also continue to help in the development of public policy options particularly at this time when public thinking has become so one dimensional. Our ability to communicate with people in positions of leadership and power on both sides is perhaps unique and essential, maybe even more than ever right now.

I believe that the possibility of a bi-lateral Israeli-Palestinian solution is further away than ever and therefore, we must turn to the international community to help. We might need for the United States to play a much more responsible leadership role. There are initial signs that this is beginning to happen, but it must not be too little because it is already too late. [In 2016, I no longer believe in the viability of any imposed solution and strongly believe that the parties have to get to the solutions primarily on their own.] Civil society, locally, in Israel and in Palestine, and internationally must become much more aggressive and determined in making demands to end the conflict first by ending the siege of Palestine and getting the Palestinian leadership to retake control of its territory and its people. Terrorism must end, but Israel must understand that the root reasons for the terrorism must be addressed and not only the symptoms. The occupation must end and if the leaders and people of Israel are incapable of seeing that just now because of the threats that they face, the international community, at the political level and at the civil society level, must drive that point home in determined and in unambiguous language. The days of constructive ambiguity are far behind us.

The people of Israel and the Government of Israel must understand that they are waging a war that cannot be won. The occupation will end and an independent State of Palestine will be established. The current destruction of the basis for future understanding between Israelis and Palestinians can and must be repaired by individual Israelis and Palestinians together. We must overcome the hatred, the anger, the fear, and the despair. That is the true task of peacemakers today. At a time when our leaders have stopped thinking about tomorrow, we must provide the tomorrow. We must create the hope through our expression of human concern for each other's welfare. We must demand that our relations be humanized when all around us tells us to dehumanize the other.

When my Palestinian friends are under siege, when they have no water, no food, are living under curfew and risk being killed, my expression of outrage is a message of my humanity and my belief that this is not being done in my name. When many Palestinians call me to express their outrage after a suicide bombing in Israel, I too know that this was not done in their name and their expression of outrage is a witness to their humanity. I will not accept that there are no partners on the other side. I know that there are many, as I know that there are many in Israel.

We in IPCRI have decided that we are not canceling any of our work plans. We may have to delay them for reasons beyond our control. We will not accept "no" as an answer from people who yesterday were willing to meet and talk and today have changed their mind. We will continue to provide the venue and the means for people to meet and talk and plan together a better future. We will continue to oppose the use of violence and force as a means of conflict resolution—this resolves no conflicts and can solve no problems.

We all live in great fear today. We all have no real idea what is in store for us each and every day. We have to remain firmly committed to our principles and to our visions. And if reality doesn't fit our vision right now, we must not accept the new reality, we must reject it and we must change it. When I first became politically involved in this conflict some 27 years ago and I supported the two-state solution—the creation of an independent State of Palestine alongside of Israel in the 1967 borders—I was called a traitor and a self-hating Jew. There may still be those who continue to say that, but I know that the majority of the people of Israel still recognize that that is what will emerge, if only we are wise enough to accept it. People might think that we are crazy and naïve. I believe that I am neither. The positions that we represent and stand by are the only sane and the most un-naïve positions possible. When the entire area has gone insane, remaining sane can sometimes seem like insanity, but there is a clear and coherent difference. Recognizing that difference is the first step in reclaiming our roles as peacemakers.

Near Death Experiences

17

THE OFFICE

There were many times over the past years when I put myself into seriously dangerous situations. Sometimes I was not fully aware of the danger in advance, other times I knew I was taking risks and did whatever I had to do, nonetheless. There were several times when I was truly scared and one time when death was literally a centimeter away.

When I rented my first office in East Jerusalem, it was in the early days of the first intifada. Jews did not venture into East Jerusalem. The only Israeli presence I saw there on a daily basis was police patrols, in cars and on horseback. This was a time when Palestinian violence against Israelis was mostly burning Israeli vehicles and stabbing people from behind. Every so often, there were cases when both of these happened, literally, outside of my office. IPCRI's first office was in the Hindiyeh Family Building, Nablus Road #1, the first building on Nablus Road directly across from the Damascus Gate of the Old City of Jerusalem. One could not select a more central location in East Jerusalem.

Israelis were afraid to come there. I bought an air conditioner from one of the leading Israeli companies. They refused to come to install it, even after I said to them that the office was located in the "undivided eternal capital of the State of Israel and the Jewish people." They were not convinced. I had to find a Palestinian technician to install the air conditioner.

I parked my car in the parking lot of *Al-Fajr* newspaper, about 250 meters from the office. Mr. Hanna Siniora, later to become cochairman of the board of IPCRI and then my co-CEO, was the publisher and editor of the newspaper and welcomed me and my car in his space. This protected my car from getting burned. Eventually my car did get the torch in East Jerusalem on a day when I didn't park in the *Al-Fajr* lot, parking closer to the office because I was only going to be there for a short time. After leaving the office, I walked around the corner and saw the Israeli fire patrol extinguishing the fire that engulfed my car. The Israeli government's insurance paid for the car, but I got a bill from the fire patrol to pay for their service.

The office I rented was quite reasonably priced, given its central location. It was quite filthy when I first rented it. I knew that it had been vacant for a while. After I moved in, the neighbors gave me some information that might have influenced me not to take the office. In 1986, a Fatah terrorist cell murdered an Israeli woman, Zahava Ben Ovadia, who was what is commonly known as a "fixer" in the office that I rented three years later. Zahava had a business that assisted Palestinians to get licenses and permits from Israeli authorities in the West Bank and in Jerusalem. The kind of work that she did and the services that she provided could only be done with very good contacts in the ISA. The rumor around town was that she was herself an agent of the ISA. She was killed by a Fatah cell led by a Jerusalemite named Ali Musalamani. It took three years before the landlord found someone who was willing to rent the office where Zahava was killed. Twenty-three years later in the course of one week, I would meet Musalamani, who was released in the prisoner exchange for Gilad Schalit that I helped to facilitate. I also met Taly Ben Ovadia, Zahava's daughter who is a well-known editor and producer for Israeli television news. Musalamani expressed a desire to meet me, and I met Taly at a conference on prisoner exchanges at the Institute for National Security Studies in Tel Aviv. I asked Musalamani if he had regrets over killing Zahava Ben Ovadia. He said that he was a soldier taking orders and that he had no regrets. I asked him if he educated his children to follow in his footsteps. He said most definitely not and that one was a lawyer and the second a doctor. When I met Taly, I told her that I had met Musalamani and asked her if she might be interested in meeting him. She said that she was not. I am glad that I have never been faced with such a difficult question. I don't know how I would respond.

Back to 1989—there were many days when I was at the office alone. I was just getting started. I didn't have money to pay salaries, my own included. I could barely cover the cost of rent. My Palestinian counterparts, first Adel Yahya and then Ghassan Abdallah, were, like me, working as volunteers. I was a full-time volunteer, and they worked part time—both coming from Ramallah and having other paying jobs.

I befriended all of my neighbors in the building. I invited them for coffee. I would stop and chat with them in the mornings. There was a dentist, a lawyer, a tailor, a sewing supplies seller, and the famous newspaper name, Abu Salam, at the entrance to the building. My security would be based on having a trusting relationship with them. I was a "street wise" New Yorker, so I knew that I had to develop patterns of behavior that would protect me on the streets of East Jerusalem. I had to make myself known to the locals. The East Jerusalem Post Office on Salah a Din Street was about half a kilometer away from my office. Along the way were many shops. I made a point of getting to know every shopkeeper along the route. I walked every day from the office to Salah a Din Street to get my face known in the area. In case someone eyed me with a knife in their pocket with the intention to kill an Israeli, I would stop about every fifty meters to greet someone, shake their hand, and have a short chat. This was my protection.

The uncle of the tailor across from my office was an old gentleman named Sheikh Mousa. Sheikh Mousa was from Silwan, south of the Old City, but he would pray in the mosque nearby the office where he would also give the sermons and read from the Quran. He would stop in my building in the mornings to visit his nephew. When we first met, he came into the office—the door was open. He introduced himself in English. He was easily seventy years old. During the British Mandate, he worked in the post office where he learned English. He loved the British, missed the Mandate days a lot, loved to reminisce about the good old times, and he loved to speak English. So every morning, Sheikh Mousa would come to visit me. He had a great smile, with the few teeth still in his mouth. He also loved to drink Nescafé instant coffee and insisted that he would make it for me. Three teaspoons of sugar was a mandatory component of Sheikh Mousa's Nescafé. Talk about taking life-threatening risks! Everyone in the building and in the neighborhood knew that I was Sheikh Mousa's friend—another life insurance policy! He was a great old man, and I loved my morning chats with him. I think that he also liked his visits with me. When Sheikh Mousa passed away in the mid-1990s (Allah Yerhamu—God have mercy on his soul), I attended the funeral. There were well over one thousand people there; I was the only Jew. It seemed that everyone there knew I was Sheikh Mousa's *hawaja* (foreign or Jewish) friend. So many people came to me to say how much they appreciated me being at the funeral.

In days of tension in East Jerusalem, of which there were many, my neighbors would tell me, "Gershon, maybe you should lock your door today." But I did not listen to them. My inner voice told me that as soon as I began to lock the door, people would begin to wonder, "What is he doing behind that closed door." In my mind, that was more dangerous than taking the risk of leaving my door open. So for seven years, all throughout the first intifada and beyond, my office was located in the heart of East Jerusalem, and every day was a new adventure. People always asked me if I was scared. I don't remember feeling scared. I felt a part of the local scene, much in the way I feel now, when I travel into Palestine in 2016.

TRAFFIC JAMS CAN BE VERY DANGEROUS

In 1995, as the Palestinian Authority was establishing itself, Palestinians from the Diaspora were encouraged to come home and invest in Palestine. Israel, as the occupying force, created new programs that would allow Palestinians to come home to Palestine and get residency rights in the West Bank and Gaza. Palestinian millionaires were taking trips to investigate investment possibilities. Some of them actually managed to create new businesses, and the new Palestinian economy was launched. IPCRI wanted to encourage the trend and thought that it would be wise to see if joint ventures between Israelis and Palestinians could be developed, strengthening peace, enhancing the peace dividend, creating more jobs, opening markets, and developing mutually beneficial links across the border. IPCRI created a business forum and was working hard to create opportunities that would make it worthwhile for the busy business people to invest their time in coming to meetings.

I befriended Daniel Isa who had set up a soft drink factory in Ramallah. Daniel was in the process of trying to become the Palestinian concession owner for Coca-Cola. The Israel Bottling company, the concession for Coca-Cola in Israel, is owned by Muzi Wertheim. Muzi has a past in the Mossad and is a close friend of almost everyone in Israel's military and political establishments, especially Ariel Sharon. A member of IPCRI's board of directors, the economist Dr. Gil Feiler launched a Middle East economic consulting firm called Info-Prod (Middle East) Research. Gil's business partner was Muzi Wertheim. This was the kind of opportunity that I yearned to advance. I went to Ramallah at the invitation of Daniel Isa and had a tour of his brand-new and very modern soft drink company, which he hoped would become Coca-Cola Palestine. It was not the first time we met. The meeting went very well. I left the factory in the Ramallah industrial zone and headed toward downtown Ramallah in order to leave the city. In downtown, near the central Manara Square I found myself stuck in what could only be called "the mother of all traffic jams." Out of nowhere, my car was surrounded by about ten "shabab"—youths, but not of the kind who are on the local little league baseball team. These guys were big and scary looking. They saw me, an Israeli, in an Israeli car with Israeli license plates, and they were on the lookout for prey like me.

They knocked on my window, I had already locked my doors when I saw them approaching. I slowly rolled down the window, not enough to allow anyone to grab me. One of the shabab said to me, "'adaish is-saea"—what is the time? I looked at my watch and with a confident voice, speaking Arabic, I said, "tenteen u'nus"—two thirty. "Shu bitsawi hon?" he asked me—what are you doing here? I said, I had a meeting with some business people, and I mentioned the name of Daniel Isa. The big guy responded, "Ok—get out of here now," which is exactly what I did, as soon as the traffic moved. This was a clear reminder that not everyone on the streets was in favor of the peace process that was just unfolding. There remained a lot of dissatisfaction and criticism about the compromises that Yasser Arafat had made and the economic situation was still such that many young people, such as those that surrounded my car were unemployed and angry. It was clear to me then, as it is now, that there must be clear "peace pays"—substances within the political process that clearly demonstrates that people's lives will improve with genuine peace.

PROTECTED BY AK-47s

Around the same time, I befriended Brigadier General Samir Siksik, the deputy military liaison of the Palestinian security forces to the Israeli Army. Samir, also known as Abu Khamis, was the first PLO military officer to cross the border from Sinai into Israel to prepare for the return of Yasser Arafat and the officers and troops of the Palestinian Liberation Army who would form the core of the Palestinian security forces in Gaza. Samir told me of his first encounter with Israelis that changed his entire worldview and converted him from a man of war into a man of peace. His job as the first Palestinian officer coming in was to escort the convoy of military equipment and people from Arafat's Presidential Guard, known as Force 17, into Gaza. The PA was allowed to bring in several armored personal carriers (APCs) fit with automatic machine guns to protect the office of President Arafat. The APCs that the Palestinians had were old, outdated, Russian made. They broke down in Sinai before reaching Gaza.

Samir arrived at the Gaza crossing, under Israeli control, riding in a jeep without the APCs. The Israeli officers awaiting his arrival were surprised to see him without the armored vehicles. They inquired and Samir told them that they were left abandoned on the side of the road in Sinai. The Israeli commanders picked up the phone and called the Multi-National Force of Observers (MFO) headquarters in Sinai. The MFO coordinated with the Egyptian forces, and the IDF sent in heavy-duty trailers into Sinai to fetch the APCs. Samir was convinced that the Israelis intended to confiscate them for use in the IDF. When the APCs crossed the border into Gaza, they told Samir that the IDF would take them to their garage, repair them, and return them like new within a week. When they were returned in perfect condition, much better than they were before their long journey, Samir was totally in shock.

This story shook up Samir's entire worldview. He was a Palestinian fighter who had spent most of the years of his adult life fighting or dreaming about fighting the Israeli-Jewish Zionist enemy. Now suddenly he found himself face to face with the enemy, officer to officer, and they were not only nice, they were fixing the weapons that he envisaged he would use to fight against them from within Gaza. His first response was simply, "These Israelis are crazy." He then began to develop personal friendships and became one of the leading peace advocates within the Palestinian security apparatus.

Abu Khamis invited me to come to Gaza to visit him. I had been in Gaza many times before, but I had never been picked up from the Erez Crossing from Israel by a Palestinian army jeep escorted by two more jeeps of Palestinian soldiers carrying AK-47 rifles—Kalashnikovs—as my body guards. This was one of the more peculiar experiences I have ever had. These young

Palestinian soldiers were there to protect me; just the thought of it blew me away. We traveled around Gaza the whole day. Samir took me to the military headquarters, to the president's office, to the headquarters of the Palestinian Preventive Security force. Samir's home in Gaza was his own headquarters, not more than a small military command post with an officer's home inside.

Samir and I became very good friends. He visited me in my home in Jerusalem and met my family. I once traveled with him to Amman and met his children and his wife. He had come to Gaza without his family and would return periodically to Amman to see them. On one of my visits to him in Gaza, after spending the whole day together, we sat down in the evening in his home/command post for dinner. I knew that something was on his mind and he was waiting for the right opportunity to tell me. "Gershon," he said, "I want you to tell Rabin that there are at least thirty-five tunnels under the Rafah crossing area, and they are smuggling weapons into Gaza." I said to Samir, if this is true, why aren't you doing something about it? He then held his two arms together in a crossed position and said, "I can't, my hands are tied, but if Israel doesn't do something about it, the situation will blow [up] in both of our faces." This was in the beginning of 1995. I reported what Samir told me to the Rabin peace team with which I was in contact. To the best of my knowledge, nothing was done with the information, and it did blow up in our faces. I was surprised that Samir gave me this information. I was less surprised that he knew that nothing would be done within his own command to prevent these smuggling tunnels from being used to smuggle in weapons and explosives.

Samir was a brave man and, as a supporter of peace with Israel, he developed a real hatred toward Hamas and the other radical Islamic groups. One day, the main Hamas-supported mosque in downtown Gaza was spewing hateful ranting from one of the local Hamas Sheikhs over the public loudspeakers. What was being said must have been really bad because Samir got out of his jeep, took his Kalashnikov rifle out, and shot down the speakers on the mosque. It was quite a scandal, and all of Gaza was speaking about it. Arafat punished Samir by putting him in prison for a week, but Samir became a legend in Gaza after that. When I asked Samir about the incident, he simply smiled from ear to ear.

Samir, his commander Major General Nasser Yusef (Abu Yusef), and Nizar Ammar, the brigadier general in charge of planning for the Palestinian Security Forces (who participated in our London Security Group back in 1992), were all very critical of the multiplicity of Palestinian forces under Arafat's command. They were most wary of Mohammed Dahlan and the preventive security force in Gaza. They all criticized the lack of democracy developing in the Palestinian Authority over the years and were concerned that without democracy there would be no peace. My many meetings with them, in their offices or in their homes, always focused on issues concerning the negative developments that they saw within their own society. Yet none of them took a step forward and raised these issues in public or faced Arafat directly. I was impressed that there were people like these three in high-level positions of authority within the Palestinian security forces, yet I was equally disappointed that they never stood up and challenged the failings that they saw so clearly.

ON A MISSION FOR THE PRIME MINISTER

One more Samir-related story (even though it is out of sequence in terms of time). In December 2000, in the third month of the second intifada, five months after the calamity of the failure of the Camp David summit in July 2000, the Israelis and Palestinians were still in the midst of negotiations, despite the bullets flying back and forth. The two sides agreed to try one more time with a negotiating summit. This time it would take place in Taba, in Sinai, on the Israeli-Egyptian border. Even though Prime Minister Barak had a government without a majority in the Knesset, he was persuaded by his foreign minister, Prof. Shlomo Ben Ami, to try and push the envelope and reach an agreement with the Palestinians. Much progress had been made in the negotiations being run by Barak's Chief of Staff Gilad Sher and by Saeb Erakat on the Palestinian side. The summit would take place about two weeks before national elections in Israel. If an agreement could be reached, some thought on the Israeli side, Barak could win a victory in the elections and fulfill the dream of securing peace.

I was asked by General Danny Yatom, the director of Barak's office, through Moshe Amirav, who Yatom enlisted to set up a committee of experts on Jerusalem, to draft some ideas on the refugee issue and on the issue of the Temple Mount. My instructions were that on the issue of refugees I should not use the terminology "right of return" and that on the Temple Mount issue I should not use the words "Palestinian Sovereignty." With those exceptions, the Israeli negotiators were willing to consider any new and creative ideas. I drafted eight pages of proposed wording on both issues. I received a call from Yatom, who wanted to know what the Palestinians thought about my proposals. I told him I would check with them.

I called Dr. Nabeel Shaath, who I had heard would be chairing the committee on refugees at the Taba summit. I knew Nabeel Shaath from the early 1990s when I would visit him in Cairo. Nabeel told me to send him the ideas, which I did, and then he asked me to come to Gaza to discuss them. He invited me to come to Gaza on Thursday, December 21, 2000, a short time before the start of the Taba summit. He wanted me to come in the evening. We are now about three months into the second intifada. On many nights, the Erez crossing between Israel and Gaza became a shooting zone. There is a half-a-kilometer gap between the Israeli and Palestinian sides of the crossing. During normal times, there were taxis that would take you from one side to the other, or you could walk through the "sleeve," which was a kind of aboveground tunnel for workers from Gaza who had jobs and permits to work in Israel. During the intifada, the "sleeve" was closed and no taxis crossed over. But before even arriving there, I had to deal with the Israeli side.

I was authorized by the Prime Minister's Office of Israel to go to Gaza in order to talk to Dr. Nabeel Shaath in a kind of prenegotiation. When I arrived at the Israeli side of the Erez crossing into Gaza, I presented my Israeli ID card to the female soldier in the office. Yes, my name was there, but then she took out the standard form for me to sign that relinquishes responsibility from the State of Israel should something happen to me. Imagine that! Unbelievable.

After being amazed by how the State of Israel had decided to relate to my mission, I then found myself standing in the middle of the road, five hundred meters long, between Israel and God knows what will greet me on the other side. Shooting could begin at any minute between the sides, and I could be targeted from both sides. There was no moon that night, total darkness. I thought to myself, would it be safer for me to walk along the outer wall of the "sleeve," which could protect me but maybe on the other side they will think that I am sneaking my way across? Or should I boldly walk in the middle so that everyone could easily see me, but then I would also be a very easy target? I think that I was so scared that I searched for a mental diversion, just so that I could get to the other side safe and as quickly as possible without panicking. I remember thinking to myself, what would Ehud Barak do? Barak is Israel's most decorated soldier, a real hero. Barak, as prime minister, was being attacked by the opposition and the media for his "zig-zag" policy decisions. I said to myself, "Barak would zig-zag his way across the five hundred meters," so that is what I actually did. It probably took me twice the time, but no one shot at me.

When I did arrive on the other side, three Palestinian soldiers were poised, facing me, with their Kalashnikov rifles pointed at me. I raised my hands in the air and said, "Don't shoot; I am coming to meet Nabeel Shaath." They escorted me into a shack and the officer in charge asked me several questions. I told him that Shaath's driver is supposed to pick me up to take me to Shaath's home. Well, we waited and waited, and no one came. It was a cold night, so they offered me tea, sweet tea with mint, of course. The commander asked me what I was going to talk to Shaath about. I told him "the refugee issue." Well, there were nine soldiers in the room; all of them were refugees, and they wanted to know what ideas I was going to present. It turned out to be a fascinating discussion. After about thirty minutes when the driver did not show up, the commander called Shaath's home. The driver answered. He had fallen asleep. He said he would be there soon. And even though under normal conditions it would take twenty to thirty minutes, he was there in less than fifteen.

In equal time, I was delivered to Nabeel Shaath's home. He was newly (re)married and had a small pet dog that was treated like the king of the home. His Sri Lankan servant offered tea, coffee, other drinks, and food. I told him that it was already quite late, after 9:00 p.m., and we had a lot of work to do. I told him that I had to report back to the Prime Minister's Office as soon as possible. We got right into the work. Shaath is very smart and a real diplomat and skilled negotiator. He was quite flexible, and I found a lot of support from him for some of the ideas I presented. I would say that if the negotiations were left to Shaath and myself, we would have found an acceptable middle point on both of these sensitive key issues, but both of us were very inclined to find agreement, and the atmosphere was much less of a tough negotiation and much more of a shared desire to find solutions.

Shaath was very serious about the proposals I drafted. He had studied them in advance and was prepared to discuss them. There were definitely ideas presented that he as a PLO leader could live with and thought that Arafat would accept as well. There were other ideas that he entirely rejected. I took notes throughout the evening in order to prepare my report for the Prime Minister's Office. It was already after midnight. The evening went by very quickly. There was no way I was going to travel back to Israel at this time of night.

I called Abu Khamis, Brig. General Samir Siksik, and he of course invited me to stay the night. Shaath's driver took me to Samir's headquarters. There were armed troops in front and a large metal gate that had to be opened for me to enter. It was after 1:00 a.m. Samir had a meal for us to eat, a light snack of salad, eggs, humus, labeneh (a kind of dried yoghurt), French fries, and fresh pita bread. We ate and drank sweet tea and talked until after 3:00 a.m. I slept for a few hours and then, at around 6:30 a.m., I was driven back to the Erez checkpoint. The jeep could not bring me to the Israeli side because it would have been shot at. So once again, I had to walk the five hundred meters, this time in broad daylight, which I am not so sure was safer. When I arrived on the Israeli side, I was not greeted with soldiers pointing their guns at me, but they were clearly confused by seeing an Israeli coming from Gaza so early that morning well into the second intifada.

STAY ON THE MAIN ROAD

In 1996, we moved our office from Jerusalem to Bethlehem. The peace process was moving forward, and more and more Palestinians were coming to

Israel. For each Israeli-Palestinian meeting we organized, we had to request permits from the Israeli Army for Palestinians to enter Israel. Palestinian vehicles were allowed, with permits, on Israeli roads, and Israeli cars were allowed into the areas controlled by the Palestinian Authority. Nonetheless, Israelis were much less likely to enter the Palestinian areas than vice versa. I thought that it would be good to create a situation where Israelis had to come to the Palestinian side. Moving our office to Bethlehem was one such way. I chose Bethlehem and not Ramallah because it was less crowded, got less attention, was smaller and easier to get to and move around in. In Bethlehem, we were also much less under the direct scrutiny of the Palestinian Authority.

Most Israelis that we invited to come to the office were afraid to come. Usually, we would convince them to come to Rachel's Tomb, which was under Israeli control—in fact, there was full Israeli control from the entrance of Bethlehem until Rachel's Tomb. The checkpoint at the entrance to Bethlehem was called Checkpoint 300, it being that many meters from there to the tomb. Most Israelis would agree to do that. Someone from the office would go and meet them there and they would follow us back to the office. Some were afraid to even come as far as Rachel's Tomb, so we would pick them up at Checkpoint 300. On their second visit to IPCRI, most people would usually come on their own, seeing how peaceful the place was.

The office was located on the border between Bethlehem and al-Doha. The following story is what people in Bethlehem told me about the history of the place where the IPCRI office had relocated. I am not completely sure about its full accuracy, but this is not a history book, and the stories that I was told are interesting and demonstrate how people see their own narratives.

South of Bethlehem before the Dheisha refugee camps was a lot of land originally owned by residents of Beit Jala. The area was part of the Beit Jala municipality. Several decades ago, there were three predominantly Christian cities in the West Bank: Bethlehem, Beit Sahour, and Beit Jala. They are adjacent to each other. With a large exodus of Christians from the West Bank over the years, the only predominantly Christian city today is Beit Sahour. There is now a Muslim majority in Beit Jala and in Bethlehem.

In the 1970s, Palestinians from the Dheisha refugee camp (Muslims) who were working in Israel and beginning to earn more significant wages began purchasing land from Beit Jala. Soon their numbers increased and a large Muslim population was beginning to build homes and settle within the Beit Jala municipality. Facing this Muslim invasion, as the local people called it, the Beit Jala municipality decided to cut out a section from their statutory boundaries and create the town of al-Doha. Palestine Street is the borderline between Beit Jala and al-Doha. IPCRI's office was on Palestine Street, about one hundred meters from the Bethlehem Muqata'a—the Palestinian Authority military headquarters—and right next to the headquarters of the infamous Palestinian Preventive Authority.

I very much enjoyed driving from my home in southwest Jerusalem to Bethlehem every day. I explored Bethlehem and its surroundings, and I was really feeling at home there. I did most of my shopping there and thought it was important to support the local economy. When we moved to Bethlehem, IPCRI opened registration files with the PA Ministries of Interior and Finance. We opened a bank account in the closet Palestinian bank, a branch of the Egyptian Arab Land Bank where one of our board members, Fouad Jabr, was the CEO. We decided to process our salaries through the Palestinian Ministry of Finance and the Palestinian bank and to pay taxes to the Palestinian Authority. The Paris Protocol, the economic agreement between Israel and the PLO, made allowances for Palestinians to continue working in Israel and their income taxes would be delivered by Israel to the Palestinian Authority, after deducting a three percent service fee. Surprisingly, there was also an arrangement for Israelis to pay the PA tax authorities and for those taxes to count against the taxes that would normally be paid to Israel. This was a concession by Israel to the Palestinians. So, my salary had its taxes deducted and paid to the PA. I had to file an additional tax return to pay my national insurance (social security) payment directly to Israel and the additional taxes I owed, because the tax structure on the Palestinian side allowed for smaller tax payments. We offered all of our Israeli workers to be paid in this way, or to be paid through an Israeli employment agency. Most of them chose to be paid through the Israeli agency. I chose to be paid through the PA tax system. I was working physically in Palestine, and I thought it was right to pay my taxes there. I thought it was also an expression of solidarity, a vote of confidence in the peace process and a demonstration to others of an example of genuine economy peacemaking.

Our office was located in a beautiful brand-new building. We had the entire floor of that building, and we were preparing to take another floor just before the outbreak of the second intifada. On October 9, 2000, eleven days after the beginning of the second intifada, I left work in Bethlehem on my way home to Jerusalem. Although the violence began on September 28, 2000, the Palestinian areas had not yet been designated off-limits to Israelis, and I could still enter Bethlehem. Since the beginning of the intifada, all other Israeli members of the staff stopped coming to the office because they thought it was too dangerous. On the morning of October 9, 2000, we had a visit from Commander Abu Iyad, the commander of Palestinian Preventive Security in Bethlehem. Knowing that there were Israelis in the office, probably the only Israelis in Bethlehem, he came to see us. We had coffee together, and he requested that until things calm down we should keep a very low profile. I suggested that perhaps I should take a break from coming to the office, or at least to stop coming in my car. He told us that I could park the car at the top of Beit Jala in the Talitha Kumi School, a private school with a large compound. The entrance to the school was on a road controlled by Israeli patrols. The back side of the school had a door leading to Beit Jala in an area controlled by the Palestinian security.

Later that day while driving to my home in Jerusalem toward Rachel's Tomb, I remembered that I left something on my desk that I needed for a meeting the next day. Before Rachel's Tomb, there was a place to make a U-turn. Since the Palestinian Authority took control of Bethlehem, the Palestinian police set up a checkpoint in that spot, just south of Rachel's Tomb. The newly opened Bethlehem Intercontinental Hotel was just before the checkpoint. Until now, the checkpoint had been there as a symbolic presence. The Palestinian police never stopped anyone, and it was normal just to drive through it without even stopping.

After I made my U-turn to return to the office, out of nowhere, eight non-uniformed armed security personal jumped out and surrounded my car. One of them opened my front door on the passenger side, jumped in, and with his AK-47 pointed at me, he said, "Drive!" My mind was racing and my reflexes responded quickly. I shut the motor, threw the keys on the floor under my foot and said, "Call Jabril Rajoub (the commander of the Preventive Security for the whole West Bank) and tell him that you are holding Gershon Baskin." I thought to myself, the safest place for me to be right now is in front of the Intercontinental Hotel on the main road some one hundred meters before Rachel's Tomb. As long as the Israeli Army didn't start shooting at the Palestinian checkpoint, or vice versa, this was the best place for me to be. The gun-pointing, non-uniformed soldier sitting next to me started asking me questions: "You know Jabril Rajoub? How do you know him? What are you doing here?" I explained to him who I was and what I was doing in Bethlehem. I told him that for the past four years I have had an office in Bethlehem, and I was on my way home and forgot something in the office. I told him that if he couldn't locate Rajoub, he should call Abu Iyad, whom I drank coffee with just that morning in my office.

We waited for what seemed an eternity. The gun-pointing, nonuniformed soldier sitting next to me, seeing that I was nervous, kept saying, "Don't be afraid." I should point out that our entire conversation took place in Arabic, which I discovered under pressure sounds a lot more like real Arabic than when I normally speak it. After about fifteen or twenty minutes, a car pulled in front of me, and another officer stepped toward the car. The gun pointing non-uniformed soldier sitting next to me opened the door and got out. The officer began asking me questions, "Are you Gershon

Baskin? Are you from IPCRI?" Yes, yes, I said. He then said that he had instructions to escort me out of Bethlehem. I started the engine and followed him while a Palestinian military jeep rode behind me as we drove to the top of Beit Jala where I left the Palestinian Authority–controlled areas. It was the last time over the course of the next five years that I would enter Bethlehem with my car.

On October 13, 2000, four days later, two Israeli reserved soldiers accidently drove into a Palestinian checkpoint at Beitunia, west of Ramallah. The Palestinian solders at the checkpoint ordered them to drive to Ramallah, to the central police station there. To their horrendously bad fortune, as they arrived at the police station, a funeral procession was passing for someone who was killed by the Israelis. The angry crowd grabbed the two soldiers from their car and dragged them into the Ramallah police station. Inside, they were lynched. In one of the most horrific scenes of violence ever filmed in this conflict, their dead bodies were thrown from the second-floor window of the police station, and their killers proudly displayed their blood-covered hands to an Italian film crew who happened to have captured the entire event on film. That could have been me, was my first thought.

Over the next two months, I continued to come to the office, doing as Abu Iyad had suggested. I parked my car at the Talitha Kumi school and either someone would pick me up and take me to the office or I would take a taxi, which were now waiting there because Israel had closed the entrances from Beit Jala into Bethlehem. I was the only Israeli on our staff who was coming into work. We would hold staff meetings once a week in my home in Jerusalem and conduct our work together by telephone and Internet while we waited and hoped that the situation would calm down and return to something closer to normalcy. It didn't appear that was happening, and more and more we began to consider the need to relocate our office to a place where Israelis and Palestinians could get to safely.

Sometime before Christmas that year, I parked my car at Talitha Kumi, as usual, and Zakaria al-Qaq came to pick me up on the "Palestinian side." When we met, he told me that he thought I should not have come that day. On the ride up from our office, he saw a group of armed young men in the road stopping cars. I listened to him and went home. Going home for me had the feeling of defeat. I hated the feeling; I was both sad and really angry. On his way back to the office, the armed men stopped Zakaria, searched the car, including the trunk, and let him go. They said to him, "We heard that there are some Israelis in the area." That was my second to last day in our wonderful office on Palestine Street, al-Doha. I came one more time to clean out my personal things and to instruct the movers on packing up the office.

Over the years, we had held many conferences at a place called Tantur, an ecumenical institute on Vatican land on the Jerusalem-Bethlehem border. The rector of Tantur, Father Michael McGarry, when once addressing one of our conferences, explained "Tantur was neutral but not indifferent." In January 2001, we met Father McGarry and appealed to his not being indifferent to allow IPCRI to move to Tantur for an interim period, until the violence ends. Tantur was very cautious in Israel's superpoliticized environment not to do anything that would anger the Israeli government against the church, but he could not turn us down, we told him that we had nowhere to go. He deeply appreciated the work of IPCRI and agreed to allow us to move in. In February 2001, we moved to our new base on Vatican land in between Jerusalem and Bethlehem.

TAKING SHELTER IN THE CHURCH

Before the huge separation wall was built cutting Bethlehem off from Jerusalem, Tantur was on the footpath used by up to one thousand Palestinians a day to get from the south of the West Bank into Jerusalem and into Israel for work. There were days when the path from Bethlehem through Tantur into Jerusalem was like a pedestrian highway. The path began about 150 meters before Checkpoint 300. If you didn't have a permit to enter Israel, there were lots of ways to simply walk around the checkpoint from the side. Tantur was one of those sides. People would walk from the main Bethlehem-Jerusalem road up the side of the hill to Tantur. Tantur is surrounded by a stone wall, a symbolic border as the land is owned by the Vatican and the compound enjoys the privileges awarded to diplomatic missions under the Vienna Convention. In other words, Tantur is off-limits to the Israeli authorities.

After the second intifada began, the Israeli police demanded that Tantur close the back door of the compound, which leads to and from Bethlehem. Father McGarry refused. He said that the door exists in the legal plans for the compound approved by the Jerusalem municipality, and additionally, if he closed it, the Palestinians would relate to Tantur as an Israeli institution and could vandalize the property or hurt the more than twenty Palestinian employees working there. So the door remained open, and the flow of Palestinians illegally entering Jerusalem continued. People needed work to feed their families, and the intifada was not going to stop them from entering Jerusalem. The economy of the West Bank was falling into ruin, which only increased the pressure for Palestinians to try and find work in Israel.

In response to Father McGarry's refusal to close the back door, the Israeli Army decided to dump a huge quantity of dirt and stones in front of the door, and in doing so, they also broke part of the surrounding wall. It didn't take more than twenty-four hours for Palestinian workers to clear the path to the door in the wall. This was an exercise that repeated itself many times. Once, the army dumped heavy grease on the boulders they put in front of the gate, and once again, twenty-four hours later the door was cleared—the workers dumped sand on the grease and then wiped it all off.

The workers kept coming up the path and through the gate. Every day sitting in my office, I would watch the parade of workers coming through, and several times a week, I would watch soldiers and border guards chasing them. I took very seriously the principle that Tantur was Vatican land and that the soldiers and border police were in violation of both Israeli law and international law, and I insisted that they know it. It was very clear to me that if they wanted to prevent Palestinian workers without permits from entering Jerusalem, they must do so in accordance with the law. They could stand and surround the Tantur compound from the northern side where the exit is to Jerusalem, but they could not come into the compound and do whatever they wanted on the church land.

I would run out of my office as I saw the soldiers and border police chasing Palestinians, and I would try to stop them. Once the Palestinian workers were inside the Tantur compound, they enjoyed the shelter of international law. I told them not to give their ID cards to the soldiers and police, and I insisted that the soldiers and police leave the compound. This happened on tens of occasions and a good part of many of my mornings were spent chasing Israeli police and soldiers around Tantur, explaining to them that if they wanted the London police to respect the rights of the Israeli Embassy there, they too had to respect the rights of Tantur, which is out of their territorial control. They could catch the Palestinians outside of Tantur, but not inside. Any of the Palestinian workers who wanted to get into Jerusalem had no choice but to go through the northern gate, which enters Jerusalem. Once they did that, they would have broken the law, and the Israeli police were completely justified in stopping them. While they were in the Tantur compound, they had broken no laws.

I was arrested seven times inside Tantur for doing this. One of the times was actually outside of Tantur, just in front of Tantur from the north across the street. One of IPCRI's employees came in the office quite upset. He said that he saw a soldier beating up a young Palestinian on the street. I ran down the hill, and all out of breath, I saw a young man on the ground protecting himself while the soldier was busy kicking him. I placed myself between the soldier and the young man and stopped what he was doing. I was able to ask the young man a few questions, and it was immediately clear to me that he was mentally handicapped. The soldier tried to push me out of the way, but I was physically bigger than him. He called his friends to help, and I protected myself. In the meantime, they lost interest in the young man on the ground and focused on me. The young man ran away and no one ran after him. With words instead of force, I managed to convince them not to hit me, but they held me and forced me to sit on the ground until the "blue police" (the regular police) came and took me to the Moriah Police Station in Talpiot, Jerusalem.

The law enables the police to hold someone for three hours without questioning them. If after three hours you are not questioned, you can demand the right to leave. During the holding period, the police were in possession of my ID card. After two hours and fifty-nine minutes, I was called. I was questioned for about ten minutes. I had debated whether or not to cooperate with the questioning. I could have used the right to refuse to answer questions. I knew my rights, and I knew that I had done nothing wrong; in fact I had prevented a soldier from committing a felony. Nonetheless, the situation is humiliating and designed to cause anxiety, even fear. I was told that if I did not cooperate, I would be charged and maybe even spend the night in jail. I was not prepared for that, so I did cooperate. I explained who I was, what I do, where I work, and how I happened to be on the street in Gilo across from Tantur trying to protect the young Palestinian man on the ground. The officer listened, wrote down every word I said, which made ten minutes of questioning take more than thirty. I signed the statement. The officer said that probably no charges would be pressed against me and that I was free to leave. They, of course, did not drive me back to Tantur.

WATCHING CAN BE DANGEROUS, TOO

On October 18, 2001, after weeks of shooting from Beit Jala into the Israeli (settlement) neighborhood of Gilo in Jerusalem, Israeli forces invaded Bethlehem and Beit Jala. Shooting had been taking place nightly from Beit Jala into Gilo, where IPCRI's office was located in the Tantur Ecumenical Institute. I could hear the shooting every night from my own home in southwest Jerusalem. In the morning, I would see the physical damage done by the shooting, both in Gilo and in Beit Jala and Bethlehem. I was so sad. I spent a lot of sleepless nights listening to the shooting. The situation was intolerable. Homes were being shot at in Jerusalem. Palestinian gunmen had taken over several of the taller buildings in Beit Jala and had a bird's eye view and a clear shot at the buildings. The Israeli Army returned fire. Each morning when I came to the office, I would see the buildings in Beit Jala that had taken fire overnight.

When the Israeli Army waged a ground invasion of Bethlehem and Beit Jala in January 2001, the tanks and armed personnel carriers rolled on the road below our office. As they entered Bethlehem, the scene in front of me was like a movie. Several members of IPCRI's staff and I went on the roof of the building, and I began filming the action. Shooting was constant, back and forth. The Paradise Hotel in Bethlehem was on fire, and Palestinian combatants were shooting from the roof of the building. We watched a battle taking place in the al-Aida refugee camp just behind the Interconti-nental Hotel. One of our staff members from Bethlehem was with us. She was concerned because the fighting had moved very close to her family home where her mother and father were. Later we found out that her house had taken some shots to the outside walls.

We were about two hundred to three hundred meters away from the battle in the refugee camp. Suddenly I felt a bullet go through my hair; I heard the whistle of the bullet next to my ear. I was literally one centimeter away from death. Even now, when I watch the video and recall the scene, I can hear that bullet go by. We crawled off the roof to safety. I don't believe that someone was aiming at us. It was probably just a stray bullet, but it almost got me.

Making Peace

On January 31, 2012, I formally launched another effort toward making peace, after experiencing firsthand Netanyahu's leadership in bringing Gilad Schalit home despite the very high price. Netanyahu placed the unwritten covenant between the State of Israel and its people—that we don't leave a soldier behind—above the principle that we don't negotiate with terrorists, and by doing so, he made a crucial leadership decision. Netanyahu proved that he was able to overcome his own position and do the right thing. I thought that Netanyahu could be the best person in Israel to lead the state into a fully comprehensive peace agreement with the Palestinians, based on the parameters for peace that are well known and have been on the table since Ehud Olmert's last efforts to make peace with Abbas in September 2008. In Israel, it is often said that you cannot make war without the support of the left, and you can't make peace without the support of the right. Well, at least the second half is true. A deal between Netanyahu and the PLO leadership would firmly secure the support of about seventy percent of Israeli society. The same deal brought by the left or the center in Israel would have the potential of tearing Israeli society into pieces. It's the old "Nixon-China" thing. You need the right wing to break down the walls that it erected.

Other than my hopes that Netanyahu would lead us toward peace, as irrational or unrealistic as some may think that would be, nonetheless, fully conscious of the obstacles in the way, I was also quite hopeful that my good relationship with David Meidan, who was Netanyahu's appointed emissary to bring Gilad Schalit home from Hamas captivity after more than five years, would enable me to have a channel to pass messages directly on to the prime minister. Meidan did give me the direct phone numbers for the PM's chief of staff, Natan Eshel, and several other people in the PM's inner circle. I had the direct fax number for Netanyahu and the way to verify that my messages would reach the top. I was also hopeful that Meidan could use his relationship and his success record to help to create what I believed was the only way forward—a secret direct channel of negotiation between Netanyahu and Abbas and their emissaries. My hope was that I could convince the leaders to enter this path and that Meidan would be selected as the emissary and I would work with him. In my dreams, I saw Meidan negotiating with a person selected by Abbas and that they would agree to accept my proposal, one in which I and a Palestinian counterpart would serve as a joint strategic mediation team that would create gap-bridging proposals when needed. I even prepared a mapping of the secret back channel (see Figure 1).

I came to this suggestion following a series of meetings with President Abbas that were facilitated by then minister of Islamic Trust Affairs, Dr. Mahmoud al-Habbash. Habbash was a former member of Hamas, and from Gaza originally. Habbash and Abbas had become quite close. I thought that Habbash brought with him the legitimacy of religion, of formerly being from Hamas but having left to join the Palestinian peace camp. I also thought that the fact that he was not very well known in Israel was also a great advantage, because the Israeli side had become so used to vetoing every Palestinian leader they had negotiated with in the past. I have heard so many times of Israeli officials disparaging people's personal integrity and honesty—the people leading the chart were Saab Arikat, Nabil Shaath, and Jabril Rajoub. I thought if we could bring some new faces to the table then perhaps the task of beginning to build trust would also be easier. That is one of the reasons I was so enthusiastic about working with Habbash and developing a relationship with him.

Habbash organized a meeting for me and himself with Abbas on January 31, 2012. The following is the summary of the meeting that I wrote (in Hebrew) and sent to Netanyahu.

Report: Meeting with President Mahmoud Abbas, January 31, 2012
Meeting Background: On January 16, 2012, I met with the Palestinian Minister for Religious Affairs Dr. Mahmoud al-Habbash, a former Hamas member who is now close to Abbas. I asked Habbash help me set up a meeting with President Abbas. The purpose of the meeting: To seek Abbas's agreement to conduct negotiations with Israel through a direct secret back channel for a comprehensive Israeli-Palestinian peace agreement. After presenting my thoughts and ideas to Habbash for an hour and a half, he was convinced that I should meet with the president, and he promised to arrange the meeting.

The meeting was held today at the Muqataa in Ramallah and lasted about thirty-five minutes. In attendance were President Abbas, Dr. Mahmoud al-Habbash, and me. I opened the meeting by thanking the president for agreeing to meet me. Because of his busy schedule, I went straight to the subject of the meeting. I spoke a few words about the secret direct back channel talks with Hamas on Schalit, and I argued that a key component to the success of those talks was their totally secret nature. We were able to conduct a direct secret back channel as an official track between the two parties for six

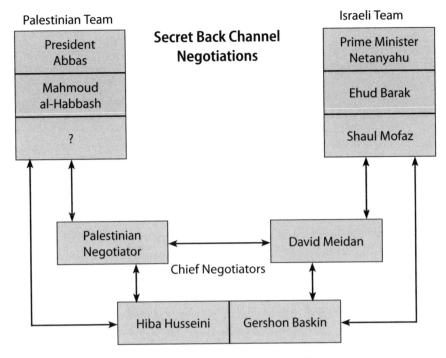

Secret Back Channel Negotiations

Palestinian Team

| President Abbas |
| Mahmoud al-Habbash |
| ? |

Israeli Team

| Prime Minister Netanyahu |
| Ehud Barak |
| Shaul Mofaz |

Chief Negotiators

Palestinian Negotiator ↔ David Meidan

Professional Bridging Assistance Team

Hiba Husseini | Gershon Baskin

months without any leaks. I then suggested that there is almost no chance that the channel of Netanyahu's appointed emissary Attorney Yitzhak Molcho and Dr. Saab Erekat, the head of the PLO Negotiations Department would be successful. Part of the reason for this is because it is a public channel. Abbas added that there is no chemistry between the two (he joked that Molcho was not the only reason why there was no chemistry).

Abbas agreed without any hesitation that the only way to succeed in negotiations on a permanent settlement is a direct secret back channel, and reinforced this position by stating that in Oslo the parties succeeded in reaching an agreement largely due to the secrecy of the talks. He said that if Prime Minister Netanyahu would agree to a direct secret back channel, Abbas said that within 48 hours he and/or his emissaries would show up for those talks.

After his in-principle agreement, our conversation went into the essence of negotiations. I brought up the need to provide for Israel's security demands and needs prior to a thorough discussion on the delineation of the borders between the two states. Abbas spoke of his deep commitment to true peace and about his daily struggle against terrorism. He said he agrees that the Palestinian state will be demilitarized, and he opposes any attempts to smuggle weapons into the area, and that he takes direct action when there are attempts to smuggle. "I will not allow even a single bullet to be smuggled and I arrest anyone attempting to do this." He said Israeli security personnel, including Amos Gilad (political-security bureau head in the Ministry of Defense), acknowledge that his actions are 100%—not only effort, but also based on the facts on the ground, and he seemed proud of this record. He said he understands the needs and the demands of Israel's security, and he is ready to talk about arrangements that separate the issues of political borders and the concept of a security border for Israel. He cannot accept the permanent presence of Israeli soldiers on the eastern border of the Palestinian state, but he does not oppose the idea of an Israeli military presence within a multilateral force. He also said that there can be additional security arrangements with the Jordanians on the Jordanian side of the border.

Abbas spoke at length about governance, including the fight without compromise against corruption. He said that today he deposed a Fatah leader, Samir Mashrawi because of corruption. He dismissed several ministers in Fayyad's government and stated that there are more on the way out.

I asked him to relate to the issue of incitement. He immediately recalled the words that the mufti of Jerusalem made earlier in the week, quoting a Hadith on the obligation of the Muslims to kill Jews. The mufti also recalled the mother and sister of the murderers of the Fogel family (Hakam and Amjad Awad who in March 2011 murdered Udi and Ruth Fogel and their three infant children—Yoav, Elad, and Hadas in the Itamar settlement). The mufti praised the killing on the Palestinian Authority official television. Abbas instructed the TV not to broadcast it, and he ordered the mufti to retract his statement. Minister Habbash said he was interviewed by media outlets in Palestine and Israel and said the PA opposes the killing of Jews and that the Hadith (ways of the Prophet) the mufti quoted was misunderstood. Habbash said, "The Quran teaches us that the Jews are People of the Book and Muslims can marry Jewish women, we can eat with Jews, and the like." Abbas quoted some verses from the Quran, and added that the Quran talks about the Jews, and that Muslims accept the Torah and the prophets of the Jews. So we talked about the need to act against incitement. Abbas said, "Incitement—yes, we have it. I admit, we are guilty, we are against it but not enough. Under Bush we had agreed to have a trilateral committee with the Americans against incitement. I propose that we now reestablish this committee. Actions against incitement should be taken on both sides. What does Netanyahu say? Mutuality—I agree [with] that now."

I told Abbas that I was seeking to achieve a formal long-term cease-fire with Hamas, including a hotline warning mechanism with Egyptian involvement. I asked him what [were] his thoughts on the issue. Abbas said he was very supportive. He said that he has put a lot of pressure on Hamas to abandon the armed struggle for nonviolent resistance. He said Khaled Mashal's recent statements on this issue were due to Abbas's pressure on him. He said that in three days he will meet Mashal in al-Doha (and it's a secret).

I told him I was contacted by Hamas people who asked me to work to secure the release of Hamas Parliamentarians in Israeli jails. I asked him what he thought about it, would this weaken his support in the West Bank. He said, again without hesitation, that he was for the release and that their retention in Israeli jails while he holds talks with Israel makes it difficult for him to have public legitimacy. He is not afraid and in fact he said it will actually weaken Hamas—a kind of reverse public psychology. He went on to say that Olmert's pledge to release prisoners detained before the Oslo Accords has not yet been kept, and their release would help him and strengthen him.

I suggested we try to link the progress in peace talks and the release of prisoners. Today there will be no chance that Israel will release political prisoners without Netanyahu seeing a justified reason for it.

The last part of our conversation focused on my request for him as president to take action against those who are threatening joint Israeli-Palestinian peace-related activities as part of the anti-normalization campaign. Abbas said he supports joint activities for peace. He stressed that the lack of progress toward peace weakens him and his claims against the Palestinian public in this regard.

In summarizing our conversation, Abbas said that he has no intention of staying in the position of president forever. If there is no real progress toward peace and quickly, he fears that he is nearing the end of his term as the Palestinian leader. If there are serious negotiations, secret and sincere, he will remain in his position because it is his life's dream to bring true peace to his people. He said that we (the Palestinians) have and they (the Israelis) have no other option. He recalled the words of Abba Eban that the Palestinians never miss an opportunity to miss an opportunity. He said, "We must not, both of us, miss the chance for peace. I'm ready and I want to do it with Netanyahu because I know that he will bring all of Israel with him." In this context, I asked him if he would bring the agreement, what would happen with Hamas and Gaza. He said, "This will be our problem," and he is convinced that the Palestinians in Gaza will not forgo the possibility of enjoying real peace. They will force the agreement on the regime there, and that is how we will bring about real Palestinian unity.

I was very encouraged by the meeting. Abbas was open, direct, honest, and trusting. I felt that he related to me as someone who could be entrusted to deliver messages to Netanyahu and to push forward toward the secret direct back channel of negotiations that I proposed. I was far less confident in my ability to get the message across to Netanyahu and to convince him to accept the Abbas offer.

I asked David Meidan to transmit the message, but I got the feeling from David that despite the very good relationship between us, he was not going to position himself alongside of me in front of Netanyahu. David at this time officially remained on the Mossad payroll, and although he had been released of all official tasks within the Mossad, he was on call for the prime minister to undertake special missions on his behalf. One of those missions was to be in charge of the file of several MIAs from past wars. I don't know what other missions he was assigned by the PM. David also tried on several occasions to push forward the proposal for me to meet Netanyahu. After Natan Eshel was forced to resign as chief of staff in January 2012, Eshel's deputy, Gil Sheffer was appointed in his place. David Meidan asked Sheffer to arrange for Netanyahu to see me. It was agreed that Sheffer would conduct a preinterview with me to clear me for the meeting with Netanyahu. The meeting with Sheffer was set, postponed, rescheduled, postponed, and rescheduled about four times before it was clear that the meeting was simply not going to take place. In the end, Meidan told me that someone inside Netanyahu's inner office convinced Sheffer to abandon the idea of arranging a meeting for me with Netanyahu.

I approached Minister Michael Eitan and had a very good meeting with him, in which I presented the idea of the secret back channel. I presented him a copy of my report of the meeting with Abbas. I asked him to carry the message forward to Netanyahu to convince him to give negotiations with Abbas a chance. Eitan responded that his own personal relations with Netanyahu were not good, and he thought that the prime minister wouldn't listen to him. He felt almost like a member of the opposition within the government, and his ability to move such an important issue forward was very limited.

I then contacted Minister Dan Meridor at the suggestion of Eitan. Meridor was the minister in charge of the intelligence and secret services. Although known as one of the Princes of the Likud, during Netanyahu's first term, he broke away from the Likud and was one of the founders of the Center Party. In the 2009 elections, Netanyahu called him to return to the Likud—to come home—and he would have a senior position in the government and would be a member of the inside security cabinet. Netanyahu kept his word to Meridor, and I hoped that Meridor would be in the position to influence Netanyahu. I had a fairly good relationship with Meridor from past encounters. A few years before, I tried to convince him to run for mayor of Jerusalem. I was not the only one, but he met with me and I made my case for him as a person who was worthy of being Jerusalem's mayor. He felt that unless the national government took itself seriously with regard to Jerusalem's special status rather than only paying the lip service that is traditionally heard, he would not have a real chance of helping Jerusalem to reach its real potential, and he did not want to go "tilting at windmills."

My meeting with Meridor was very good. He listened, asked questions, but his position was that Abbas has proven over and over again that he is not a partner. Meridor said that he would go and convince Netanyahu to enter a secret back channel if Abu Mazen would be willing to state that he understands that there will be no effective right of return of Palestinian refugees to Israel. I told Meridor that outside of the context of negotiations it is very unlikely that Abbas would state something like that so explicitly. Meridor said that for him to be convinced that Abbas was really ready for peace he would have to hear that. So I contacted Abbas again.

MARCH 12, 2012
President Mahmoud Abbas
Dear Abu Mazen,
I hope you are well. I met this morning with Minister Dan Meridor about the possibility of opening a secret back channel [for] negotiations with you as we discussed in our meeting in the end of January. Following our meeting, I wrote a report for Netanyahu, and the report was delivered by Meridor to him. I decided that the best way to push for this proposal, which I completely believe in, is to enlist Meridor as the primary person who could influence Netanyahu to accept it. I had a long and challenging meeting with him in which he raised a lot of questions and issues.

I have to be completely frank with you, Meridor, who I believe represents the majority of the ministers in Netanyahu's government, is basically convinced that you do not want to reach an agreement with Israel. I say this from the outset because Meridor has more Palestinian negotiation experience than most of the other ministers, and he is also the most liberal minister in his personal views. It is important for you to understand the Israeli assessment of your position.

From his point of view, without accepting the principle that the right of return will be exercised in the State of Palestine and not in Israel, there can be no agreement with Israel. There is of course room for some symbolic return on a humanitarian basis, but the most fundamental Israeli red line is this one concerning the right of return. You know this. You heard it from Tzipi Livni and Ehud Olmert as well. Because the Israeli side believes that you are not prepared and will never be prepared to accept this concession, the assessment is that it is impossible to reach an agreement with you that will be an end-of-conflict agreement. Is this true? Are you ready to negotiate on the basis that the right of return will be to the State of Palestine? I understand that with this as a principle, it means that you will have more leverage on Israel regarding other issues, including on Palestinian rights in Jerusalem.

Meridor asked if you are ready to accept the Olmert proposal. I would not speak in your, name and I know that there are problems with the Olmert proposal from the Palestinian side, but his question is legitimate. How far are you willing to go to reach an agreement? If you want to open the Olmert offer, what are the points that you would want to change? If it is opened, then Meridor said that Israel would also want to change it—so this is a catch.

If Meridor was convinced that you are prepared to reach a full comprehensive agreement on all issues including end of conflict and accept the basic idea that the Palestinian state is the homeland of the Palestinian people and not Israel—that the return of refugees will be to the Palestinian state, then Meridor would go and work on convincing Netanyahu to run the secret back channel to conclude the agreement. Meridor would be willing to be the head negotiator himself or anyone else Netanyahu would select. Personally, I would work to be part of the team to help to develop bridging proposals, and I know that David Meidan, who I worked with to bring about the prisoner exchange, would work to be part of the Israeli team.

I don't know if these conditions are acceptable to you. I would understand if they are not, to which I would conclude that Israel and Palestine cannot come to a negotiated agreement at this time. This might be a real possibility, but if you have come to terms with the non-implementability of the right of return to Israel proper, then it will be possible to reach an agreement.

I am putting this direct and upfront. This would be the most telling position regarding the possibility of reaching an agreement. Every other issue will be possible to reach agreements on, including Jerusalem.

I would be happy to meet with you once again to discuss this and to give you my firsthand impressions from the Israeli side.

If there is a secret back channel, then only a very select few can know about it. Dan Meridor said that he would be willing to negotiate directly with you, of course that would require Netanyahu's agreement, but all options are open and possible.

Please let me know how to proceed.

Best wishes

Gershon Baskin

Dr. Habbash delivered the letter to Abbas and said that he would schedule another meeting with me soon. I had to travel abroad, and Abbas was also traveling so the first time that we managed to arrange a meeting was in May.

This is the summary of my meeting with Abbas, which I also sent to Prime Minister Netanyahu.

MAY 22, 2012, 1:00 P.M., RAMALLAH

Present: President Mahmoud Abbas, Minister of Religious Affairs Mahmoud al-Habbash, Dr. Gershon Baskin

Abbas was under considerable distress and pressure resulting from a lack of political and economic achievements (both internal and externally). Mahmoud Abbas remains committed as ever to achieving peace with Israel and stands by the fight against terrorism and against those who advocate the armed struggle. He does not feel that Israel appreciates all that he is doing in his counterterrorism efforts and in his genuine devotion to peace between the two peoples. He added, "They have to believe me. If they do not trust us, there's no point in trying to promote peace between us. I am doing everything possible against terrorism and I think I am worthy of their trust."

Abu Mazen highlighted some immediate needs from Israel, without which it would be very difficult to continue the security cooperation that exists today:

There are four thousand guns and ammunition being held back in Jordan that Israel approved through the US security coordinator, Lt. Gen. Michael Moeller, but have not allowed to enter the West Bank. Mazen said that only one of every twelve Palestinian security officers has a gun. He cannot go on like this. He refuses to smuggle weapons as suggested by various factions both within the West Bank and neighboring countries. (He also noted that there are Israeli criminal elements who are willing to sell weapons to the Palestinian Authority and to Palestinian civilians). He insists that the weapons for the Palestinian security forces must be approved by Israel and enter into the West Bank with the approval and consent of Israel. He noted that recently the PA arrested ninety-one people in the Jenin district, including many Fatah members. Abu Mazen repeated that he does not agree that terrorism will once again raise its head, but cannot do the job without weapons.

Fifty APCs (armored personnel carriers) in Jordan were also approved through the US security coordinator, and Israel is preventing them from entering the West Bank. Abu Mazen emphasized that if did not get the guns and armored personnel carriers he would have to dismantle the new battalions trained in Jordan (by the Americans). If Israel will not allow them to enter the West Bank, he has nothing to do with them if they are not able to operate in the field. As a result of the desperate situation developing, if he cannot act against terror, he would have to consider stopping the security cooperation with Israel. He said the calm of the last five years is there because of his vigorous work against terrorism and the cooperation with Israel and that without this, the area would burst into flames once again.

The release of 131 prisoners from before 1993—he said, and repeated it several times, that Olmert promised that the prisoners that were arrested prior to Oslo, prior to 1994, would all be released. He said that Olmert promised him that more prisoners than were released in the Schalit deal would be released to Abu Mazen under the framework of negotiations for peace. Abu Mazen said that many people in Fatah were encouraging him to capture an Israeli soldier and to hold him for the release of Palestinian prisoners. They tell him that this is the only way you will release the prisoners. Abu Mazen said that he is absolutely opposed to this; he also said that if anyone in the West Bank were to kidnap an Israeli soldier or civilian, he would personally kill them. He added that Israel must keep its word in this matter even though Olmert is no longer the prime minister—that was the promise of the prime minister of Israel and Netanyahu has to honor it.

Our conversation turned to the topic of my proposed secret back channel. As we discussed earlier, Abu Mazen continues to support this channel without hesitation, but said he would only open this channel after getting a positive response to the immediate needs listed above. He does not believe that we can achieve peace through the channel of Netanyahu's special emissary Attorney Yitzhak Molcho and Palestinian Negotiations Chief Saeb Arikat.

Abu Mazen said after these needs are met in the affirmative he would be willing to meet with the prime minister secretly or publicly, whatever Netanyahu prefers. He said that these needs are not preconditions, but without them it is most difficult for him to function.

He wants to promote the secret back channel. I asked him who will head his staff (after I showed him my drawings of a proposed covert channel structure), and he said that he will decide after receiving the weapons, armored personnel carriers, and prisoners. I told him it would be difficult for Prime Minister Netanyahu to give him these things without getting something in return (you give, you receive), and he replied: "If Israel does not give these things we will have to stop the security cooperation and our fight against terrorism. It's not a threat, this is reality."

I asked him about his agreement with Hamas on a unity government. He said there will not be a unity government but a transitional government whose task will be to prepare elections. He stressed that in any interim government there will be no minister from Hamas and no ministers at all who will not swear to respect the principles of recognizing Israel, the signed agreements, and total opposition to terrorism and violence. "As long as I am President, I will not allow a government to be formed that does not accept these principles."

He said that when the secret channel is opened, the negotiations will deal with security and borders first and then other issues, and we will work on reaching agreement on all of the issues. He asked me to present all of these messages to Prime Minister Netanyahu.

Netanyahu rejected the initiative and refused to meet with Abbas. I tried to appeal to Netanyahu through his national security advisor, Yaacov Amidror. I spoke directly to Amidror on July 4, 2012, at the home of the US ambassador to Israel. Amidror claimed that Abbas made unacceptable preconditions for negotiations and that Netanyahu would not agree. I suggested that he (Amidror) meet with Abbas or allow someone else to meet to see if a secret back channel could be opened. Amidror was less than interested, especially after US Secretary of State John Kerry announced that he would be launching a new initiative. After Kerry announced his initiative, I saw Abu Mazen once again, who said that he still believes that a direct secret back channel with Netanyahu would have a better chance of success than negotiations facilitated by Kerry. But since Kerry made his announcement, Abbas could not open a secret back channel without the approval of Kerry. This is what Amidror told me as well. The Americans would probably not agree, and Netanyahu couldn't do it without the American approval.

I then contacted someone from Kerry's team to inform Secretary Kerry that I was trying to arrange a secret direct meeting between Abbas and Netanyahu. The message I got back from Washington was to cease and desist—Kerry vetoed any such meeting and informed Abbas and Netanyahu both that he did not want any meetings between them to take place outside of his facilitated process. I was told by the American side that if such a meeting were to take place and it were to fail, it would put an early end to his own initiative.

Eight days stand between us and the end of the nine-month period Secretary of State John Kerry allocated for Israeli-Palestinian negotiations. Peace seems more elusive and fleeting than ever. The nine-month pregnancy of peace is not ending with a stillborn baby but rather it now seems evident that it was entirely a false pregnancy.

After twenty years of negotiating, it is not really the issues themselves or the solutions that are impossibly complex. It is not even the internal political alliances and coalitions on each side that makes the process so difficult. If both of the leaders were successful at reaching an agreement, they would be able to sell it at home and have enough political support to carry a referendum in support of the deal.

The fundamental difficulty remains in the total mistrust between the parties, and particularly between the leaders. In their heart of hearts, most Israelis, and most Palestinians, including the two leaders, really believe that the other side is planning to destroy them. Palestinians believe that Israelis are constantly working to cleanse the land of them and that settlements are the tool being used to achieve that aim. Now they even speak adamantly of concrete Israeli plans to remove Muslims from Jerusalem and to destroy the mosques on the Haram al-Sharif / the Temple Mount. Israelis believe that the unwillingness of the Palestinians to recognize Israel as the Jewish nation-state is a clear expression of Palestinian plans to destroy Israel. These beliefs are held by both Benjamin Netanyahu and Mahmoud Abbas.

It is quite amazing that even after more than eight months of negotiations the two leaders have not held face-to-face talks. It may sound rather simplistic, but no Israeli-Palestinian permanent peace agreement will ever be possible unless the leaders begin to trust each other. That trust must be built by the leaders getting to know each other on a personal basis and perhaps even liking each other.

I say this from my own personal experience of negotiating with Hamas. The release of Gilad Schalit became possible because basic trust developed between me and my negotiating partner, Dr. Ghazi Hamad—the product of five years of direct contact.

Mr. Abbas and Mr. Netanyahu do not need five years of negotiating time, but they must be brought together for intensive, continuous, and direct bilateral negotiations. Without building trust, it is difficult to imagine a deal emerging any time soon.

Ari Shavit, in his seminal book *My Promised Land: The Triumph and Tragedy of Israel*, claims that peace is not possible, not because of the settlers and the settlements and not because of the occupation or territorial disputes. His claim is that the nakba—the catastrophe that happened to the Palestinians with the birth of Israel—is the ultimate defining moment, the essence of the Palestinian collective memory that will never enable the Palestinians to accept Israel's existence. The Palestinian refugees will never forget where they came from and will never end their dream to return to their homes—which is now Israel. According to Shavit, it is not the occupation of 1967 but the existence of Israel from 1948 which drove the Palestinians from their home that prevents them from recognizing Israel and making peace. And now, even almost seven decades later, three and four generations gone by, those descendants of the refugees keep the dream of return, with their keys, their overblown stories of their wealth and riches and large villas and tracks of unending land with rich soil that could grow anything. The memories are so much more vivid and green than the reality ever was prior to 1948, but it is the memory that shapes their identity and their struggle. Their suffering under Israel's hands for more than sixty-seven years has kept the memory alive and has given life to the fire that burns from within to undo history with Israel's ultimate destruction. And therefore, they will never really, existentially recognize Israel's RIGHT to exist. This is the crux of Shavit's argument.

And who can better understand them and identify with them than us, the Jewish people living in the Land of Israel. Especially when we read the passages from the Pesach Hagadah that in every generation we must tell the story that we were slaves in Egypt and today we are free. We are a people based on memory of thousands of years, never forgetting who we are, who we were, and where we came from. Of course we understand the Palestinians and, as we transpose ourselves and our own collective memory onto them, we are convinced that true peace between us is never possible. Even though we work overtime to deny what we have done to the Palestinians and even reject the legitimacy of the word "nakba" (for how could our own birth be a catastrophe?), in our inner conscious world we understand the Palestinian memory more than we will ever be willing to admit to ourselves.

But that makes life too easy.

No, the Palestinian refugees will never forget their homes, their villages, the places they came from that no longer exist, except in the stories that they have been told from their grandmothers and grandfathers to their mothers and fathers and now from themselves to their own children. Collective memories don't die. We Jews know that so well. The central thread of Palestinian collective identity is the nakba, being transformed from a peaceful people on their land into homeless, possessionless, wandering suffering refugees. Even those who remained in Palestine and were crammed into refugee camps became the iconic symbol of that catastrophe. Even though the refugee camps are no longer camps of tent cities and today they are urban slums, the memory stays alive and vivid, and the Palestinian political system has worked very diligently to ensure that the memory will continue. All over Palestine, in the West Bank, Gaza, and in East Jerusalem, the graffiti on the walls brings back the daunting memories of the homes lost.

Palestinians come from a traditional society where the family—the multigenerational extended clan, the tribe, still remain the source of identity. So many Palestinians are defined by where they came from. For so many of them, their family names are the place where they came from. Their identity is shaped by the virtue of having come from one place where they lived for generations, were born there, and died there. And even if the facts of history don't always mesh with the legend, it is the legends that define the identity. It is clear that people with the name Hijazi, for example, came from the Hijaz—the Saudi peninsula—yet the Hijazis of Palestine have been in Palestine since the Muslim conquest, and they are Palestinians, not Hijazis. And even for more recent comers like the Masris who came from *Masr*—Egypt— they have been in Palestine for hundreds of years and have not been Egyptians in any way for a very long time. Yes, many Palestinians immigrated to Palestine when Jews were also immigrating, at the turn of the nineteenth century and in the twentieth century. But they define themselves and are accepted as Palestinians, natives of this land who belong here just as all other Palestinians who suffered the nakba. It is the experience of the nakba that defines who they are as a people. It was that moment of history that has shaped their collective memory and their national struggle.

So then is Ari Shavit right—is real peace never possible—only a messianic dream? I believe that he is wrong. He is not wrong in the understanding that they will never forget where they came from. He is not wrong in comprehending that their dream of return will live on forever. The stories of what was will never end, and they will probably continue to be enhanced and embellished with the passing of time. But peace is possible because the memory of suffering and loss can be transformed by the task of building a new dream and a new reality. In Israel, we went from the disaster of the Holocaust to the building of a nation and a state. It is similar to what the Palestinians will have to do as well. But it is not only a task of building, of doing something positive on their own. Former Palestinian Prime Minister Dr. Salam

Fayyad understood quite well how to inspire a nation to undertake the tasks of state building. But he also understood quite well that the redemption of dignity requires something from the other side.

The birth of Israel is not the only element responsible for the nakba. There were other owners of responsibility, including Palestinian leaders themselves. Amongst the others were the British, the Arab leaders, and even the institutions of the international community which failed to implement their own resolutions. But Israel will have a key role to play in finding the path toward the kind of reconciliation that will help to heal the wounds and to enable the Palestinians to truly move forward, beyond nakba, in shaping their collective memory for the future. The acknowledgement by Israel and by Israelis of their role in the nakba will be an essential element of peacemaking. It will not be easy for Israelis to acknowledge that their birth, which was clearly a moral imperative, especially after the Holocaust, caused the cataclysmic suffering of the Palestinian people. It was not solely the rejectionism of the Palestinian leadership that created the nakba. Israel cannot escape its own very dominating role in actively bringing about the evacuation of more than 800,000 people from their homes and in destroying their lives. Maybe it was unavoidable, maybe it was necessary, as people like Ari Shavit claim, but it will also require Israel to look deep into its historical mirror and come to terms with that reality and to convey an element of sorrow and compassion to the Palestinian people.

The Palestinian dream of return will live on in their imaginations, and when they close their eyes and recall their pasts, they will continue to see a land from the River to the Sea with orange groves and olive trees, and springs and sheep wandering under the figs trees. Their Palestinian utopia will continue to be one in which there are no Israelis and where Israel does not exist and has never existed. But when they open their eyes, Israel does exist. Tel Aviv continues to be a magnet of attraction to the world and even for them. Israel is an undeniable fact that they cannot ignore. Israel is also, in a bizarre way, their very best chance of creating a state that will be democratic and even prosperous.

In order for both the Israelis and the Palestinians to overcome their collective memories that sanctify the past at the expense of the future, the basic relationship between the two peoples will have to change fundamentally. There are people on both sides and in the international community already working on trying to conceptualize an Israeli-Palestinian version of the South African Truth and Reconciliations Commission. The South African model was based deeply on

African values and traditions merged with their modern day Christian foundations. In Israel and Palestine, we will need a localized version of how to confront some of the horrific things that were done in the name of Zionism, Palestinian nationalism, religion—Judaism and Islam—fear, hope, survival, and ignorance. Some have suggested using the Arab cultural model of *Sulha*, which is relevant both in times of joy and celebration and in times of mourning and tragedy. In both societies, there is an extremely high value to honor and dignity—both in the individual sense and in the national pride. This also has to be addressed.

I don't have a particular model that will be relevant and employed when the time comes. I know that there will have to be some way to address the pains of the past. I am more concerned with the opportunities of the future. We will be able to overcome the pains of the past if we build a future that gives dignity and honor, and provides the opportunities for building a new relationship between Israelis and Palestinians.

The essence of the new relationship is the end of the occupation and Israeli control. But it is not solely the political end of the occupation—the relationship between the occupier and the occupied—but also the consciousness of occupation, control, and subjugation. The new relationship must be based on the eventual removal of the physical obstacles that prevent free movement and access to all parts of Israel/Palestine. Each side will have their own state, under their own sovereignty with their own territorial expression of their national identity. The rights of citizenship and residency will be limited by the boundaries of sovereignty, but the rights to enter and move around freely within each other's sovereign areas must be incorporated into future peace agreements, as soon as possible, when security allows for it. This will help to heal the wounds of the past. Palestinians will have the ability to move around the entire land from the River to the Sea and so will Jews. Israeli Jews will be able to visit Jewish holy places within the Palestinian state. The ability to have access, to move freely, the removal of barriers and checkpoints and the sense of security provided through arrangements that will have to be the joint responsibility of both sides must be a central element of peace building and reconciliation between the parties. If the future peace agreements will be based on walls, fences, barbed wire, and checkpoints, the basis of the relationships on both sides will not change and even if the political occupation will come to an end, the psychological occupation will continue.

Shavit turns the peace movement in Israel and those who worked for peace into messianics struggling to bring a false messiah, no different from the moral equation he makes with the settlers and their supporters. Peace is not redemption, and it is not the messianic era. In truth, the really hard work for peace begins the day after the peace treaty is signed because it is then that the relations between the two peoples can begin to change.

The Oslo process was initially designed with the conceptual model of cross-boundary cooperation. The framers of Oslo, Yair Hirschfeld and Ron Pundak led by Yossi Beilin, and on the Palestinian side, Ahmed Qurie (Abu Ala) and Maher el Kurd, supported strongly by Mahmoud Abbas, saw the development of Israeli-Palestinian peace based on strengthening economic cooperation that would create Palestinian independence and then build interdependence and interaction between the two societies. The Israeli political and military elites (strongly backed by the Israeli settler movement) viewed the first Oslo agreement as being naïve. Prime Minister Rabin did not have confidence in Beilin's team, and he was equally suspicious of his Foreign Minister and longtime rival, Shimon Peres. Rabin only had confidence in the army and security forces. All future Israeli-Palestinian negotiations on the road to the failure of Oslo were dominated by the Israeli military and security elites. The conceptualization of peace fostered by those people was the separation model.

The one exception is the dominant role that IDF Chief of Staff Amnon Shahak played in the negotiations for the Israeli-Palestinian Interim Agreement on the West Bank and the Gaza Strip signed in Washington on September 28, 1995. General Shahak developed trusting relationships with several of the key Palestinian negotiators, including the head of the Palestinian Preventive Security Forces Jabril Rajoub in the West Bank and Mohammed Dahlan in Gaza. It turns out that the head security folks on both sides spoke the same language. Shahak also developed a trusting relationship with Nabeel Shaath, who was one of the leading Palestinian civilian negotiators. This agreement produced with it some twenty-six joint bodies between the sides that aimed to create the cooperation across the boundaries that could have changed the nature of the relationships between the parties. But two months later, Rabin was assassinated by an extremist Israeli, and the peace process began its rapid demise.

After Israeli elections in 1996, Benyamin Netanyahu was elected, and although he told the electorate that he would continue to implement the Oslo agreements, he did not. In fact, he worked very hard to freeze the entire process. In response to Palestinian terrorism, Netanyahu refused to implement the primary element of the agreement, which was turning more territory over to the Palestinian Authority, although he did sign the Hebron Agreement on January 17, 1997, and the Wye River Memorandum on October 23, 1998. Under Netanyahu, there was a strong sense that the Oslo process was frozen and the element of territorial withdrawal by Israel was not going to progress.

The Interim agreement from September 1995 stated that all of the territory of the West Bank and Gaza would be transferred to the Palestinian Authority except for specified military location and settlements. The exact wording of the agreement was:

Article X Paragraph 2: "Further redeployments of Israeli military forces to specified military locations will commence after the inauguration of the Council and will be gradually implemented commensurate with the assumption of responsibility for public order and internal security by the Palestinian Police, to be completed within eighteen months from the date of the inauguration of the Council."

Article XI Paragraph 2: "The two sides agree that West Bank and Gaza Strip territory, except for issues that will be negotiated in the permanent status negotiations, will come under the jurisdiction of the Palestinian Council in a phased manner, to be completed within eighteen months from the date of the inauguration of the Council."

From these two paragraphs, the Palestinians were correct to understand that even before permanent status negotiations commenced they would be in control of at least ninety percent of the West Bank and even more of Gaza. The total land area of all of the specified military locations in the West Bank at that time accounted for less than one percent of the West Bank. But when Netanyahu came along, he had his government and military interpret these words not as specified military locations—which include military bases and early warning stations—but rather as "security zones." From Netanyahu's perspective, the entire Jordan Valley (accounting for twenty percent of the West Bank) is such a zone as well as a strip of land adjacent to the Green Line and surrounding the West Bank. The section regarding "the issues that will be negotiated in the permanent status negotiations" refers to the Israeli settlements. The total physical "footprint" of all of the settlements in the West Bank accounted for less than three percent of the area at that time. Nonetheless, the Israeli government under Netanyahu decided that the land areas of concern were the artificially created statutory boundaries of the settlements and not just the built-up areas. That area accounted for more than twenty percent of the West Bank. Today, in 2017, twenty-two years later, area "c" of the West Bank—the area under full Israeli control—accounts for sixty-two percent of the West Bank. Until the Israeli disengagement from Gaza in 2005, Israel was in full control of thirty percent of Gaza.

In 1997, while Netanyahu was fresh in his first term, I was privy to a document written by the Legal Department of the Israeli Foreign Ministry. That document clearly stated that the Israeli interpretation of these two paragraphs of the agreement was wrong and that the Palestinian claim that Israel was obligated to withdraw from more than ninety percent of the West Bank and Gaza prior to permanent status negotiations was correct. That document was obviously buried deep in the safe of the Prime Minister's Office or in the trash bin of history and never referred to again.

The Palestinian basis for entering the Oslo process was their understanding of their own historic compromise taken by President Arafat giving up their claim over seventy-eight percent of historic Palestine—the land that the State of Israel conquered in the war of 1948. Arafat could have easily demanded that the future map and negotiations be based on the UN Resolution 181 partition plan, which would have granted the Palestinians far more land. The recognition of Israel by Arafat under Oslo left the Palestinians with the belief that they would get twenty-two percent of the land between the River and the Sea, and they had no idea that they would be forced to negotiate that remaining small part of the land with Israel.

Not only was the land transference issue a major breach of the understandings between the parties, the implementation of the agreements was taken over by the Israeli military and security elites on both sides. Since the military/security takeover of the Oslo peace process, the conceptual implementation of peace with the Palestinians, from the Israeli side, was based on the separation model. The military had no conceptual ability to understand cooperation with former enemies. No military knows how to make peace. They can prepare for war, they can wage war, they can defend their country and its borders, but militaries by definition are not mechanisms of peace-making organizations. In addition to this, with the implementation of Oslo, the Israeli Civil Administration (formerly the Israeli Military Government), which was in fact an arm of Israel's military, was empowered to be the primary body for engagement by the Palestinian civilian government and its security forces. The Palestinian public did not engage with Israel's civilian government and agencies but rather with the Civil Administration. The name "civil administration" is misleading. The only "civil" thing about it is that it was formed to provide services to the Palestinian civilians, but it is entirely a military operation under military rule and law and headed by military officers.

Sometime in 1998, I was invited to participate in a meeting in the Israeli Ministry of Finance. The purpose of the meeting was to brainstorm on ideas for a meeting that was being planned between the finance ministers of Israel, Jordan, and Palestine. There were about twenty people in the room sitting around a large table. Almost all of the participants were civil servants from the relevant ministries: Foreign Ministry, Finance, Agriculture, Tourism, and Industry and Trade. There were a couple of NGO people in the room like myself. There were also two IDF officers sitting on the side listening and taking notes. The meeting lasted nearly two hours, and a lot of very constructive ideas were raised for improving the economic cooperation between the three parties. At the end of the meeting, one of the IDF officers stood up and gave the official summary of the meeting. I was shocked. To me it seemed that what just happened was a military coup. Who empowered the IDF to take control of the meeting and its summary? Who put them in charge of a civilian operation that was convened to plan a meeting of three finance ministers from three neighboring countries? I was the only person shocked in the room. It seemed quite normal for this to have happened to most everyone else in the room.

In my view, it is this attitude that mainly led to the total collapse of the peace process later with the reemergence of Palestinian violence. Ehud Barak was elected to replace the sense of the Israeli public that peace was still possible, but that Netanyahu would not be capable of making a deal with the Palestinian leaders. But with a sharp military mind and security gestalt, Barak's conceptual view of peace with the Palestinians was total separation with continued Israeli control, complete with walls, fences, and barbed wire. Many politicians and public leaders called it "a divorce from the Palestinians" and rejected the cooperation modality that was fostered first in the Oslo model. Barak called it "us here and them there."

Barak refused to implement further territorial withdrawals that were previously agreed upon. Barak said that since permanent status talks would soon begin, why give the Palestinians extra land prior to negotiations. Barak viewed previous agreements as an additional bargaining chip in the negotiations that he would conduct with Arafat. With the completion of settler bypass roads enabling settlers to dwell in their own separate kingdom without encountering

Palestinians, Israeli support for settlement expansion continued at an even more rapid pace under Barak than his predecessor. The entire internal rationale of Oslo imploded, being based on territorial withdrawals leading to Palestinian statehood in exchange for Palestinians engaging in counterterrorism. But when the withdrawals ceased, Palestinian security officials began to ask themselves on whose behalf were they actually fighting against terrorism? The logic of Oslo was that the Palestinians would fight against terrorism, or resistance to Israeli control and occupation, because they would be creating a state of the rule of law which would become theirs when Israel withdrew. As it became increasingly clear that Israel was not going to withdraw, that its control was becoming harsher and that settlements were expanding, the logic of security cooperation went out the window and with it the spirit of Oslo. That is why the first violence of the second intifada came from armed Palestinian security personnel and the first Israeli killed in the second intifada was the Israeli commander of a "joint" Israeli-Palestinian patrol.

Benyamin Netanyahu first came to power in mid-1996. In that period, as I would ride to work every morning going through Beit Jala to my office in Bethlehem, I would often see joint Israeli-Palestinian military patrols on the road. The joint patrol system was established under the interim agreement. It was a mechanism set up mainly to provide security for Israeli settlers before all of the bypass roads were built. The deal was that a patrol consisting of two jeeps would ride together—one Israeli, one Palestinian. When they rode through areas under Israeli security control (most of the West Bank—areas "b" and "c"), the Israeli jeep would lead and the Palestinian jeep would follow. As they entered area "a" under full Palestinian control, the Palestinian jeep would lead and the Israeli one would follow.

At first, I would see the two jeeps stopping for a coffee break and the soldiers on both sides were sharing coffee, sandwiches, and small talk. Suddenly toward the end of the summer 1996, I noticed that the jeeps had parked about on hundred meters apart during their coffee breaks, and the interaction between them ended. This was very curious to me.

As a lecturer in the College for the Training Education of Officers as part of my reserve duty in the IDF, I was invited to speak to officers of joint Israeli-Palestinian patrols. I was shocked to learn that they had actually been given orders not to associate and socialize with their Palestinian counterparts. I could not think of a more ridiculous and dangerous order to give these young soldiers.

Lessons Learned

19

JOINT STAKEHOLDER COFACILITATION TEAM

One of the most important lessons I have learned over the past thirty-eight years of being engaged in bringing Israelis and Palestinians to sit together, trying to design a better future, is that we are best off when we are left on our own. The best negotiations that have taken place between Israelis and Palestinians have been those in which there was no third-party mediator. Those include the original Oslo negotiations where the Norwegians provided the platform and the facilities but only offered bridging proposals when requested. The negotiations between Prime Minister Olmert and President Abbas are the second example of good negotiations without a third party. Olmert and Abbas met forty-two times and came closer to an agreement than ever before. They did not conclude those negotiations, mainly because Olmert was indicted for corruption and had to step down as leader of his party, following which Abbas was told by Israelis and by Secretary of State Rice to wait for Tzipi Livni to become prime minister—something she was never able to achieve.

Since the very early years of IPCRI, I began to develop what I call "joint stakeholder mediators" or "cofacilitators," meaning a team comprised of an Israeli and a Palestinian who facilitate and mediate negotiations between Israel and Palestine, rather than a third party. A third party is usually labeled "a trusted third party" or "a neutral third party." It is a nice idea, but in reality there is no such thing. Over the decades of failed negotiations, the United States has assumed the role of the trusted third party. Palestinians have claimed that the United States is not unbiased and always favors Israel's interests over those of Palestine, but Palestinians have also said that the United States is the only third party that can be effective—meaning that only the United States can apply effective pressure on Israel. The problem with that statement is that until now they have not applied effective pressure on either side.

The additional problem with the United States taking the role of mediating and negotiating is that in this trilateral framework, the Israelis speak with the Americans, the Palestinians speak with the Americans, and the Israelis and the Palestinians don't speak with each other. Ambassador Martin Indyk, who was charged with running the negotiations under Secretary of State John Kerry from July 2012 to April 2013, told me that sometime in the first months of negotiations he left the room with the Israelis and

Palestinians inside to allow them to speak freely with each other. When he returned to the room he discovered that they sat there mostly in silence waiting for him to return. I claim that the dependence on the third party limits the Israeli-Palestinian direct conversation.

There are those that claim that because the Israeli-Palestinian conflict is so asymmetrical, the Palestinians need a pro-Palestinian mediator to level the playing field. That is a nice idea, but very unlikely to happen, unless there are predetermined understandings on outcomes between the third party and Israel—also something that seems out of reach at the present time.

In IPCRI we had developed and perfected the idea of the "joint stakeholder mediator team." Over the years, I had organized, run, facilitated, and mediated more than two thousand Israeli-Palestinian meetings, mainly focused on problem-solving and negotiations. It is a great challenge for two people from the conflict to step outside their traditional roles and alliances, and rise above their own identities to serve as a team of negotiators whose job is to get the conflicting parties to reach agreements. It requires the two stakeholders from both sides of the conflict to focus on reaching agreements and not on achieving their own side's interests. It means that they must be willing to challenge members of their own side and call them out when they are being conflictual and avoiding confronting perspectives outside of their worldview and understanding.

I have seen this model work, and when the two mediators are capable of working together as a team focused on reaching agreement, there is no better model of negotiations. This is the model that eventually worked to secure the release of Gilad Schalit from Hamas. No one is more sensitive to the needs, interests, and threats of the parties in the conflict than people from the conflict zone. No one is more aware of the "chemistry" between people around the table than those who come from the same places and societies.

In 2003, at the height of the horrendous violence of the second intifada, we in IPCRI succeeded in organizing a high-level delegation from both sides to fly to Istanbul for a meeting whose aim was to reach agreement on a cease-fire of hostilities. We worked extremely hard to select people who were well connected to the highest level of decision makers on both sides. We did not have the financial resources to convene this meeting, so we approached a political NGO in Sweden that was associated with the ruling Social Democratic Party there. We had worked with them in the past, and they immediately agreed to provide the finances for this meeting. They did, however, make their support conditional on the meeting being facilitated and mediated by a member of Parliament (MP) from their party. Against my better judgement, we agreed. The whole delegation flew together to Istanbul from the Israeli Ben Gurion Airport. The entire trip to Istanbul was very tense. As was my custom, I remained in the security area with the Palestinian participants for more than three hours as they cleared the Israeli security. One of the Israeli delegates was a recently retired Israeli general. The whole procedure could have been much swifter if he had intervened, but he did not—a sign of the animosity that existed during that very tense period.

After arriving at the hotel in Istanbul, checking in, and having lunch—mostly sitting at separate tables, we convened in our meeting room for the opening discussion. In the first five minutes of the meeting, the Swedish MP managed to insult the head of the Palestinian delegation, who got up and stormed out of the meeting, never to return despite the pleading of members of his own team and the Swedish MP himself. The Palestinian senior official simply wanted the right to open the meeting with a positive statement of his own hopes and the hopes of President Arafat for the meeting. The Swedish MP silenced him stating that he was talking now and he would call on the Palestinian gentleman in turn. The head of the Palestinian delegation insisted on his right to make an opening statement, but the Swedish MP insisted that he was running the meeting and would decide who would speak and when. It was a clear cultural misunderstanding, but an insult was an insult and the damage was done. This senior Palestinian, an elderly gentleman who had received the explicit permission and direction of the Palestinian president to be at this meeting was made to feel like a young school boy being reprimanded by the school principal and that was not going to pass. Perhaps if it had not been during that very violent period, the end results might have been different. That event reinforced for me what I had already understood: the incident would not have happened had I and a Palestinian colleague been cofacilitating the meeting.

The following are a set of lessons that I have learned over the years from negotiating, facilitating, observing, and creating policy proposals in attempts to advance Israeli-Palestinian peace.

LESSON LEARNED: *In protracted conflicts, it is not sufficient to only detail the beginning of the process; it is important, and perhaps essential to reach agreement on at least the principles of long-term final or permanent status issues.*

The Israeli-Palestinian Declaration of Principles (DOP) signed on September 13, 1993, provided a framework for mutual recognition between the State of Israel and the PLO. This agreement, it was hoped, would provide the sides with the framework and the mechanism to begin a process of normalization, mutual recognition, and mutual confidence building, which would lead to future negotiations. The DOP also listed the main issues in conflict that must be resolved for the permanent status between the two sides. The DOP dealt with procedural issues for the short term, focusing on temporary status issues and leaving the core issues of the conflict for later stages.

The two sides adopted the Kissengerian notion of "constructive ambiguity" in order to "sell" the agreements to their own constituencies. In doing so, each side was also allowed to interpret what they perceived to be unwritten agreements regarding the final or permanent status that will emerge at the end of the process.

The main issues of the conflict (i.e., borders, Palestinian sovereignty or statehood, Jerusalem, Israeli settlements, refugees, etc.) were not included at all in the initial negotiations. They were left out of the agreement to be dealt with at a later stage. These issues are the heart of the conflict. By not reaching at least a declaration of principles on these issues at the beginning of the process, each side was free to develop amongst their own constituencies disparate understandings of what the final outcome would be. Rather than coming closer together on most of the core issues, the gaps in understandings grew throughout the years when no negotiations took place regarding the final status of the agreement.

LESSON LEARNED: *Dates are holy but so is performance.*
The DOP set up a timeline for implementation. The basic timeline determined that there would an interim period of five years and that negotiations on permanent status "will commence as soon as possible, but not later than the beginning of the third year of the interim period."

The DOP also set forth a schedule for Palestinian elections and Israeli redeployments or withdrawals from Palestinian territories. The second Oslo agreement set up a more rigid schedule for further implementation of Israeli withdrawals. In early 1995, Prime Minister Yitzhak Rabin, following a series of terrorist attacks, assured the Israeli Knesset that there are "no holy dates" and that further Israeli redeployments would not be implemented according to the schedule set forth in the agreements.

From that time on, throughout the peace process, implementation timelines established in the agreements were not honored. A process of mutual breaching of the agreements began as each side came to understand that if the other side did not comply with the signed agreement, then they too are not bound to what they signed.

The entire process was predicated on the understanding that each side fulfill its part of the deal on time. A unilateral Israeli decision to breach the agreement on the implementation timetable led the Palestinians to breach other elements of the agreement. The Israeli decision was based on the belief that the Palestinians were not undertaking a sincere battle against terrorism. The Palestinians argued that their best weapon against terrorism is the progress of the peace process and the Israeli withdrawals from Palestinian territories, and thus a catch-22 cycle of breaches following breaches ensued and progressed until the final breakdown at the end of 2000.

Permanent status negotiations did not begin as scheduled. Israeli withdrawals did not take place on schedule, while at the same time violence increased, opposition on both sides gathered support, and breaching the agreements became the norm.

LESSON LEARNED: *Political violence cannot be tolerated. The Oslo process was marked from the outset by a continuation of Palestinian violence and terrorism.*
With the signing of the agreement in September 1993, there was a huge drop in the number of attacks; however, they never completely ended. Additionally, during Purim 1994, a Jewish terrorist massacred Muslims praying in the Ibrahimia Mosque in Hebron. In 1995 we were witness to many acts of fundamentalist Islamic suicide bombers who murdered Israelis indiscriminately.

These acts of violence created an impossible situation for the political leaders on both sides who stood behind the peace process. There is no simple formula for what leaders should do when their citizens fall victim to terrorism aimed at halting a peace process. Ceasing the process would only award those who seek through their terror to achieve precisely that result. It was Prime Minister Rabin who articulated the policy that the fight against terror would continue as if there were no negotiations and that the negotiations would continue as if there was no terror. Other than agreeing with that basic formula, there are probably at least two additional points that could be raised and may point to some lessons that should be learned.

First, it was a mistake to call the victims of terror "the casualties of peace." This is wrong—they were casualties of continued warfare and not casualties of peace. The notion that these victims of terrorism suffered as a result of a peace process only served to strengthen the opposition to the peace process in both publics. Words are very important and very powerful.

Second, at almost no time during the peace process did the two sides work honestly and sincerely together, in partnership, to confront the problem of terrorism and violent opposition to the peace process. Had the two sides worked together against the problem, rather than the two sides working against each other, there is a chance that the results could have been more positive.

More often than not, Arafat was blamed by the Israelis for not preventing terrorism emanating from areas that were not even under his security control and thus not his responsibility. Without opening the argument of whether or not Arafat was ever really sincere in fighting against terrorism, the likelihood of a real Palestinian effort against its own extremists could have been enhanced through a cooperative approach rather than the antagonistic approach that was employed. The more that Israel blamed the Palestinian Authority, its leaders, and its security chiefs for failing to prevent terrorism, the more these same people were presented in their own media as agents of Israel, as they suddenly responded to Israeli demands to "round up" some extremists and imprison them.

There is no doubt that the leaders on both sides failed to find a positive and effective way of confronting the spoilers, the extremists, and the killers on both sides. This is not a problem that has surfaced only in the Israeli-Palestinian context—it is a problem that has become one of the most significant dangers to peacemaking around the globe.

No security service in the world can give their people a 100 percent guarantee of security in the world of global terrorism. The essential element that needs to be in focus is the cooperative struggle in the fight against terrorism and the extent of genuine efforts being made by both sides. Extending universally applied standards for enforcement, including punishment of violators, is also an essential element of the fight against terrorism and cooperation across the conflict lines. In the Israeli-Palestinian context, that means engaging the same high level of consistent force, deterrence, and application to all terrorists, on both sides of the conflict, regardless of their nationality.

LESSON LEARNED: *Protracted conflicts in which there is little or no trust and confidence require external mechanisms to verify implementation of the agreements, to ensure compliance, and to offer external dispute resolution.*
The Israeli-Palestinian agreements did not have any external mechanisms to verify implementation, to ensure compliance, and to offer dispute resolution. The DOP stated: "Disputes arising out of the application or interpretation of this Declaration of Principles, or any subsequent agreements pertaining to the interim period, shall be resolved by negotiations through the Joint Liaison Committee (JLC) to be established. . . . Disputes which cannot be settled by negotiations may be resolved by a mechanism of conciliation to be agreed upon by the parties."

What happens when the sides cannot agree on how to resolve the disputes or disparate interpretations of the agreements? What happens if the sides are not capable of reaching an agreement on the mechanism of conciliation?

This is precisely what happened. Each side breached the agreements, or interpreted their obligations or the obligations of the other side in different ways, and then issued statements against the other side. The JLC was incapable of resolving the disputes because it became the forum through which each side raised it claims against the other—not for the purpose of resolving the dispute but to "score points" against the other side.

When the breaches piled up so high, the JLC ceased to function, as did most of the joint bodies that were formed through the agreements. There was no mechanism established that could fairly determine which claims were valid and which were less so. There was no external mechanism to help the sides comply with the commitments they had made. There was no external mechanism that could help bring about resolution of the disputes; and thus, once the process of breaching the agreement became the norm, there was little or no value in signing new agreements.

Signing new agreements nevertheless became part of the process—these agreements mainly stated that the sides would undertake the implementation of agreements already signed in the past. At least two formal agreements were subsequently signed that were aimed at repairing the damages of formerly breached agreements (the Wye River Memorandum and the Sharm e-Sheikh Agreement), yet these agreements were also breached. Throughout the process, the failure to resolve the disputes also emanating from a lack of external mechanisms led to further breakdowns in trust and confidence, which further limited the ability of the sides to continue negotiations on the core issues.

It seems that had the sides invented mechanisms involving acceptable third parties for processes of implementation verification, compliance assurance, and dispute resolution, perhaps breaches of the agreement would have been resolved from the start, and future disputes would have been contained and resolved. Leaving the verification, compliance assurance, and dispute resolution means to the two disputing parties alone sabotaged the process from within.

LESSON LEARNED: *Agreements must be as explicit as possible.*
Too much of the Oslo Agreement was open to too many varied and opposing interpretations. Several of the best examples relate to territorial and settlement issues. Palestinians understood that upon signing the DOP Israeli settlement activity would cease in the West Bank, Gaza Strip, and East Jerusalem.

The Palestinians believed that the Israeli agreement to specify that the process was based on UN Security Council Resolution 242, that the process would not prejudice the outcome of final status agreements, that the Israelis agreed to mention the integrity of Palestinian territories, and that the Palestinian Council would have authority over all areas of the West Bank and Gaza "except external security, settlements, Israelis, foreign relations" meant that Israel would refrain from the construction of new settlements or from expanding existing ones. This, however, did not happen.

The Israelis claimed that nowhere in any of the agreements did Israel agree to cease settlement construction. Israel further claimed that the construction of new settlements, bypass roads, or the enlargement of existing settlements did not prejudice the outcome of the permanent status agreements because their construction did not impinge on the possibility that they would either remain under Israeli sovereignty by agreement, or be transferred to Palestinian sovereignty by agreement. According to the letter of the agreements, Israel is correct.

On the other hand, there is little doubt that the continuation of settlement construction, the continued confiscation of Palestinian lands and the construction of bypass roads was one of the major factors that led to the end of the Oslo process. One can only ponder: Why, then, did the Palestinians not demand an explicit reference to the cessation of all settlement construction in writing as part of the agreement?

There is no problem in providing additional examples where nonexplicit language may have made the signing of an agreement possible, but in fact made its amenable implementation impossible.

LESSON LEARNED: *Peace must pay—peace must have a constituency. There were many promises that peace would pay.*
Shimon Peres spoke about a new Middle East that would flourish with the fruits of peace. A lot of money was pumped into the process, and economic development projects and large-scale infrastructure development projects were launched. At the same time, in response to a continuation of terrorism, various Israeli governments imposed new systems of closures limiting Palestinian access to Israel and to Israeli markets.

The most affected sector was that of the export of Palestinian labor to Israel. Economic data point to the fact that the losses to the Palestinian economy equaled and even surpassed the total amount of donor funds that were pumped into the process. The result on the ground was a continual shrinking of the Palestinian economy (with the exception of 1999–2000). The common Palestinian citizen became poorer, and the Palestinian economy actually suffered significant losses after September 1993. In short, the fruits of peace were never delivered to the plates of the average Palestinian citizen.

LESSON LEARNED: *Mediators must be ready and prepared -to play bridging roles when required.*
For most of the Oslo peace process, the Americans were perceived as a kind of mediator. Israeli and Palestinian negotiators more often than not

requested that the Americans serve a convener role and not a mediator role. There was great reluctance to invite the Americans or others to submit bridging proposals. The Palestinians feared that the Americans were too close to the Israeli positions, and the Israelis feared too much intervention by any outside parties. As such, both sides forfeited the valuable roles that credible mediators can play.

Peace processes that are as entrenched and complex as the Israeli-Palestinian example require outside intervention by credible neutral parties that are ready to back their proposals with political and economic weight. The peace process would have benefited greatly by the active participation of credible and experienced mediators who were prepared to put bridging proposals on the table.

LESSON LEARNED: *Peace processes must be "civilized"*
—the role of the military must be reduced.
The Oslo peace process, after the first stage of negotiations, was controlled primarily by military and security personnel on both sides. As time passed, the role of the military-security forces in controlling the relations between the sides became more and more entrenched and institutionalized. All of the joint committees and bodies had high-level participation from the military-security forces.

The "civil affairs" coordination between Israel and the Palestinians was controlled by the office of the Coordinator of Government Affairs in the Territories—a military officer at the rank of general. Even though the coordinator dressed in civilian clothes for meetings with the Palestinians, it was clear that it was still the IDF and the Ministry of Defense on the front line. In the end, the role of the civilian ministries and officials was minimized in favor of the military.

Military personnel are not usually trained in the arts of peacemaking. They usually lack the sensitivities necessary for transforming relations that were based on conflict and animosity into relations of peaceful neighbors. The heavy-handed, continuous presence of the military also signaled to Israelis and Palestinians alike that the basic dynamics of the relations did not change after signing peace process agreements. The military occupation simply changed its clothes, as was stated by many Israeli and Palestinian civilians.

There were great expectations that the peace process would end the occupation and the mentality of occupation. There should have been a conscious decision to transfer all coordination and cooperation outside of direct military-security matters to civilian ministries. Coordination of agricultural affairs should have been dealt with by the two ministries of agriculture, tourism by the ministries of tourism, and so on, without a military presence overriding decisions and setting the tone.

LESSON LEARNED: *Personal relationship building is important.*
It might sound a bit too obvious, but it must nonetheless be stated
explicitly—peace is built first and foremost from the personal
relationships of individuals.

The Oslo process created a mechanism called "joint patrols." Usually, personal relations between the Israeli and Palestinian soldiers did not develop. The Israelis traveled in their own jeeps and the Palestinians in theirs. Not all of the officers in the joint patrols even knew the names of their colleagues from the other side, with whom they patrolled every day. When crises occurred and violence broke out, even before September 2000, in many cases, the joint patrols ceased to function. When these joint patrols were most needed—for the exact circumstances for which they were created—they were unable to function.

There were, of course, exceptions to the rule. It has been reported that the joint patrol that worked in the Jenin area until September 2000 continued to function throughout all of the prior crises, even when joint patrols in other areas were not. A researcher who looked into the workings of the joint patrols discovered that the commanders of the Jenin joint patrol on both sides had become close personal friends. They had visited each other at home after work and on holidays. Their families knew each other, and they liked each other. When crises occurred, they picked up the phone and spoke with each other. They were able to raise their complaints with each other and then continue to work together, and their work was much more effective.

LESSON LEARNED: *Ongoing contact between leaders is essential.*
There was never a "hotline" between the office of the Israeli prime minister and the president of the Palestinian Authority. The hotline is not only the technology of a special phone line—it is a concept. When there is an emergency, pick up the hotline and deal with the crisis quickly and directly. Crises brewed, percolated, and then exploded. They were then allowed to fester until "enough" suffering had occurred or until the international community intervened and pushed the sides to end the crisis.

Even during the beginning of the events of September–October 2000, there was no direct contact between Ehud Barak and Yasser Arafat. At the time when direct contact could have been the most potentially powerful means of putting an end to the crisis and the violence, their resistance to making contact due to the total lack of trust and confidence between them meant that the leaders essentially preferred to escalate the conflict through vociferous mutual criticisms rather than overcome their mutual dislikes of each in favor of the larger interests of their people.

LESSON LEARNED: *Peace education must be undertaken seriously, and incitement against peace must end.*
Throughout the years of the Oslo peace process, peace education was tremendously undervalued, while at the same time, incitement against peace in the media on both sides and in Palestinian educational textbooks continued and grew.

Education for peace is an essential part of peacemaking. Equal attention to reaching agreements should be placed on the development of peace education tools, on teacher training, and on insuring that the materials and the trained teachers reach the classroom.

When the Palestinian Authority limited and even prevented the participation of Palestinian students and teachers in peace education program, a giant red light should have flashed brightly for policy makers warning them that the peace process itself was in danger.

LESSON LEARNED: *Peace processes must also take place from the bottom up.*
The Oslo peace process was largely framed as a top-down strategy for achieving peace between Israel and the Palestinians. The strategy was based on reaching political agreements between the government of Israel and the PLO. The expectation was that political agreements between the leaders would significantly change the realities on the ground, and the peoples of both sides would almost automatically support the process.

As an afterthought, the sides added to the Oslo II agreement an annex calling for the institution of people-to-people projects as a means of strengthening peace between the two populations. The international community embraced the agreements and the idea of people-to-people projects. However, during all of the years of the peace process (until September 2000), only an estimated $20 to $25 million was allocated for funding people-to-people projects. In the final assessment, the people-to-people process was not taken seriously, not by the donors and not by the Israeli government or the Palestinian Authority, which allocated almost no funding at all to this process and paid only lip service to it politically.

Most Israelis and Palestinians never participated in a people-to-people program. Most Israelis and Palestinians never even knew about people-to-people programs and activities. However, some successful people-to-people programs did continue into the intifada and have been sustained up to today.

At the time of the outbreak of violence, most of the donors froze their support for these projects, taking a "time-out" for assessment and evaluation. Just when these funds were needed more than ever, they became more and more difficult to find.

The people-to-people NGOs have played a significant role in the past by keeping contacts between the sides alive and viable. Without them, there would be almost no positive contacts at all today between Israelis and Palestinians. There must be recognition by the governments and representatives of the value of this work, and when the sides come back to the negotiating table, they should invest a lot more energy and thought into how to integrate the bottom-up peacemaking process into their overall strategies.

Why the Kerry Initiative Failed

20 On March 3, 2013, Prime Minister Netanyahu held a stormy meeting with President Obama in Washington. Netanyahu pressured Obama on Iran, threatening that if the United States did not increase sanctions against Iran that Israel would be forced to attack the Iranian nuclear facilities, even on its own. Netanyahu brought with him substantial intelligence information demonstrating that Iran had increased its enrichment program and that the hard water plutonium reactor was advancing at rapid speed. Obama was angry at Netanyahu for accusing the United States of not taking the Iranian threat seriously enough and of not making any progress on the Palestinian track, causing headaches for the United States throughout the Arab and Muslim world. Relations were quite tense.

On March 17 and 18, 2013, another round of the P5+1 (UN Security Council Members: United States, Russia, China, United Kingdom, and France, plus Germany) was held with the Iranians. At this meeting, the United States saw that the pressure of sanctions on Iran was working and came away with the assessment that a deal could be reached with the Islamic Republic that would move it away from becoming a nuclear breakout state without military aggression.

Immediately after the March P5+1 round, President Obama had his enormously successful visit in Israel. Obama was received with the kind of warmth and support that Clinton had received before him. It was the first time since Obama came to office that the Israeli public got a sense that the president had a warm spot in his heart for the Jewish state. Until then, most Israelis probably bought into the lie, or at least thought it might be partially true, that Barack Hussein Obama was really a Muslim and harbored contempt toward the State of Israel. The problematic relations between Netanyahu and Obama were demonstrated vividly in their May 2009 White House meeting when Netanyahu lectured Obama on Jewish history.

When Obama visited Israel in March 2013, I had the privilege of sitting in the Jerusalem Conference Center when he spoke to hundreds of young Israelis. Obama wanted to speak directly to the people of Israel. His speech was masterfully designed. He wanted to appeal to the people of Israel to trust him and his desire to help Israel to march forward to peace with the Palestinians. Here are some excerpts from his speech that demonstrate his attempts to touch the Israeli soul and psyche:

I also know that I come to Israel on the eve of a sacred holiday—the celebration of Passover. . . . Just a few days from now, Jews here in Israel and around the world will sit with family and friends at the Seder table, and celebrate with songs, wine, and symbolic foods. . . . I'm proud to have brought this tradition into the White House. I did so because I wanted my daughters to experience the Haggadah, and the story at the center of Passover that makes this time of year so powerful. . . . It is a story of centuries of slavery, and years of wandering in the desert; a story of perseverance amidst persecution, and faith in God and the Torah. It is a story about finding freedom in your own land. . . . And it is a story that has inspired communities around the globe, including me and my fellow Americans.

When I consider Israel's security, I think about children like Osher Twito, who I met in Sderot—children, the same age as my own daughters, who went to bed at night fearful that a rocket would land in their bedroom simply because of who they are and where they live. That's why we've invested in the Iron Dome system to save countless lives—because those children deserve to sleep better at night. That's why we have made it clear, time and again, that Israel cannot accept rocket attacks from Gaza, and have stood up for Israel's right to defend itself. And that's why Israel has a right to expect Hamas to renounce violence and recognize Israel's right to exist. . . . When I consider Israel's security, I also think about a people who have a living memory of the Holocaust, faced with the prospect of a nuclear-armed Iranian government that has called for Israel's destruction. It's no wonder Israelis view this as an existential threat. But this is not simply a challenge for Israel—it is a danger for the entire world, including the United States. . . . That is why America has built a coalition to increase the cost to Iran of failing to meet their obligations. . . . As president, I have said to the world that all options are on the table for achieving our objectives. America will do what we must to prevent a nuclear-armed Iran. . . .

The Palestinian people's right to self-determination and justice must also be recognized. Put yourself in their shoes—look at the world through their eyes. It is not fair that a Palestinian child cannot grow up in a state of her own, and lives with the presence of a foreign army that controls the movements of her parents every single day. It is not just when settler violence against Palestinians goes unpunished. . . . Only you can determine what kind of democracy you will have. But remember that as you make these decisions, you will define not simply the future of your relationship with the Palestinians—you will define the future of Israel as well.

Negotiations will be necessary, but there is little secret about where they must lead—two states for two peoples. There will be differences about how to get there, and hard choices along the way. Arab States must adapt to a world that has changed. . . . Now is the time for the Arab World to take steps toward normalized relations with Israel. Meanwhile, Palestinians must recognize that Israel will be a Jewish state, and that Israelis have the right to insist upon their security. Israelis must recognize that continued settlement activity is counter-productive to the cause of peace, and that an independent Palestine must be viable– that real borders will have to be drawn.

On the basis of Obama's successful visit and the lengthy time Obama and Netanyahu spent together, an alliance of understanding was built between the two leaders. Obama left Israel only after paving the way for an Israeli-Turkish understanding and, more importantly, a framework of understanding on the two most central issues facing both sides: for Israel, Iran; for the United States, Palestine.

Netanyahu laid out four demands: that Iran stop enriching uranium; that its stockpiles of enriched uranium be removed from the country; that a fortified underground enrichment facility be closed; and that Iran not make plutonium, another possible path toward nuclear weapons. Obama demanded that Netanyahu agree to renew the peace process with the Palestinians. The president appointed Secretary of State John Kerry to take charge and to plot a course together with Netanyahu on moving forward.

In return, Obama gave an outpouring of warmth and support of his own to the people of Israel and even to Prime Minister Netanyahu. It was at the private meetings between Obama and Netanyahu that a deal was struck between the two. Obama promised Netanyahu that the United States would guarantee that Iran would not become a breakout state with capabilities for reaching nuclear bomb status within months and that in exchange Netanyahu would deliver a deal with the Palestinians that would lead to the end of the occupation and Palestinian statehood. Obama prom-ised Netanyahu that if needed, the United States would be prepared to use military force against Iran.

The deal, sealed between Obama and Netanyahu, was finalized on June 27 and 28 in a four-hour meeting that went beyond midnight in the prime minister's residence in Jerusalem. Obama wasn't in the room, John Kerry was, but Obama was on the phone throughout the evening. The deal was Iran for Palestine! Obama promised Netanyahu that Iran would not become a nuclear threshold state with the ability to build a bomb in under one year. Netanyahu promised Obama that he would negotiate seriously the creation of a Palestinian state next to Israel. Obama promised increased military aid, including additional spending on Israel's rocket defense systems and upgraded intelligence cooperation covering the whole region, including Iran. Kerry promised to try to seal a deal within nine months.

The official Israeli-Palestinian negotiations got underway on July 29, 2013, one month after the Iran for Palestine deal.

Then enters Secretary of State John Kerry, who has to bring the Palestinians to the table and begins to set up his nine-month negotiations strategy—based on the Iran for Palestine understanding between Obama and Netanyahu. But the Palestinians were not so easy to deliver. The Palestinians demanded the famous prisoner release of all of the remaining Palestinian prisoners who had been in prison since before Oslo in 1993—some 104 people—and the freeze of all settlement building before they would even consider joining the table. Kerry balked at the settlement freeze, knowing that Netanyahu would not agree and that, the last time it happened, the Palestinians didn't believe that the settlement building had stopped. Israel did, in fact, continue to build in East Jerusalem, and only after nine out of the ten months of the building freeze did the Palestinians come to the table. He tried to offer them increased US economic aid, which they gladly accepted, but they would not budge without the prisoner release. So Kerry successfully got Netanyahu to agree—to the United States, not to the Palestinians—that Israel would release all of the pre-Oslo prisoners based on progress in the talks. The issue of Israeli-Arab prisoners was not fully known at this point and only became problematic when it became public that 14 of the 104 prisoners held Israeli citizenship. What is important here is that the promise to release prisoners was made by Netanyahu to the United States and not to the Palestinians.

Kerry began making a record-breaking number of visits to the region. At first, Kerry attempted to get Abbas and Netanyahu to conduct a series of direct face-to-face meetings. Netanyahu balked and refused to meet directly with Abbas. In the end, Netanyahu agreed that a team of Tzipi Livni and his private lawyer and confidant Attorney Yitzhak Molcho would conduct direct negotiations with a Palestinian team headed by Dr. Saeb Arikat. It was decided that the negotiations would last for nine months and would be direct Israeli-Palestinian negotiations with American mediation and facilitation.

The Israeli-Palestinian-US talks got underway in July 2013. At the table were three delegations: Israel, Palestine, and the United States. From July until mid-November, it seemed that real progress was being made. From conversations I was having with people from all three sides, I understood that the atmosphere in the room was positive and constructive. I learned that all of the core issues were on the table: borders, Jerusalem, security, and refugees. The Israeli and Palestinian sides were presenting new ideas, and the Americans were already putting bridging proposals on the table. The parties also stayed committed to the US demand that there be no leaks to the press and that only the US reports would go to the media. During this period, I commented in my column and in lectures that the fact that the meetings were continuing—they kept scheduling additional meetings, which is not to be taken for granted because the talks could have exploded on any single issue—and because they were keeping to the no leaks policy, I was optimistic that real progress was in fact being made. That was also the rumor that most of the analysts and experts were hearing.

By all accounts that I heard personally from members of the negotiating team, the talks were very serious. I was requested by a member of the US team to submit recommendations. I did this on a regular basis. I also shared my recommendations with the Israeli and Palestinian teams. I wrote tens of pages of recommendations, which I heard were well received and many adopted or supported.

At this point of the negotiations, I was feeling quite optimistic. The reports I was getting were quite positive. Despite official statements coming from Saeb Arikat that there was little progress, I was actually hearing the opposite from the Israelis and the Americans. To substantiate the positive sense, the three waves of pre-Oslo prisoner releases occurred. Despite the public outcry in Israel and the significant public pressure against Netanyahu and the government not to release them, Netanyahu kept to schedule and released tens of Palestinians who had been convicted of terrorism and killing Israelis. No one from the Israeli side bothered to inform the public that they were being released as part of previous promises that had been breached. Instead the Israeli public was led to believe that they were being released as a form of prepayment or blackmail simply to get Abbas to come to the table. If releasing murderers is the payment for negotiations, many Israelis were opposed to those negotiations. That is also the sense that Netanyahu delivered to the public. Key Israeli leaders, such as Netanyahu, Lieberman, and Defense Minister Yaalon, made it clear that Abbas would stay in the negotiations only as long as the prisoners were released. Netanyahu said that the prisoners would only be released if the Palestinians were serious about negotiations.

Then on November 4, 2013, the P5+1 reached an interim agreement with Iran. Netanyahu was angry; he felt that the interim nuclear agreement signed with Iran legitimized the Islamic Republic for no reason. Netanyahu said, "Iran has given practically nothing, but gets international legitimacy." According to Netanyahu, the interim deal only delayed Tehran's nuclear program by four weeks, while the Islamic Republic continues to develop more effective centrifuges that would allow them to reach a bomb faster. From Netanyahu's perspective, the deal that he made with Obama (Iran for Palestine) was breached by Obama. Netanyahu felt betrayed by Washington and also believed that he was released from the Iran for Palestine agreement.

Netanyahu publicly savaged the Geneva interim accord with Iran as a "historic mistake" and immediately said Israel does not see itself as bound by it. Netanyahu and other members of the Israeli government said that Obama had betrayed Israel. Officials in Jerusalem repeatedly castigated President Obama for overseeing a failed negotiating process with Iran under which Iran's nuclear weapons drive would not be thwarted while the sanctions pressure against Iran were collapsing. Netanyahu stated:

> What was achieved last night in Geneva is not a historic agreement; it is a historic mistake. Today the world has become a much more dangerous place because the most dangerous regime in the world has taken a significant step toward attaining the most dangerous weapon in the world. This agreement and what it means endangers many countries including, of course, Israel. Israel is not bound by this agreement. The Iranian regime is committed to the destruction of Israel, and Israel has the right and the obligation to defend itself, by itself, against any threat. As prime minister of Israel, I would like to make it clear: Israel will not allow Iran to develop a military nuclear capability.

In an address to the foreign press several days later, Netanyahu added that Israel had the right and obligation to tell its allies when it disagreed. "Israel has a lot of friends and allies, but when they are mistaken, it is my duty and obligation to say so."

Feeling betrayed by President Obama, Prime Minister Netanyahu felt himself released from his side of the interim deal. From the end of November 2013 until the end of the nine months on April 29, 2014, the trilateral negotiations essentially ended. From that point on, the American negotiating team led by Ambassador Martin Indyk moved from direct negotiations, in which the Israeli, Palestinian, and American negotiators were in the same room, to shuttle diplomacy, in which the American mediators traveled back and forth between Jerusalem and Ramallah, meeting with each delegation separately. At that point, the negotiations lost their momentum, and all sides lost their internal drive to come up with bridging proposals. The Israeli public became increasingly angry at the idea that Palestinians who had murdered Israelis were being released so that negotiations could take place. The public and the media, seeing the end of direct negotiations and the shuttling of Indyk with the frequent visits of Kerry to the region lost the little hope that had existed that a deal could be found.

At this stage and in the months leading up the deadline at the end of April, Kerry and Indyk were spending more than double the amount of time with Netanyahu that they were spending with Abu Mazen. It was clear that the Americans were trying to push Netanyahu to demonstrate more flexibility in order to be able to at least present a framework agreement—far short of what they had hoped for at the outset of the talks.

The increasing animosity between Netanyahu and Obama rooted in Israel's dissatisfaction with the Iran interim agreement put an end to the Israeli-Palestinian negotiations way before they reached their end on April 29, 2014. The Americans tried to convince Netanyahu that the interim agreement with Iran was working. They said that Iran had slowed down its enrichment program. They emphasized that the verification regime in place, which is independent from Iranian compliance, was enabling the international inspectors to have full freedom to verify compliance all over Iran without prior notification. They asserted that the successful verification regime would guarantee Iran's implementation of the terms of a final agreement. Netanyahu was not buying what Obama was selling.

The negotiations ended after nine months. No agreement was reached. The Palestinians began their international diplomatic offensive of signing on to international conventions and joining international organizations, including the Rome Statutes for entrance into the International Criminal Court as the State of Palestine. Since that time, until the writing of this book, no Israeli-Palestinian negotiations have taken place.

A Plan to Replace the Netanyahu Government

I tried to meet Netanyahu after the completion of the Schalit deal in October 2011. I was informed that I would be receiving an invitation to come to the Prime Minister's Office. The invitation never came. David Meidan, the Mossad officer who I worked with in the secret back channel to negotiate the Schalit deal, told me that someone in Netanyahu's office blocked my invitation. Instead, I received a letter of thanks from Netanyahu on October 26, 2011, eight days after Gilad Schalit came home.

When my book about those negotiations was published in Hebrew, I went to the Knesset with a copy of the book, hoping I would be able to hand it to Netanyahu. I was sitting in the VIP gallery of the Knesset and could see Netanyahu some fifty meters away from me. His Chief of Staff Gil Sheffer was sitting across from me in the VIP gallery on the opposite side of the Knesset plenary. I texted Sheffer that I was sitting there across from him and that I had a copy of my book that I wanted to give to the prime minister. I saw him look at his telephone reading my message. I saw him look up at me and then he continued to ignore me. I then sent a text message to Liran Dan, Netanyahu's spokesperson, telling him that I was in the Knesset and wanted to give his boss my book. He explained to me that for various reasons the book had to be sent to the Prime Minister's Office and then it would reach him. I told him that from my experience the book would never actually get to Netanyahu. So he told me to deliver the book to the Prime Minister's Office and put his name on it, and he promised me that he would personally deliver the book to the prime minister. He then told me that he would try to arrange for Netanyahu to shake my hand when he left the plenary to go down to his office in the Knesset building.

I saw Netanyahu stand up and leave, and I left the VIP gallery. I went downstairs and saw Netanyahu in a photo-op with some guests. Liran Dan came up to me and told me to wait a few minutes. He then whispered into the ear of Gil Sheffer who was standing next to Netanyahu. Sheffer then whispered in Netanyahu's ear. I saw Netanyahu glance over to me and then shake his head with a definitive "no" and then disappeared into his office with his chief of staff and security detail. Liran Dan came over to me to apologize.

After coming to terms with the fact that Netanyahu refused at least three offers from Abu Mazen to participate in a secret direct channel of genuine negotiations, a proposal that I delivered to him both through his national security advisor, through Minister Dan Meridor, and by direct fax to his office, I fully understood that Netanyahu was not going to turn into the great statesman that he could have been. As the old saying goes, rather than making history, Netanyahu chose to become history. Months of frustration followed for me without a strategy in hand to help to advance peace. The Americans failed miserably with the Kerry initiative, falling into the same old patterns and traps that they fell into previously. Kerry ended up accepting most of Israel's positions and tried to strong-arm the Palestinians into accepting them. Abu Mazen said that he was almost dumbfounded when he read the Kerry plan in his meeting with Kerry in Paris in February 2014. Rather than coming up with some genuine bridging proposals, it seems that the Americans caved to Israeli pressure and put that to bear on the Palestinians, who once again were presented as the rejectionists in the story.

The US team led by Martin Indyk claims that in April 2014 Kerry submitted another document to Abbas reflecting the adoption of more bridging proposals that they believed the Palestinians could accept. According to the Americans, Abbas never responded. My understanding is that the Americans decided to focus on a document of principles on five issues: borders, security, refugees, Jerusalem, and mutual recognition. I was told by a member of the American team that they had secured agreement on two of the five—borders and one other issue. I find this claim very hard to accept. Agreement on borders would mean that Netanyahu agreed that the Palestinians would end up with a state on twenty-two percent of the land between the River and the Sea—with an Israeli annexation of significant size, big enough to leave most of the settlers where they are and a one-to-one territorial swap with land on the Israeli side of the border. I cannot believe that Netanyahu agreed to this. The parties agreed, according to my American source, that the Kerry document would not be published or leaked, so we have no way to know what it actually contained. Surprisingly, no document has yet been leaked.

A new strategy began to develop in my mind after I attended a small dinner gathering at the home of Alice Krieger in Tel Aviv. Long ago, Alice worked for Ariel Sharon and was also a fundraiser for the Jewish National Fund in the UK before moving from there to Israel. Alice convenes Friday dinner gatherings for Israelis that she likes with members of the diplomatic community. At the dinner on April 3, 2014, I attended along with representatives of the Egyptian and Jordanian embassies in Tel Aviv. I was positioned by Alice to sit next to Yitzhak "Buji" Herzog, the head of the Labour Party and Israel's opposition in the Knesset. Throughout the dinner, I listened carefully to Herzog and watched his interaction with the other dinner guests. I spoke to him in private about some of my attempts to get Netanyahu together with Abu Mazen. The following day, I sent him a text message telling him that he impressed me very much. I then began sending regular messages to Herzog. On April 7, 2014, I texted him the following:

Now it is clear that Abu Mazen has suggested a secret meeting with the prime minister and the one who refuses is Netanyahu. The prime minister demands that Abbas withdraws the letters that he signed to join fifteen international conventions and organizations. This will not happen. Now we are facing more unilateral steps on both sides. The negotiations under the American mediation are empty of content and the Americans have adopted most of the Israeli positions. They have proven that they are not impartial mediators. This will not lead to an agreement, and you know that there is no Palestinian who can accept a state under Israeli control of its external borders and no capital in Jerusalem. The prime minister is proving that he is not the leader who will make history. This is a great pity, but we must face the reality that we must find a different way to lead Israel to safety. I had hopes that my colleagues in the peace camp were wrong in their not supporting negotiations under Kerry but I admit, it was I who was wrong. Now is the time for fixing that.

Herzog answered me that he would support a secret meeting between Netanyahu and Abbas, but in the end, he said, "What is for sure—Bibi (Netanyahu's nickname) is not able to deliver." On May 29, 2014, I raised the idea to Herzog that he and perhaps Tzipi Livni enter into a direct secret back channel with Abu Mazen to try and produce an agreement that would prove that the real obstacle was Netanyahu and not Abbas. I followed it up with a texted message on May 30, 2014:

Shabbat Shalom. When I proposed to you to enter into a direct secret back channel with Abu Mazen with the goal of reaching a permanent status agreement, I know that this is completely outside of the box and it does hold within it some political risks, but since we are talking about saving the country, we must also consider moves like this even with the risks involved. If you were to succeed in reaching an agreement with Abu Mazen, even an agreement of principles, it would be enough to turn to the people and state that the real obstacle to peace is Benyamin Netanyahu and therefore we must go to new elections. We need a move like this because it is a time of emergency. I am prepared to check with Abu Mazen if he would give a green light for this move.

Herzog told me we would meet and talk about the idea. Herzog then went on holiday and it took another few weeks before we were able to schedule a meeting. On June 14, 2014, I had a long conversation with Dr. Mahmoud al-Habbash, the Minister of Religious Affairs and one of Abbas's closest confidants. I had been developing a relationship with Habbash since I first met him in the end of 2011. Habbash has arranged all of my private meetings with Abu Mazen and has participated in them. I have gone to see him in his Ramallah office regularly, and we chat several times a week on Facebook. We have developed a relationship of trust. Our talk was mostly about the dead-end negotiations of the Americans and the common opinion of both of us that Abu Mazen had offered significant compromises to the Americans but in return got regurgitated Israeli positions that Abu Mazen could not accept. We agreed that with Netanyahu in power there was little if no chance of reaching an agreement.

Dr. Habbash and I spent a lot of time discussing the issues in conflict. It was important for me to understand from him how far he—and more importantly, how far Abu Mazen—was willing and able to go in order to reach agreements with Herzog on all the main core issues. We discussed everything—Jerusalem, borders, refugees, settlements, security, economic relations, Jewish state recognition, education, and even issues of religion, Islam, sharia, and Judaism. At all points of our discussion, I asked him if the views he was presenting reflected those of Abu Mazen, as well. This has been a long process because when I first met him and he took me several times to meet with Abu Mazen, I raised the idea of a direct secret back channel between Abu Mazen and Netanyahu. Netanyahu of course rejected all of these overtures, but in the process, I got to know Abu Mazen's positions in depth. When Abu Mazen first agreed to conduct a direct secret back channel with Netanyahu, my hopes were that the negotiations would be conducted by Habbash on the Palestinian side and by David Meidan on the Israeli side. David liked the idea, and I even arranged for him and Habbash to meet, which took place in March 2013 at the King David Hotel. For two hours we sat together and in Arabic discussed all of the issues and the idea of a secret direct back channel. I was very optimistic after that meeting, but later disappointed when it became clear that Netanyahu was not interested, and David was hesitant to try to convince Netanyahu to accept the idea.

On June 30, 2014, I decided to test the waters, and I presented the idea of a secret back channel with Herzog to Habbash. He immediately agreed and agreed to take it to Abu Mazen and said that he believed with great confidence that Abu Mazen would agree. Later that night, he told me that Abu Mazen gave the green light. Abu Mazen thought that it could be possible to reach an agreement with Herzog. He understood the political risks, but thought it was worth the try because there would be no progress with Netanyahu, and things would otherwise only get worse. Now it was time to push Herzog.

I finally met Herzog in the Knesset on July 9, 2014. He was hesitant and cautious. He needed time to think about it. He was not convinced that Abu Mazen was ready to make an agreement. He believed, as the myth goes, that Israel had already offered him everything possible, and that he had turned it down. The prevailing thinking in Israel, from both insiders and outsiders, is that Abu Mazen is not capable of signing an agreement. The reasons behind his assumed lack of ability or desire to sign agreements are his fear to make a real concession on the right of return of Palestinian refugees and also because many Israeli analysts have come to believe that the Palestinians are not really interested in having a state. These people claim that Palestinians are much more comfortable being in the state of victimhood rather than having to take responsibility for actually building and running a state.

I claim that they are wrong on both counts. Abu Mazen cannot give up the right of return. That is correct. But the misunderstanding of this position is that when the Palestinians say that no Palestinian leader has the right to give up the right of return it is because this right, they claim is not a collective right, but an individual right. Abu Mazen gave up the right of return for himself. He did it on Israeli television on November 2, 2012, stating, "I want to see Safad. It's my right to see it. But not to live there." Abu Mazen did not and cannot give up the right of return for all Palestinian refugees and their descendants. The Palestinian position on refugees has been that every single refugee must be given the choice to make their own decision.

Herzog and many other Israelis believe the statement that the Palestinian rejection of Israeli offers up until now signals that they do not want a state. This reflects a lack of understanding of the facts regarding the Israeli offers made thus far, which have been less than what any Palestinian leader can accept. Rather than coming to terms with the faults of the Israeli proposals, many Israelis seek to place the blame for no agreement on the shoulders of the Palestinians. I still contend that it is possible to reach an agreement and that the Palestinians are prepared to take on statehood.

Many Israelis also claim that the Palestinian leader will never agree to end the conflict and to end all claims. I have heard Abbas state explicitly, in private and in public, that a full agreement with Israel would mean the end of conflict and the end of claims.

In order to push the negotiations between Herzog and Abbas forward, Herzog requested a private meeting with Abbas. I immediately spoke to Habbash and he spoke with Abbas. Abbas suggested that Herzog meet first with Habbash and prepare the meeting between him and Abbas. I proposed that they both come to my house in Jerusalem. The meeting took place on September 2, 2014.

The meeting in my home was open and frank. Both participants tried to judge the seriousness of the other and whether or not there was in fact a chance of reaching agreement between Herzog and Abbas. I stated to both in my opening remarks that what was at stake here was the entire future of Israel and Palestine. If Abbas and Herzog could reach an agreement, it could change history. It would be something that Herzog could use to demonstrate that there was a Palestinian partner for peace and that the primary obstacle to reaching peace was Netanyahu. I had printed out for the meeting the draft of the agreement that I had prepared for Martin Indyk and the Kerry team several months before. We never got into that level of detail, but they took my draft with them. There was good chemistry between Habbash and Herzog. Habbash assured Herzog that Abbas was very serious about wanting to reach a negotiated agreement with Israel that would end the conflict and all claims. Habbash said he would arrange the meeting with Abbas. I told them that I would soon be going on holiday and requested that the meeting be postponed until I come back. That was not agreed. Herzog wanted to meet Abbas as soon as possible, but he also told me that he wanted to find someone he trusted who would represent him in meetings with whoever Abbas selected to conduct the talks. He needed time to think about who would be the right person. Herzog also told me that he would send me a copy of the peace plan that he had prepared, which he did later that day.

On September 5, 2014, Herzog met Abbas in Ramallah. Abbas reiterated his position that the Israelis and Palestinians return to the negotiating table primarily to determine, under a strict timeline, the borders of a future independent Palestinian state. According to the press reports, Abbas said, "The time has come for Israel to determine how it envisions the borders of the Palestinian state." Herzog told Abbas that the Palestinian leader should avoid taking unilateral steps that could damage the possibility of diplomatic dialogue. Herzog also stated to the press at the end of his meeting, "We have a partner that is ready to go the distance for peace and take original, brave steps on core issues."

What was not reported was that Herzog and Abbas agreed to try to reach a negotiated agreement between them through a secret direct back channel. They agreed that they would each appoint one person to represent them. No one, aside from the leaders, the two emissaries, and myself, would know about this channel. It was agreed that it would be kept in complete secrecy. Abbas appointed Habbash to be his representative, as I hoped that he would. Herzog requested time to think about who he would like to represent him. While I was on holiday, Habbash contacted me and told me that he would be meeting Dr. Ephraim Sneh as Herzog's representative. Sneh was a good choice—he was moderate, had deep knowledge of the situation, had negotiated in secret with the Palestinians in the past, and seemed to be someone who knew how to reach agreements with the Palestinians. Sneh had a long record of senior military positions and served as deputy minister of defense in Barak's government.

I contacted Sneh and told him that I wanted to meet. I met Sneh and we discussed the framework and the issues. I presented him with a copy of the peace treaty that I wrote for Martin Indyk. During our discussion, it was clear that Sneh and I saw eye to eye on most issues. I was confident that Sneh was a good choice. I told Habbash that Sneh was a security "hawk" and a political "dove." I stressed the importance of winning his confidence by first tackling the security issues. I told Habbash that I thought the best approach would be to stress the importance of joint Israeli-Palestinian command and control operations and put less emphasis on what has been the Palestinian plan until now of relying on third party forces, such as NATO. I knew that Sneh did not think that any third party could relieve Israel of its threat perceptions or its assessment that Israel could never be secured by third parties, only by the IDF. In general, I shared Sneh's position on the need for continued Israeli presence inside the future Palestinian state, but only as part of joint Israeli-Palestinian and regional security mechanisms.

The first negotiations meeting between Sneh and Habbash took place in mid-October. Both reported to me that it was a very good meeting. They agreed on the process and on the issues they would address. They agreed to first draft a protocol on security issues. Sneh commented to me in private at our next meeting that he was impressed by Habbash's intelligence and his deep understanding of the issues. Both Sneh and Habbash told me that they were confident in their ability to reach full agreement on all of the issues. Habbash was certain that whatever he presented and agreed to would be accepted by Abbas, as well. He also said that he was sharing with Abbas on a regular basis the progress being made and when drafted text was prepared, he spent time going over the texts with Abbas, in private, without the knowledge of anyone else.

I proposed to Sneh and to Habbash the idea of going abroad to some isolated place for several days to work intensively on the document so that we could complete our mission quickly and then move it into the political arena. Habbash liked the idea; Sneh did not. I was not sure why Sneh hesitated and why he didn't want to move forward in this way. I was not privy to the talks although I did get updates and met with each of them privately on a regular basis. Herzog and Abbas agreed that only they would conduct the talks, and they did not want anyone else involved. Sneh was deeply suspicious of security breaches and was convinced that if Netanyahu knew about the initiative, he would do everything to destroy the process and Herzog along with it. Sneh insisted on a total digital blackout—nothing in email, texts, telephone calls, faxes—nothing. Even when we met together in his Herzliyah office, Sneh insisted that I leave my telephones outside of his room, turned off. He told me that I should not speak about this in Habbash's office, believing that his office and phones were bugged by the Israel security. Sneh was totally convinced that if the Shin Bet got word of these talks and our progress, they would report it to Netanyahu, causing irreparable damage, and then we would be finished.

As Sneh and Habbash began their series of meetings and found agreement on almost everything, they made progress drafting the security protocol. As I pushed to be directly involved in the talks, Sneh said that if they would agree to add another team member, I would be added on the Israeli side. In light of the fact that I was not sitting in the meetings with them, I made sure to meet with both of them separately at least every other week. Not only was I trying to put the pieces together in order to make sure that they were not encountering obstacles in their negotiations, I used each meeting to push hard against the clock, hoping that we could make quick and effective use of the agreement between Herzog and Abbas. One of my main concerns was that on the security protocol they would chose to base their proposal on the concept of "third-party peacekeeping forces" led by the United States, either through NATO or in a special multinational force such as the one working in Sinai. I am completely against this model and tried to convince Habbash and Sneh to work toward a model based on joint Israeli-Palestinian forces—command and control in designated areas with designated tasks. This is the surest way to ensure the security and peace of both states and places the direct responsibility for the most fundamental aspect of peace on the shoulders of the two sides together.

On December 3, 2014, in a surprise move by Netanyahu, the Knesset voted to disband itself and to head for new elections. We had not anticipated the sudden fall of the Israeli government. We had hoped that a draft Israeli-Palestinian peace agreement between Herzog and Abbas would help to bring down the government on the most crucial issue facing the future of the State of Israel, but instead, Israel was heading to elections on issues of almost no consequence to the future of both peoples. I knew that once Herzog began organizing his campaign, it would be more difficult to convince him to make use of whatever agreement would unfold. He would be doubly cautious when told by his strategic advisors that any discussion of specific issues in the agreement would most likely lead to losing votes rather than gaining them. I did not agree with those advisors, but I knew that Herzog would agree with them over me.

While it seemed quite clear to me that the main issue that always faces the Israeli electorate is security and peace, Herzog would be extremely cautious not to push a security and peace agenda because the Israeli public simply doesn't believe that peace is possible. The Israeli society has become so convinced that there is no Palestinian partner that any promises of peace by politicians are perceived as no more than empty words. They would have to stand up to the threats and fearmongering of Netanyahu, which play on real threats and real fears in a very unstable and dangerous region and time. Herzog would have little ammunition to contest Netanyahu as "Mr. Security." That was the entire hope behind my initiative—to disprove the notion that there is no partner for peace.

In a move that most Israelis would portray as strengthening the idea that there is no Palestinian partner for peace, in the end of December 2014 the Palestinians tried once again to submit a draft resolution to the United Nations Security Council. It was submitted by Jordan. It was mostly a good resolution but nonetheless perceived and presented both by Israel and the United States as another Palestinian unilateral step aimed at having the international community impose a solution rather than going through negotiations. This was certainly the impression held by Herzog and Netanyahu, and strengthened Herzog's decision to steer far away from the Palestinian issue in the election campaign. This was wrong, but the Palestinian draft resolution was voted down by the Security Council with the Americans once again using their veto against the Palestinians.

The Palestinian decision to submit the resolution begs the question of why they submitted it at that time for an immediate vote. They must have known that the resolution would not pass. The Palestinians must have been aware that pushing a UN resolution on ending the Israeli-Palestinian conflict through the Security Council demands a lot of preparation work and drafting, with the engagement of the various parties, in order to pass it. My sense is that the Palestinians put down a draft to place a benchmark of their baseline positions—look at what we are demanding. We (the Palestinians) want the world to know that our demands are such and such and that they are reasonable. That is a kind of starting point for the Palestinians.

For the most part, the resolution was a call to the international community to preserve the viability of the two-state solution, to end the occupation, and to break Israel's hold over millions of Palestinians. Many of the parties in the international community and especially in Israel say that the Palestinians continue to never miss an opportunity to miss an opportunity. I do think that they made a mistake by bringing it to a vote without guaranteeing its acceptance. Nonetheless, I think it is important to examine the text to understand what exactly they wanted from the world. There are many positive statements in the text. There are a couple of changes I would have made, but most of the text, I would leave as is. I was pleased to see the Palestinians declaring that "the final status agreement shall put an end to the occupation and an end to all claims and lead to immediate mutual recognition." This paragraph makes it clear that this is in fact their intention—on the condition that the Israeli occupation of the lands conquered by Israel in 1967 comes to an end based on agreed upon borders.

The draft resolution was also positive in its adoption of the need to address incitement: "Urges both parties to engage seriously in the work of building trust and to act together in the pursuit of peace by negotiating in good faith and refraining from all acts of incitement and provocative acts or statements, and also calls upon all States and international organizations to support the parties in confidence-building measures and to contribute to an atmosphere conducive to negotiations."[1]

DESPITE THE ISRAELI CLAIM THAT THE DRAFT resolution was an act of Palestinian unilateralism, the draft itself states otherwise and calls for the parties to return to negotiations in order to reach an agreement to end the occupation, end the conflict, and make peace. The draft

> calls for a renewed negotiation framework that ensures the close involvement, alongside the parties, of major stakeholders to help the parties reach an agreement within the established timeframe and implement all aspects of the final status, including through the provision of political support as well as tangible support for post-conflict and peace-building arrangements, and welcomes the proposition to hold an international conference that would launch the negotiations; calls upon both parties to abstain from any unilateral and illegal actions, as well as all provocations and incitement, that could escalate tensions and undermine the viability and attainability of a two-state solution on the basis of the parameters defined in this resolution.

This resolution, with a few amendments, could have been a very positive development toward real peacemaking. I am quite sure it will be revisited in the future. If I were drafting the resolution, I would have made the following changes: The timetable in the resolution is problematic. Even if the resolution passed, I do not think it would have been possible to fully implement an agreement by the end of 2017, as the resolution called for—two years is not enough time to implement such a complicated agreement. Furthermore, future agreements must be predicated on performance and full implementation of treaty obligations, which must be measured gradually and over time, in order to mitigate the risks and chances of failure. One of the main lessons from the failures of the past is that we must create a system of implementation whereby there are clear, performance-based benchmarks on the basis of which it is possible to monitor and verify the implementation of treaty obligations. Those monitored and verified benchmarks would be required to determine if the parties were prepared to move from one phase to the next.

This means that territorial withdrawals and transfers would be phased over time and implemented once both sides have completely fulfilled their obligations. The number one obligation of both sides would be in the development and implementation of iron-clad security mechanisms based on Israeli-Palestinian cooperation. Security responsibilities must be undertaken by the Israelis and the Palestinians together, not by foreigners from NATO or the UN. I also believe that there must be a firm and decisive undertaking by both sides to address incitement and to remove it from all public life, and with equal decisiveness, to undertake the integration of peace education into the school systems in both Israel and Palestine.

On Tuesday, December 30, 2014, the draft proposal in the UN failed to secure enough votes to pass. Following the Palestinian failure to have the Security Council adopt their resolution, Abbas made the decision to sign onto more international conventions—the most important being the Statues of Rome, which governs the International Criminal Court in The Hague. On Wednesday, December 31, 2014, Abbas ratified the Rome Statute, thereby opening the Palestinian Authority territory (or the State of Palestine as referred to by the UN) to International Criminal Court (ICC) investigations. The Hague-based court has jurisdiction to prosecute individuals for war crimes, crimes against humanity, and genocide.

Herzog was furious. On January 3, 2015, he sent me a text message: "I must win the elections—that is everything and if the Palestinians support Netanyahu, which is already clear as the sun light, then I am against them with all of my might and nothing else matters to me now. It is clear that Abu Mazen is coordinating with Bibi."

I saw Habbash that evening in his home in Ramallah and told him what Herzog was feeling. He assured me that Herzog was wrong and from his house I wrote to Herzog the following "You are wrong. What you are saying is so untrue. Don't fall into this trap—it won't help you. It is possible for you to be in coordination with the Palestinians. I am telling you with full responsibility that they are in favor of you and understand that the continuation of the Netanyahu-led government is a disaster for them and for us." Herzog responded immediately. "In the meantime everything they are doing, one for one, is helping Bibi and in a big way. That is the reason for his gains in the polls."

I wrote back, "You cannot compete with Bibi as Likud 'b.' You must present the alternative. Netanyahu promises more conflict. You must bring the hope. The boss of our friend [referring to Abbas and Habbash] reviewed the document in the works and made some small comments and believes that your friend [meaning Sneh] and he can reach an agreement within days. We have already begun speaking about what to do with an agreement in order to advance your campaign. This plan still remains the biggest hope for your victory. Don't be Bibi 'b'—rescue us from him."

I went to visit Habbash once again in his home in Ramallah on Saturday night January 31, 2015. He was sick and had just came back from Amman where he dropped off his oldest son, Mohammed, to fly to London where he was to begin his studies. Habbash had met with Sneh for another meeting on Thursday. They are very close to an agreement. Sneh told me that they needed to complete the security protocol. I went to once again push the urgency. We were about forty-five days away from elections. If we did reach an agreement, it would take time to convince Herzog to use it, and we and the election strategists would need time to figure out how to make the best use of it. The security (or lack of security) events in the north (in Syria and Lebanon) following the killing of Jihad Murghnieh, the son of a previously killed Hezbollah military commander, and an Iranian general in what was reported to be an Israeli attack on January 18, 2015, and the attack in Israel that killed two soldiers later the following week assisted Netanyahu in closing the gap, eliminating the temporary lead in the polls that Herzog briefly enjoyed. Herzog was clearly afraid to use the Palestinian issue directly for fear that it would drive voters away.

Throughout the elections of March 2015, my contention was that Herzog could not win on the economic social issues alone, although the polls showed that it was the economy and the cost of living that was on the minds of most Israelis during the campaign season. I contended that at the end of the day the driving force in voting decisions in Israel is ultimately the security and peace issues and not the economy. But it was impossible to convince Herzog and his advisors, particularly when he had such little trust in Abu Mazen.

I went to Habbash again to emphasize the positive messages that the Israeli public has to hear from Abu Mazen. I told him how important it is that Abu Mazen repeat what he had already told Egyptian President Sisi the previous week, which was that the Palestinians would freeze their steps in the ICC against Israeli officers and politicians for war crimes if there were serious negotiations taking place. Strangely, this announcement should have been front-page news in Israel, but it was only reported by one news agency—the NRG web site, which is one of the least read news sources in Israel. I told Habbash that Herzog believes that what the Palestinians have done since the elections only strengthens Netanyahu. Habbash said that it is clear that Abu Mazen wants Herzog to win, but that the Palestinians have to be very careful not to appear to be interfering in the Israeli elections. I said this is why it is essential that we finish the agreement as soon as possible. He told me that Abu Mazen reviewed the entire agreement that has been drafted so far. He repeated what he told me previously—that there are no major differences. He said that Ephraim Sneh has all of their comments and must now come back with Herzog's responses on the whole document.

I spoke about the possibility of convening a joint press conference with Abbas and Herzog to announce that they had reached an agreement, or alternatively two parallel press conferences, one in Jerusalem and one in Ramallah. Habbash trashed the idea. He said it was too close to elections to do that, and the Palestinians would be accused of intervening in the Israeli elections. Habbash then said that once there is an agreement, if Herzog would announce that he had reached an understanding with Abu Mazen on the principles of an agreement for comprehensive peace, then Abu Mazen would verify that information and state that it would be possible to reach a full peace agreement a short time after the next Israeli government is elected. That seemed viable if Herzog would agree and if they could complete the agreement in time.

I then started presenting some ideas of additional steps that could be useful. I proposed to him that through V15 (Victory 15—the civil society organization spontaneously founded prior to elections, supported by One Voice, which is an organization on whose board I sit), we organize a large delegation of Israeli activists to come to Ramallah to meet Abu Mazen and to hear the positive message from him in public with all of the Israeli media present. Habbash responded that Abu Mazen would be willing to do that if the request came from Herzog. I told him that I would convey that to Sneh so he could check with Herzog. It was important, once again, to show to the Israeli public that the main obstacle to peace is Netanyahu and not the Palestinian leader. The lack of a partner in the eyes of the Israelis is the main reason why most Israelis believe that peace is impossible. But, according to the public opinion studies that we know, if the public thought they had a partner in peace, they would support the parameters that would make a deal possible.

I was deeply concerned about the lack of trust and suspicion that Herzog felt toward Abu Mazen. I proposed that perhaps we should organize a private phone call between Abu Mazen and Herzog for them to talk things out and so that Herzog might have more confidence in Abu Mazen and his true desire to see Herzog as the next Israeli prime minister. I was not sure that Herzog would agree, but I told Habbash I would present the idea to Sneh and have Sneh bring it to Herzog. I thought that it was badly needed at that point. Herzog needed to use the Palestinian issue to distinguish himself from Netanyahu as someone who brings hope, not the despair that Netanyahu promises.

The main issue outstanding in the Habbash-Sneh talks was that of the refugees. Abbas wanted the fulfillment of the statement from the Arab Peace Initiative (API): "Achievement of a just solution to the Palestinian refugee problem to be agreed upon in accordance with UN General Assembly Resolution 194." Everyone knows that the reference to UNGA 194 is what the Palestinians use to base their claim for the "right of return" for Palestinian refugees. The resolution states: "Resolves that the refugees wishing to return to their homes and live at peace with their neighbors should be permitted to do so at the earliest practicable date, and that compensation should be paid for the property of those choosing not to return and for the loss or damage to property which, under principles of international law or in equity, should be made good by the Governments and authorities responsible." Sneh wanted to find alternative wording and did not give his immediate agreement to the proposed text, which left this one issue unresolved. Abbas did not want to shy away from the API on the refugee issue, noting that with the word "agreed" as the Arabs insisted on including in the text, there is an implicit understanding that the issue would be negotiated between the Palestinians and Israel.

I remembered that in Clinton's principles he found an interesting way of dealing with UNGA 194. Clinton made mention of 194 but presented it as the end result—in other words, whatever agreement the parties reached on refugees they would then consider that solution to be the fulfillment of UNGA 194. Clinton Parameters on Refugees states:[2]

Refugees:
I sense that the differences are more relating to formulations and less to what will happen on a practical level.
I believe that Israel is prepared to acknowledge the moral and material suffering caused to the Palestinian people as a result of the 1948 war and the need to assist the international community in addressing the problem. . . .
The fundamental gap is on how to handle the concept of the right of return. I know the history of the issue and how hard it will be for the Palestinian leadership to appear to be abandoning the principle.
The Israeli side could not accept any reference to a right of return that would imply a right to immigrate to Israel in defiance of Israel's sovereign policies and admission or that would threaten the Jewish character of the state.

Any solution must address both needs.

The solution will have to be consistent with the two-state approach . . .
the state of Palestine as the homeland of the Palestinian people
and the state of Israel as the homeland of the Jewish people.

Under the two-state solution, the guiding principle should be that
the Palestinian state should be the focal point for the Palestinians
who choose to return to the area without ruling out that Israel will
accept some of these refugees.

I believe that we need to adopt a formulation on the right of return
that will make clear that there is no specific right of return to Israel
itself but that does not negate the aspiration of the Palestinian
people to return to the area.

I propose two alternatives: (1) both sides recognize the right of
Palestinian refugees to return to historic Palestine, or (2) both
sides recognize the right of Palestinian refugees to return to their
homeland.

The agreement will define the implementation of this general right in
a way that is consistent with the two-state solution. It would list
the five possible homes for the refugees:

1. The State of Palestine
2. Areas in Israel being transferred to Palestine in the land swap
3. Rehabilitation in host country
4. Resettlement in third country
5. Admission to Israel

In listing these options, the agreement will make clear that the return
to the West Bank, Gaza Strip, and area acquired in the land swap
would be the right of all Palestinian refugees, while rehabilitation
in host countries, resettlement in third countries and absorption
into Israel will depend upon the policies of those countries.

Israel could indicate in the agreement that it intends to establish a
policy so that some of the refugees would be absorbed into Israel
consistent with Israel's sovereign decision.

I believe that priority should be given to the refugee population in
Lebanon.

The parties would agree that this implements Resolution 194.

Clinton's approach put UN Resolution 194 at the end, as the fulfillment according to whatever the parties agreed to implement as accepted by Habbash and Sneh.

Even if Habbash and Sneh completed the agreement, and Herzog and Abbas agreed on the text, it was quite clear that, with only six weeks left before elections, the text would not be used, and Herzog would not identify this as the opportunity that would push him over the top. Not only that, Sneh showed me a draft of the party platform for the Zionist Camp (the Herzog-Livni joint list) for the Palestinian issue. Sneh drafted it, and it was quite good. It mentioned the June 4, 1967, lines as the basis for Palestinian agreement with land swaps enabling the annexation of large settlement blocks. It talked about the Arab Peace Initiative as the basis for regional agreements. It mentioned Jerusalem as the capital of both states. But the party chiefs on the security issues, General Amos Yadlin and Omer Barlev knocked it down and castrated the platform together with Nahman Shai, who represented Tzipi Livni in the discussions, so that it basically said nothing other than that the party supported the idea of two states for two people as a solution to the conflict through negotiations with the Palestinian leadership. The party's decision not to take any real realistic positions on these issues made it clear that there was little hope that Herzog would stand up to the challenge of being a candidate who would promise to take genuine steps toward peace and the end of the occupation. As he told me, the most important thing is to get elected; afterward he could advance the peace agenda. I was already skeptical about the possibility of him winning, but still I hoped that we could get Abbas to strengthen the image of being a real partner.

I then sent an email to US Ambassador Dan Shapiro:

FEBRUARY 1, 2015

Dan, you know that Abu Mazen made a statement during his meeting with President Sisi that if they returned to serious negotiations the Palestinians would freeze their steps in the ICC? It was reported in Israel only by NRG and did not get much play. I know that he would be willing to repeat the statement, and I think that a win-win for everyone could be gained if there was a phone conversation between Abu Mazen and the president in which, when asked by the president, Abu Mazen would respond positively saying, "Yes, we will freeze all steps in the ICC if there are serious negotiations with Israeli taking place." That conversation could then be made public by the White House and it would go online all over the world.
Gershon Baskin

Ambassador Shapiro responded that he would pass on the request to the White House. He did not think it would happen because he said these statements had already been made. This did not leave me particularly optimistic.

More ideas kept coming up on how to help Herzog to win the elections:

Something I wanted to discuss with you and I suggested to E [Ephraim Sneh]. It is important to strengthen the personal relationship and contact between AM [Abu Mazen] and H [Herzog]. I suggested a phone call—E said absolutely no phone contact—it will be reported immediately to Bibi. I thought that it could be really helpful if AM would write a personal letter to H by hand—not on the computer—so it won't be traced—and even in Arabic. We would then have it hand delivered. It is so important that we strengthen the confidence of H in AM and in their mutual commitment to peace. The letter would emphasize AM commitment and help to return to serious negotiations—what do you think?

Habbash said he didn't think Abbas would go for it, but he would try.

MARCH 5, 2015, TO HABBASH FROM ME IN SWEDEN
WHERE I WAS LECTURING:
Good morning—I am coming home tonight and will be in Jerusalem tomorrow. It is twelve days until elections in Israel and it is still too close for comfort. Netanyahu must not win the elections. We need to be very thoughtful on what can be done to persuade the Israeli public to put their support behind peace. The remaining days are crucial. I think it is essential that the three of us [me, Sneh, and Habbash] meet together with the president as soon as possible to propose some ideas that could help. Really there is no time to lose.

One month before the elections, Sneh and Habbash reached full agreement on two documents—principles for resolving all of the core issues and a security protocol—but Abbas was out of the country and would not return until the elections. Herzog would not stand by the agreement and would make any mention of it in the elections. We were out of suggestions and out of options. Herzog was destined to lose the elections.

Netanyahu Wins, Hands Down

22 Netanyahu's knockout seemed to have put the final nail in the coffin of a possible negotiated peace agreement with the Palestinian people in the coming years. Israel appears to be on the road to international isolation. My assessment after the elections was that Israel would find itself in deep conflict with 21 percent of its citizens—the Palestinian Arab minority—who despite their own victory in the polls would face the most anti-Arab government that Israel has ever had. I still believe that without a genuine renewed peace process, Israel will be on a collision course with the US government, not only on the Palestinian issue, but around the international negotiations with Iran, which would create deep divisions and animosity between the White House and Jerusalem.

Israel would also face a European Union that will go directly against its policies of settlement and non-negotiations with the Palestinians with greater vigor than ever before. The EU will continue to strengthen its resolve to play a direct role in the question of Israel and Palestine, and they will be very active over the issue of continued settlement building. Israel would also face the next round of violence, not only in Gaza but from the West Bank and East Jerusalem, as well.

At the time, my sense was that the new government of Israel led by Netanyahu and the right wing would offer no hope to Israel. Minor adjustments to the economy and bureaucratic manipulations could bring down the price of housing, but poverty would increase, the health care system would continue to flounder, the educational system would be even more unsuccessful, and the costs of security and defense would increase as Netanyahu's threats become self-fulfilling prophecies. Israel's economic woes can only be resolved through economic growth that is entirely dependent on Israel ending the conflict with the Palestinians—but with Netanyahu's victory, Israel would move even further away from that possibility.

The day before the elections, I was in Ramallah and had a very serious discussion with one of the top leaders there about the possible outcome of the elections. When discussing the scenario that has since unfolded, he said that their first objective would be to continue, with even greater resolve, the international diplomatic strategy that the PLO has advanced since the complete collapse of negotiations in the end of April 2014, but now at even a faster pace. The strategy aims at advancing recognition of the existence of the State of Palestine, which is occupied by Israel, a member state of the United Nations. The strategy is also aimed at pushing the inter-national community to confront what they call Israel's culture of impunity, regarding its Teflon-like ability to disregard international law, and to end Israel's occupation over the Palestinian people and their state. The State of Palestine, recognized by some 135 countries and by the United Nations, will continue to join every international forum and convention possible and will continue to place their claims against Israel in those forums, especially in the ICC in The Hague. Palestine will make the case that the occupation of the lands occupied by Israel after 1967 is illegal and that the international community must use its diplomatic and legal tools to force Israel to withdraw from their state.

The Palestinian strategy, more than ever will encourage and advance boycotts, sanctions, and divestments. But unlike the original BDS—Boycott, Divestment, and Sanctions campaign—which has largely been based on the de-legitimation of Israel and its right to exist, the BDS campaign officially supported by the State of Palestine will focus on the illegitimacy of occupation, not Israel's existence, making it clear that their attack on occupation refers to 1967 and not 1948. Their campaign will become increasingly successful and Israelis will feel it.

While most Israelis will view the Palestinian strategy as being anti-Israel, the Palestinians will try to make the point that they are not calling for Israel's destruction and are not opposed to Israel's existence, but only to Israel's refusal to recognize the right of existence of the Palestinian people in a state of their own on lands occupied by Israel in 1967. The government of Palestine led by President Abbas will also continue to work very hard to prevent the outbreak of the next round of violence, and where they have control, they will be quite effective, in those areas. The areas under their control are, however, very limited, and there will be violence against Israelis in those areas and from those areas where Israel holds complete security responsibility.

If the Palestinian strategy fails, the leadership of President Abbas will come to an end and a leadership struggle will emerge in Palestine. The contest over the next period of Palestinian governance will not be between competing individuals on the basis of moderation and the call to make peace with Israel. For many Palestinians, perhaps most, the eventual end of the era of Abbas will end the era of the two-state option. The next generation of Palestinian leaders is much more likely to adopt a call for "one person, one vote" for all of the people living between the River and the Sea. When that happens, eventually the international community will also drop its own support of a two-state solution and will adopt the Palestinian demands for democracy.

Israel will not be a better place to live following these elections. But this is what the majority of Israelis voted for and this is what they will get. Netanyahu won the elections largely because of the real fears and the real threats that Israelis face in a very unstable region. The victory went to the man who the people believe will protect them more. The opposition offered no real solutions to any of these problems and instead focused mainly on the price of housing and the cost of living. The elections were not really about the economy, as the Labour Party leader (which ran under the name "Zionist Union") Yitzhak Herzog believed. Israelis don't believe that peace is possible and those who believe in peace made no real effort to disprove this (false) truism. That is why we lost, and that was what these elections were about. Netanyahu's victory came because in the face of Netanyahu's threats and generation of fears about Iran, the region, and the Palestinians, the Zionist Union offered nothing concrete. The issues of peace and security were hidden in the campaign and buried by the politicians who were advised by the strategists that talking about peace would drive the electorate away. But when Netanyahu talked about war and threats, and there was nothing to confront him with on the other side, the people flocked to Netanyahu.

The public continues to believe that peace is not possible and our side did nothing concrete to contest that. It was clear to me that we need a new strategy, and we need it quickly.

Where to from Here?

THE FASTEST PATH FROM DESPAIR
TO HOPE IS ACTION

After recovering from the election results, I immediately began to think, "What's next?" I maintain that there is no room for despair. The idea that there is no solution to the Israeli-Palestinian conflict at this time does come up every so often, knowing that the longer we wait without a resolution, the more difficult it will be to accept and implement it. We do not have the luxury to not try and do something that can increase the will and the ability of the decision makers to move forward toward resolution. I still believe that the best chances for moving forward remain in secret back channels. This conflict can only be ended through a negotiated agreement between Israel and Palestine and with the difficult political constellations on both sides of the conflict line, it seems quite impossible for both leaders to be able to negotiate in good faith if the negotiations are taking place in public. Each side has such significant constituencies that oppose an agreement, or even negotiations, that they would each have to spend most of their time negotiating at home within their own society.

International pressure could be effective, but there are many dilemmas surrounding this issue for anyone, like myself, who is a Zionist and supports Israel's right to exist. The international pressure is beginning to have an impact, and it will increase. The price to Israel will be more moral and psychological than economic. The global economic system and the strengths of the Israeli economy shield Israel, to a great extent, from any real economic harm caused by potential boycotts and sanctions. Individual companies can be hurt, and we have seen several, such as Bagel-Bagel, Barkan Winery, and Sodastream, move out of the West Bank into Israel proper. More factories in settlements will be hurt from the international boycotts—next in line is probably the Ahava Cosmetics company, which produces Dead Sea products—but Israel's economy at the macro level is quite strong and quite insulated from the damage that boycotts can create.

The isolation of Israel politically and socially can have a big impact on Israeli society. This can be seen in the almost hysteric way the Israeli government and the Jewish establishment (mainly in the United States) relates to it. The tactics employed convince the Israeli people and the Jewish world that all of the calls for boycotts, divestments, and sanctions are evidence of anti-Semitism. They are calling it the new anti-Semitism. There may be elements of anti-Semitism behind parts of the BDS movement, but it is a grave error to call all criticism of Israel and its policies anti-Semitism. There is a question regarding whether or not the de-legitimation of Israel is anti-Semitic. I am not sure about it. Is questioning whether or not the Jews are a people and have a legitimate right to self-determination automatically anti-Semitic? The question is appearing more and more on the international stage both because of the occupation and Israel's denial of the right to self-determination of the Palestinian people, but also because of the rise of racism within Israel proper and the lack of equality between Jewish and Palestinian-Israeli citizens. While Israel is recognized as a vibrant democracy, the questions regarding the extent of that democracy to non-Israeli Jews are relevant and legitimate. This is not only with regard to the Palestinian citizens of Israel, it is also evident regarding migrant workers, refuge seekers, and even a quarter of a million of the people who immigrated to Israel from the former Soviet Union who are not *halachically* Jewish. There are second- and third-class citizens in Israel, and their lower-class status is based first and foremost on their not being Jewish, or not being recognized as Jews by the monopolistic Jewish Orthodox establishment in Israel or by Israeli government institutions—and here we clearly have a problem. A person can emigrate from one country to another and receive citizenship in that country. It is theoretically possible for a non-Jew to immigrate to Israel and to receive Israeli citizenship; however, without converting to Judaism, it is very unlikely. The complex identity of being Jewish means not only being part of a national group, but also being a member of the same religious faith. That is where the problem exists, and it might be legitimate to question Israel's own legitimacy in light of its policies. It is even problematic for Israeli Jews who marry outside of Judaism and try to bring their new spouses to the State of Israel and for them to receive citizenship. Palestinian citizens of Israel have even greater problems "citizenizing" their spouses from abroad, and if they happen to be Palestinians, either from the West Bank, Gaza, or abroad, it is next to impossible to get their state to grant them citizenship.

The Israeli tactic of trying to deflect all criticism by labeling it anti-Semitism will work initially. There is already a growing sense amongst many Israelis that the whole world hates us and is against us because they are anti-Semites. Jewish historical memory is used to substantiate these claims. No responsibility is taken on by the government of Israel, and for the time being, by the people of Israel. But as international pressure will surely increase, there will be many countries, in particular governments which will clarify their positions and state that they are not against Israel's legitimate right to exist and to defend itself. They are opposed to the occupation and the settlements. This is true of the twenty-eight countries that comprise the European Union. It is true of other countries around the world. There will also be increasing numbers of Jews, particularly in the United States who will verbalize their dissatisfaction with Israel's policies and even call for boycotts. One clear example is the rapidly growing organization Jewish Voices for Peace. It is difficult to call this organization anti-Semitic. I have serious problems with a lot of the public statements and positions held by Jewish Voices for Peace, but it is clear to me that they are not an anti-Semitic organization or "self-hating Jews" as they are sometimes labeled. They are anti-Zionists. They question Israel's legitimacy.

There have always been groups of Jews, especially ultra-Orthodox Jews who have also never recognized the legitimacy of Israel and have always been anti-Zionist. Their reasoning was based on the idea that only God could create the State of Israel and the creation of a secular Jewish state in the Land of Israel is essentially against God's will. My great-grandfather Rabbi Yehuda Rosenblatt was an anti-Zionist ultra-Orthodox Jew. He was not anti-Semitic or a self-hating Jew. He held his beliefs that Israel should not exist without God's direct will and intervention. Perhaps if he was alive today, he would have changed his position, but his views exist today within the Jewish world.

The BDS phenomenon is of great concern. The initiators and founders of the campaign are very sophisticated and make no statements regarding their genuine political positions. From my knowledge of the people who launched the campaign and who have been behind it, I know that almost all of them are "one staters." They have never supported the two-state solution, and they never supported the Oslo process. For many of these people, the occupation began in 1948 and not in 1967. Many of those who launched the campaign and who do speak about a two-state solution see it emerging as a Palestinian-dominated state on the west side of the Green Line and a Palestinian state on the east side of the Green Line. In this version of the two-state solution, there is no room for a Jewish nation-state. When I meet these people, or people who have adopted their arguments and philosophy, the main question that I asked them is: When does it end? When will you stop boycotting Israel? If their answer is when the occupation of the 1967 lands ends and the Palestinians have established their state, then we have something in common and a basis for dialogue. If their answer is when Israel as a Jewish nation-state no longer exists, then we have nothing in common, and they are not my compatriots in a common struggle.

The phenomenon of BDS goes way beyond the campaign itself. My sense is that most of the calls for boycotts, divestments, and sanctions against Israel are really against the occupation and not against the existence of the

State of Israel. It is difficult to differentiate, but I believe that it is essential that we do so. The idea that international pressure exerted on Israel will impact political change is not without logic.

I remain a Zionist and believe that the Jewish people have the right to self-determination and to a nation-state of their own—with a large and important Palestinian Arab minority. But the reality of Israel is a complex one and the large Palestinian minority within the State of Israel requires us to be explicitly willing to acknowledge that the State of Israel also belongs to them and they belong to the State. It also requires us to end the occupation and to allow the Palestinians to achieve their self-determination in a state of their own next to Israel. I believe very strongly that the State of Palestine should have a Jewish minority, both because Jews should have the right to live in Judea and Samaria, which is where the State of Palestine will be formally recognized, but also because it is healthy for democratic states to have to confront the reality of minorities. Real democracy is not measured by "majority rules," but by the rights granted to the minorities within those states. So it would be positive for the Palestinian people to confront the reality of a Jewish minority. I once proposed to Dr. Salam Fayyad when he was the Palestinian prime minister that the Palestinians should declare that they recognize the rights of Jews to live in Judea and Samaria under Palestinian sovereignty and Palestinian law and that the State of Palestine would guarantee the rights of the Jewish citizens of Palestine at the exact same level of rights that the State of Israel guarantees the rights of its Palestinian citizens. I thought that this might also provide incentives for Israel to improve the way it treats its Palestinian citizens.

Israel must change its own definition to be the "democratic nation-state of the Jewish people and all of its citizens." Israel must allow for the creation of the State of Palestine next to Israel and end its occupation over the Palestinian people. I make this argument not because of the so-called "demographic threat." I have never been comfortable with this expression, so often verbalized by Israeli Jews who support peace with the Palestinians. It is a racist statement. How can citizens of the State of Israel be considered a demographic threat? This is the same concept that gave birth to the formula expressed by people like Ehud Barak, Israel's former prime minister and former leader of the Labour Party, "Us here and them there." This was Barak's vision of peace, which he believed would convince the public that peace was a necessity or at least something that is possible. The same people talk about "divorce" from the Palestinians—but I say that we were never married. Today there is also talk from some who state that since peace is not possible, let us at least end the occupation— unilaterally drawing a border but leaving the IDF (and occupation) in the West Bank.

This is the "pragmatists" argument, which places the primary blame for the absence of peace on the Palestinian side. It is the same argument as "there is no partner on the Palestinian side" or "Abu Mazen is not a partner."

Yes, we have to end the occupation and make peace with the Palestinians, but not because of a demographic threat. We have to do it because controlling the lives of the Palestinians, occupying them, and denying them the same rights we demand for ourselves has created a binational reality, one state for two unequal people. This has led to the destruction of Israel's moral soul. The reality of occupation has forced our young people to be policemen of occupation and has created systems of oppression and violence that are unacceptable in any truly democratic society. In order to survive, we have blinded ourselves to the reality of occupation. We develop hatred toward those who tell us the truth, like *Haaretz* journalists Amira Haas and Gideon Levy. We slander organizations like Breaking the Silence and call them traitors. These groups and individuals force Israelis to look in the mirror, something that many Israelis do not want to do, so sometimes they break the mirror and other times they lock the mirror away in a dark room.

Occupation is bad for Israel not because it creates a demographic threat, it is bad for Israel because it prevents Israel from being the kind of state that it imagines that it is and would really like to be. Occupation is bad for Israel because it also contributes to keeping the Palestinian citizens of Israel in a second-class status. Yes, it is true that Israel will only be the nation-state of the Jewish people if there is a clear Jewish majority in the state, but a serious question arises from that statement: What is the state willing to do to ensure that there is a Jewish majority? Is the state prepared to expel Palestinian citizens? Is the state prepared to use violence against Palestinian citizens? Is the state willing to use economic pressure to encourage Palestinian citizens to emigrate? Is the state prepared to deny citizenship to Palestinian citizens by trying to negotiate away segments of the Palestinian-Israel population in a peace deal with the State of Palestine? This last option might be legitimate, but only if a large majority of those in question agreed to it. Otherwise, Israel does not have the legitimate right to remove citizens from the state through the adjustment of the border.

If the Palestinian minority in Israel were to grow in numbers and challenge the Jewish majority, then Israel will not be the nation-state of the Jewish people. Already now it should be the nation-state of the Jewish people and all of its citizens, and ways should be found now to provide that definition with real content. One clear way is for the Palestinian citizens of Israel to have a lot more direct control over the education system for the Palestinian citizens of Israel. There must be a core curricula for all students in Israel, but with such diversity in Israeli society, individual communities must be able to find a real voice for their own values and subidentities. Why shouldn't Palestinian students who are citizens of Israel study Palestinian history, the Palestinian narrative, Palestinian literature and culture? How is it legitimate for them today to study more about Jewish history than their own? Yes, there must be a common basis of citizenship for all citizens of Israel, but Israel must recognize the need for Palestinian citizens of Israel to have a greater ability to express their own identity within the Israeli system.

There is no demographic threat to the Jewish majority in Israel today from the Palestinian citizens of Israel. Israeli Jews and Zionist political parties would be wise to stop verbalizing this racist expression of their own desires to ensure that Israel remains the nation-state of the Jewish people. Young people today in the Palestinian community of Israel want smaller families. They are more educated and are part of the twenty-first century where they know that large families are usually a recipe for sustaining poverty. This is good, because it is good for them, and it is by their choice. Now Israel needs to relate to them as full citizens and not as a threat.

Israel needs to end the occupation because the occupation is destroying Israel. The damage to Israel is done every single day and it must end quickly. The only way to end it that ensures Israel's safety and security is through peace, through negotiations, and through the development of partnership across the conflict divide.

SO WHAT CAN BE DONE?

I never accept no as an answer and will never stop trying to make peace a reality.

I wrote to my old friend David Meidan—Netanyahu's point man from the Mossad (now retired) for the return of Gilad Schalit:

FRIDAY MARCH 20, 2015

David,

Netanyahu returned big time and it's really bad news for us all. I don't have much hope right now, but as you know me, I'm not giving in to despair and if there is any possibility, any chance to make a difference, we should not cease trying. Netanyahu has said in the past that if the Palestinians recognize Israel as the nation-state of the Jewish people, he would demonstrate genuine flexibility in negotiations with them. I don't believe him, but we cannot allow ourselves not to examine this in depth and explore it anyway.

My proposal is that you contact him (you know that he will agree to see you and to listen to you) and suggest that you conduct a number of meetings with Abu Mazen in secret as a personal emissary of the prime minister to test the willingness of Mahmoud Abbas to move forward in negotiations—even to examine the possibility of partial agreements rather than the usual permanent full agreement. In one of my talks with Abu Mazen, I explored with him various possible formulas for the recognition of the right of the Jewish people to a state of their own. We explored various ideas and one that he seemed to like suggested that if the Palestinians achieved in negotiations satisfaction on all the core issues, and adding an Israeli commitment to ensure the equality the Palestinian citizens of Israel, he would be ready to consider recognizing Israel as the Jewish nation-state. We also talked about the possibility of this being reflected in a Security Council's resolution in which the State of Israel would be recognized as the national homeland of the Jewish people and Palestine as the national homeland of the Palestinian people. What I am saying is that in a calm and coherent way without the normal intimidation in negotiations, you can find a way to satisfy the demand of Netanyahu and open hope for possible real negotiations between Netanyahu and Abbas.

I don't know anyone else who can do it. There is no trust between Abu Mazen and Yitzhak Molcho (Netanyahu's regular emissary to Abbas). With your experience and knowledge, I think you could have that serious conversation with Abbas and find the right formula which would then put the challenge back into Netanyahu's court. I suggest you try to convince Netanyahu to try this path.

You know I am with you every step of the way.

Gershon

David answered, saying that he was surprised by the election results. His insights were clear: the Israeli public is largely on the right and therefore, Israeli leadership for years to come will be held by the right. In short, if you want to lead and influence in Israel, join the right.

He told me that he hadn't talked to Netanyahu in a long time. He said that he made sure not to speak out in public against him and to avoid media exposure. David said that Netanyahu knows his opinions and positions and that he seriously doubted he would agree to do anything that would look like weakening Molcho. David didn't think that Netanyahu was interested in starting a political process and that he would call David and ask for his help.

David believed that Obama would apply huge pressure on Netanyahu. The Security Council might put forward resolutions against Israel, and the

United States might avoid using its veto to push Netanyahu into a corner. David appraised that there would be no negotiations and no real process. The international community would try to act where the Israeli democracy failed. Unfortunately, as David saw it, there was then no place for a new initiative. He said to me, "All the power to you on your persistence."

I responded:

Hi David, I want to ask you to reconsider my request.

Few people in the country have accumulated the experience of understanding the Arab world with strategic vision to enable them to do what I am requesting of you. I have seen how you know to create a relationship of trust with the partner/rival in front of you. You speak their language and understand the cultural codes and the codes of the conflict. I share your pessimism about the prime minister, however, we cannot afford to succumb to despair or to doing nothing, as long as there is even the smallest possibility to change direction.

Yesterday the prime minister said that he would be flexible on the Palestinian issue if the Palestinians agree that their state be demilitarized (and there is no real controversy on this issue) and that they recognize the State of Israel as the nation-state of the Jewish people. This is a very complex issue, but I believe there's room to maneuver and with Abu Mazen, in the right circumstances—in secret negotiations, it is possible to reach a formula that would be a possible solution.

Your prediction about the deterioration of the situation is the same as mine. The deterioration is dangerous and may lead to more violent outbursts, in which many innocent people will pay with their lives for no reason and with no political benefits. This should not be allowed to happen, and if there is any way, small as it may be, to prevent it, we must not give up.

I don't know other people who can reach the prime minister and present him this "life saver" for the State of Israel as you can. And of course he won't ask it from you. There is no escaping the need to initiate this ourselves. For so many years you give yourself totally to the country. What motivated you then hasn't changed, I'd say you have several new good reasons to continue to serve the country since the birth of your grandchildren. It is important that we take action quickly during the first days of the new government. I ask you to rise above the obstacles and rethink your willingness to contribute to changing the situation.

He responded immediately:

> Gershon my friend, I don't see how Bibi with a government that
> includes Bennett and Lieberman can agree on evacuation of 100,000
> settlers. There is no way to move them, which means there is no real
> chance for negotiations and no chance for the Arab Peace Initiative.
> Without a true leader's willingness to make difficult moves, everything
> we do will be useless. If I were to identify the smallest signs of him
> being Begin, I would be prepared to do everything humanly possible
> to offer my service. I don't see that. There's nothing left for me to do
> but to continue with my own economic peacemaking. I remain a
> patriot and I have no intention to move to Berlin, I will continue to
> follow developments closely, hope that I'm wrong.
>
> Call and we'll talk.
>
> David

Needless to say, I was disappointed that I could not convince David to
join this new initiative. I will continue to try to persuade him and see in
what way he can use his relationship with Netanyahu to pull Israel off the
cliff—hoping it won't be too late. So now what?, I ask myself. Who else can
get to Netanyahu and not only get in the door but also have Netanyahu
listen and consider positively this initiative. The one name I came up
with was Lucy Aharish. Aharish was born in 1981 in the southern Israeli
town of Dimona, to Maaruf and Salwa Aharish, Muslim parents originally
from Nazareth in the north. Growing up, she was the only Arab student
at her school. On Purim, she dressed up as Queen Esther, and on Israeli
Independence Day she wore blue and white. When she was six years old,
she was slightly injured by a Molotov cocktail thrown at her family's car
by Palestinians while driving in the Gaza Strip. More recently Lucy was
chosen to light one of the torches at the official Israel Independence Day
ceremony on Mount Herzl. This created a media storm, mainly in the social
media, with thousands of responses from both Israelis and Palestinians.
Lucy stood firm in her positive decision to honor her country—Israel—as
a proud Palestinian citizen of Israel. I met Lucy in Tel Aviv on March 25,
2015. I spoke to her in confidence about my idea of having her approach the
prime minister. She was definitely interested and said she would take up
the challenge. She said she needed the proper pretext to ask for the meeting. She would try to interview him. I was excited about the possibility, but
Netanyahu's office never gave her a chance, and she never got a meeting. I
was quite disappointed that this channel did not pan out at all.

I met with Dr. Mahmoud Habbash several times in the aftermath of the
elections. I could only describe his mood as angry and frustrated. He was

also reflecting the mood of Abu Mazen, whom he described to me on several occasions as "fed up." After Israeli elections, the Palestinians' choice was to move forward with their internationalization steps both in the ICC and in the UN Security Council. I heard this directly from Habbash; Jabril Rajoub, the former head of Preventive Security in the West Bank and currently the Palestinian commissioner for sports—football (soccer) and the representative of Palestine to the Olympic Committee; Dr. Riad Malki, the Foreign Minister of Palestine; and Majed Faraj, the Head of the Palestinian Intelligence Force. All of these people are senior Palestinian officials I would describe as friends of mine, and all of them are very close to President Abbas. Despite their anger and despondence, I heard from them a continued commitment to peace with Israel based on the two-state solution and a commitment to ensure that no violence would take place in areas under control of the Palestinian security forces.

On July 8, 2015, I met MK Tzahi Hangebi in the Knesset members' dining room. I proposed to him that we meet shortly after the elections. He responded immediately that he wanted to wait until after the government was formed. He was involved in the negotiations for the government, and he was hoping that he would be appointed to a senior ministerial portfolio. He was appointed to the government finally in August 2016, after serving as head of the powerful Foreign and Security Affairs Committee of the Knesset and the chairman of the coalition (the "whip" of the coalition in the Knesset). Hanegbi has become more moderate over time yet continued to be very loyal to Netanyahu. Netanyahu needs strong moderate voices in the Likud today, especially because of the significant presence of much more extreme right-wing voices in positions of power in his government and within his own party.

With this in mind, I thought, because I can't get to Netanyahu and he won't listen to me, perhaps he will listen to Hanegbi. My message was quite simple: with the proper approach and attitude I believed it would be possible to hear from Abu Mazen positive responses to all of Netanyahu's concerns—primarily, the issue of the definition of Israel as the nation-state of the Jewish people and issues concerning security. If Netanyahu was willing to demonstrate that he was serious about attempting a new round of concentrated negotiations aimed at success, and not just talking for talking's sake, then he would find on the Palestinian side reasonableness and a willingness to move forward.

I waited several weeks to get a response from Hanegbi. I met him in the Knesset in passing and asked about progress, and he responded, "nothing yet." I spoke with his advisor who also attended our meeting. Hanegbi was abroad and the advisor told me that when he came back he would give me an answer.

On August 6, 2015, I went to see Habbash in his office in Ramallah in order to hear developments on the Palestinian side. I told him that I would soon be meeting with Yitzhak Herzog, the head of the opposition, and I would propose to him another meeting with Abu Mazen to see if they could still make use of the agreement that Habbash had negotiated with Ephraim Sneh on behalf of Abu Mazen and Herzog. Habbash assured me Abu Mazen wanted to meet Herzog and that they had a positive attitude toward making use of the documents that he and Sneh had drafted. I informed him of my talks with Hangebi as a way to get to Netanyahu. Habbash then surprised me and proposed that he and Hanegbi open a secret back channel to explore gaps and possible agreements. He said it was not negotiations but more of an exploratory track. I asked if Abu Mazen would support it, and he assured me that he would, but he also said it must be kept in total secret and no one from either side, except the two leaders, should know about it. I told him I would propose the idea to Hangebi. Later that evening, after returning to Jerusalem, I sent the following text message to Hangebi:

> Shalom Tzahi, I just met with Dr. Mahmoud al-Habbash, the President of the High Sharia Court in Palestine and one of the closest people to Abu Mazen. We have been friends for quite some time and have a relationship of trust between us. I told him that I had met with you. He immediately proposed that we arrange for a secret back channel of exploratory talks between him and you to check gaps and areas of agreement between the two sides. He emphasized that he was not proposing a channel for negotiations. He also stressed the importance of the talks being totally secretive with the exception of the two leaders.

On August 15, 2015, Tzahi answered me: "The sole address is Silvan Shalom. He has already met Saeb Arikat [the chief Palestinian negotiator] and I think that that's the place for these talks."

I responded, "Between us, Abu Mazen has about as much trust in Arikat that Netanyahu has in Silvan Shalom. Habbash is one of the closest people to Abu Mazen. He proposed exploratory talks and not negotiations. He is not doing this without the agreement of Abu Mazen."

Hanegbi responded, "I went to the person I need to talk to [Netanyahu] and this was the answer I was given."

I wrote back, "So I then ask: who is not the partner?"

Back to the drawing board, as they say, and back to Herzog. On July 21, 2015, I met once again with Herzog. It took a while to coordinate the meeting, and I wanted to allow some time after the elections to see how Herzog filled the role of head of the opposition. I also wanted to see if anything could develop with the Netanyahu government. I met with Ephraim Sneh on July 6 to discuss with him whether or not he thought Herzog would now embrace the plan of presenting to the public that he had reached agreements with Abbas on all of the permanent status issues. Sneh had met several times with Herzog following the elections to discuss the same issue. He was not sure that Herzog would be courageous enough to do something so bold. It pretty much goes against his public image and record. Ephraim was in full support of the idea that I meet with Herzog and try to persuade him to meet with Abu Mazen and to pick up the agreement and go forward. If I was right in my assertion that the majority of Israelis and Palestinians support peace but do not believe it is possible to achieve because they do not think there is a partner on the other side, then it is essential to demonstrate partnership. Herzog and Abu Mazen have the ability and the historic responsibility to do just that. Before entering Herzog's office in the Knesset, I called Habbash just to make sure that when I propose that Herzog meet Abbas, Abbas is willing to meet Herzog, and we can move forward. Habbash assured me Abbas was anxious to see Herzog and that he supported the idea of seeing what could be done with the joint documents negotiated by Habbash and Sneh on behalf of Herzog and Abbas.

Herzog was surprisingly in favor. He said, "Yes, I want to do something bold, and I want to meet Abbas." He questioned whether I thought Abbas was prepared to really make an agreement. He was concerned about what could be done regarding Gaza and the problem of extremists on the Palestinian side, in the West Bank, and in Gaza. I told him I thought there were solutions for all of the issues and the most important thing was to confront the challenges together—openly and honestly with Abbas. I told him what Abbas had told me regarding Gaza—if there was a fair agreement for ending the occupation and creating a Palestinian state that would include the West Bank and Gaza, but that would only be implemented in Gaza when the regime controlling Gaza accepted the terms of the agreement, then the people of Gaza would rise up in support of the agreement and against Hamas. I also spoke about the regional approach that was being supported by so many in Israel, and that the key to the regional approach was Israeli acceptance of the Arab Peace Initiative as the basis for Israeli-Palestinian negotiations. With that key, it would be possible to deposit the problems of Gaza on the table of the moderate Arab states within the Arab League.

On Wednesday, August 18, 2015, Herzog went to Ramallah to meet Abu Mazen. Their meeting got a positive review in the newspapers, but nothing operative came from it. The meeting took place only between Abbas and Herzog—all of the advisors left the room. I wanted to be there, but Herzog insisted that I not pressure him. "Let me do it my own way!" he said. As far as I could tell, that buried the initiative. Herzog would not use the documents, and Abu Mazen would not disclose them without Herzog's agreement. Later I learned that Herzog spoke to Abbas about the possibility of him joining Netanyahu's coalition. I was shocked when I learned that, but I shouldn't have been. Instead of fostering a peace option aimed at replacing Netanyahu, Herzog actually went to tell Abbas that he would like to join Netanyahu.

Because so much had been done and achieved in reaching agreement between Sneh and Habbash representing Herzog and Abbas, it was a pity to allow it to disappear with no effect. I thought the best way to proceed was to begin to apply pressure within the Labour party on their leader. I began to inform a number of Labour MK's about the process and the documents. On Wednesday, December 16, 2015, I had a meeting scheduled to talk to MK Merav Michaeli, the chairwoman of the party faction in the Knesset. The evening before, I received a phone call from a journalist I did not know, Zeev Kam, who worked for NRG. I thought that NRG had ceased to exist. It used to be the web page for the daily *Maariv* newspaper. Later I found out that NRG had been purchased by Makor Rishon—the right-wing newspaper belonging to the settlements movement.

In my meeting with Merav Michaeli, I gave her the background and then informed her about the journalist. With her small "p" political instincts she picked up the phone to a political strategist who immediately advised her to bury the story with denials. I knew immediately that is what Herzog would do. When I first proposed the initiative, I told him he had the option of deniability. I could already see the death of the initiative—another lost opportunity.

I suggested to Merav and later to Sneh and Herzog that they grab the exposure of the story as an opportunity to finally expose that there is a real chance to reach an agreement with the Palestinians. Abbas is prepared and Netanyahu is the real obstacle. But since the renewal of Palestinian violence three months before, Herzog had been attacking the government from the right and claiming that Netanyahu did not know how to defend the country. Herzog's calls for a renewed peace process were hardly heard—lip service that no one took seriously.

The story came out on the front page of Makor Rishon's NGR on Friday December 18, 2015: "On the Eve of Elections Herzog Reached a Secret Political Agreement with Abu Mazen":

> People in the know in the Labour Party exposed to Makor Rishon
> that prior to the elections representatives of Herzog conducted secret
> political talks with the PA chairman which resulted with an agreement
> of principles from which the chairman of the opposition pulled back
> at the last moment. Imagine to yourselves two weeks before the last

elections for the Knesset the chairman of the Palestinian Authority and the chairman of the Labour Party holding a press conference together stating that they are happy to announce that they have just completed an agreement of principles for peace and that if Herzog wins the elections and will become the Prime Minister they intend to turn their understandings into a detailed signed peace agreement. How would the outcome of the elections look in Israel? Would the Zionist Camp have taken with it all of the left in Israel and perhaps a large part of the political center? Or perhaps that would have pushed right-wing voters and right-center voters to push Netanyahu's party to become even more than the thirty seats it got? Perhaps it would have been a combination of both—two very large parties—Labour and Likud? Impossible to know.

This dramatic political development shortly before the elections came from the well-known peace activist Gershon Baskin who was involved in arranging the Schalit deal with Hamas. Baskin turned to Herzog and to people close to Abbas and proposed that trusted representatives of each would sit together on a regular basis and would discuss all of the core conflict issues under negotiations between Israel and the Palestinians. The end result of these contacts, as Baskin proposed according to the senior people in the Labour Party, would be presented to the Israeli public before the elections with an obligation that if Herzog wins the elections he would seek to sign a full comprehensive peace agreement based on the understandings reached with Abbas. The senior officials added that it took Baskin about one and a half months to convince Herzog to go for the initiative and that afterwards during months Herzog's and Abbas's representatives conducted negotiations. . . .

People who were part of the secret talks claim that part of the early agreement was that the process and its results should be kept in total secrecy and that no one should disclose the process or its contents. The conclusion was to allow for Herzog to withdraw from the process at the last moment and that both sides could claim full deniability. Herzog did withdraw from it at the last moment and the whole story remained secret for a year. The agreement reached between the two leaders was put away in a drawer. Gershon Baskin responded that he is not prepared to discuss it and does not wish to respond to any details that were published.

From Herzog's office the response was, "We see high importance in separating from the Palestinians. As expected from all leaders who are prepared to fight for this goal, Herzog met Abu Mazen several times beginning when he was head of the opposition. Herzog does not need mediators or shadow people for a dialogue with Abu Mazen. And said that when he is elected as Prime Minister he will go to Ramallah to speak before the Palestinian Parliament and present his vision and hope that will change the reality in the Middle East. Gershon Baskin did come to MK Herzog a long time before the elections, as many come to him with many political proposals and presented a plan for a solution to the conflict which was rejected by Herzog. With that, Herzog clarified that he is listening to every new and original idea that can bring about separation from the Palestinians, as he is trying to do with other individuals who propose solutions. During the elections, Herzog did not meet Baskin or anyone on his behalf, he did not reach a document which could be comprehended from this article.

Sources in Abu Mazen's office denied the reports of secret meetings between Abu Mazen's representatives and Herzog's, "There were several meetings between Abu Mazen and Herzog. Those meetings were publicized in the media. In those meetings, the sides spoke about future negotiations and on the issues that were raised by officials on both sides in order to end the Israeli-Palestinian conflict.

In June 2016, the Herzog-Abbas understandings once again were disclosed to the public. This time Ephraim Sneh was interviewed and acknowledged that he conducted those talks on behalf of Herzog. Sneh described the agreements as having an emphasis on Israel's security needs and taking the Olmert-Abbas negotiations forward by closing the gaps that existed between them. I was interviewed by the media and appeared on Israeli television where I expressed my deep disappointment in the failed leadership of the head of the opposition, Herzog. I emphasized that it was still possible to reach an agreement with the Palestinians on all of the core issues and to strengthen Israel's security through that agreement.

That initiative died, but more are being tried.

What Does Peace Look Like?

24 I began my search for peace between Israelis and Palestinians way back in 1976 with my meeting with the PLO representative to the United Nations. His response, "over my dead body," to the request that the PLO recognize Israel and its right to exist and agree to accept the two-states-for-two-peoples solution postponed my efforts for twelve years until the first intifada's agenda led to an acceptance of the two-state formula. At the time when I launched a joint Israeli-Palestinian public policy think and do tank (IPCRI) in 1988, I claimed it would be almost impossible for the Palestinians to accept the moral right of Israel to exist because in doing so they would be engaging in a form of self-denial regarding their own narrative. I posed the question then: Does mutual recognition have to be based on a moral equation of rights, or is a functional recognition sufficient to move forward to make peace? The question becomes more complicated, as pointed out by Prof. Shlomo Avinary, when it is taken into consideration that the Palestinians have never recognized the Jews as a people who would, as a nation, enjoy the inalienable right to self-determination.[1] The Palestinians, according to Prof. Avinary (and probably a majority of Israelis), still relate to the Jews as members of a religious faith and to their national movement, Zionism, as an illegitimate colonialist movement destined to be annihilated.

It is true that while most Israelis and Jews around the world recognize the Palestinians as a people and their inalienable right to self-determination, the Palestinians do not relate in the same way to the Jews. The basic question is does this lack of reciprocity and mutuality have to mean that peace is not possible? Do we have to come to terms with all of the narrative questions that bring us back to 1948 and the birth of the State of Israel and the Palestinian refugee problem in order to reach real peace between these two peoples? There are those who claim that without resolving the 1948 narrative issues there can be no peace (and many of them believe that these issues are not resolvable—meaning that peace will never exist).

I believe that it is possible to reach peace based on political agreements that do not resolve all of the narrative issues yet provide a strong enough basis on which it is possible to change the reality on the ground between these two peoples to the extent that it would become possible to begin to confront the narrative issues, not as a condition for reaching peace, but as a product of peaceful normalcy. While the conflict is still bloody and painful, with a lot more pain and blood on the weaker side (the Palestinians), it is much more difficult for them to confront the moral context of national rights and legitimacy. It has to be enough, at this time, for the Palestinians to come to terms with Israel's existence (which they have done) and their willingness to make peace without achieving the ultimate goal of implementing the right of return for the refugees who will not be able to return to their original homes. It takes a great deal of political and national maturity to be able to confront one's own national myths and to completely transform the national ethos from one based on the sense of historical injustice to one based on writing a new national identity. The Palestinians are not yet there because they are still engaged in the daily struggle for survival and recognition of their own national rights.

Peace between Israel and Palestine at this time has to be based on the power of normalcy and daily life focused on the mission of nation building and creating opportunities for the young generation of Palestinians to achieve their potential as equal members of the community of nations. The constant focus by Israel and Jews on the moral equation of recognizing Israel's legitimacy as an expression of the Jewish people's inalienable right to self-determination will not speed the process of Palestinian acceptance. Quite the opposite, I would claim.

The focus of making peace real must be placed on changing the basic relationships between Israelis and Palestinians—from occupied and occupiers to partners in building a new reality on the ground. This is not a simple task, and, although it is focused on developing real and mutual interests in advancing peace, the power of life itself and desire of normal people to improve their own existence is quite significant. The challenge before us is for both Israelis and Palestinians to step out of their mode of victimhood and for the Israelis to step away from their position of domination and control.

Partnership comes from a decision and from that decision must come a dedicated and difficult course of building relations based on common cause and purpose, which would normalize relations after generations of conflict and death. This does not mean normalizing the occupation but continuing to oppose occupation and domination and completely rejecting the use of violence as a tool to prompt political changes.

Oslo did not enable the process of normalizing relations to advance because we never reached the permanent status agreement that would have ended the occupation. Oslo was a process, not peace. Israelis and Palestinians agreed on how they intended to make peace; they never agreed on the terms of peace. The Palestinian popular movement against normalization is more dominant today than ever because of the understanding of the power of normalization and their demand that normalization only take place after the occupation ends. The change in the Israeli-Palestinian relationship that becomes possible after resolving the political issues that would be expressed in a peace agreement is the force that will have the greatest impact on the lives of Israelis and Palestinians throughout the land. Change will take time, but the more focused the emerging peace is on personal relationships and building partnerships across the borders, the more powerful the process of normalization will become. Peoples' lives must improve—peace must pay and must affect them so significantly that the option of moving backward toward violence would be abandoned forever.

For most Israelis and Palestinians, peace is actually unimaginable. They simply have no idea how to conceptualize it. Even the peace treaties that exist between Israel and Egypt, and Israel and Jordan do not inspire an enlightening vision. It seems so far away, so intangible, so unrealistic. Israelis live in a psychological island that is disconnected from the rest of the neighborhood; they live with a constant sense of having to prove their legitimacy and value. Palestinians, while more connected to the neighborhood, have no sense of welcome anywhere they go. Only three countries in the world offer Palestinians visa-free entrance (Cuba, Venezuela, and Malaysia) and none of them are Arab countries. Those Palestinians who hold Jordanian passports know they are holding a document that has a lower-class status than what are called "Jordanian Jordanians." Neither Israelis nor Palestinians live with a sense of peace or security. Neither side has reached the "promised land"—the safe shores where they can focus their lives' energies on maximizing their potential and self-worth and concentrate on creating quality of life for themselves and for future generations. There is always, either in the back of their minds or right in front of them, a sense of threat and existential questions of survival. Living with this sense of constant peril, both peoples still, amazingly, live life to the fullest. Despite the negative views of each other's societies, both Israel and Palestine are vibrant societies that embrace life and cherish family. Both societies are mosaics of very strong subcultures, interwoven with a high-level sense of social cohesion. Despite what seems often to be deep conflicts within each society, overall both societies have relatively high degrees of social and political solidarity.

Both societies live in fear of the other—despite the numerous similarities between them. The conflict's impact on both is deep, with very apparent traumatic psychological wounds. With the rise of violence every few years, most Israelis and Palestinians have retreated into their own spaces, limited their contact with the other side. The road of fear leads very rapidly to the path of racism and hatred. When violence is acute, the distance between fear and hatred is very short. The violence of the past decade and a half—since the second intifada, which exploded in the end of 2000—created psychological walls of fear and physical barriers that have led to a reality in which young Israelis and young Palestinians have almost no contact with one another at all.

Crossing borders without fear is part of my everyday reality. I am not totally without fear when I drive through some Palestinian towns, villages, and refugee camps, but, for the most part, I feel comfortable on the Palestinian side of the conflict lines. When I travel across conflict lines, I do it in peace and I feel at peace as I am welcomed wherever I go. This is not some naïve statement devoid of grounded reality. I have been doing this for more than thirty years and have had tens of thousands of encounters with people that many Israelis would call "the enemy." I refer to them as my neighbors, partners, and friends.

Real peace will exist when Israelis and Palestinians are free to cross those borders in a normal way, without fear. Genuine peace cannot be built on the concepts of separation, walls, and fences that our leaders have become accustomed to reminding us of every day. "Us here and them there." Those five words encapsulate the "vision" of peace offered to the Israeli people by their leaders. That is not peace and not a vision worth fighting for. It is separation, and that is what they are seeking to create. Perhaps they don't really want to imagine peace, to plan for it, and to make it happen. Divorce is much easier to imagine. The concept of peace through separation has been largely advanced by political strategists who have told their clients—the politicians—that the Israeli public does not want to live together with the Arabs. It is better to talk about separation, with the Arabs living on the other side of walls so that we never have to see them again. Along with this, Israeli politicians speak about the demographic threat. Imagine what the Palestinian citizens of Israel think and feel when referred to as a demographic threat! It sounds like a kind of disease—and that is exactly what it is. The disease is called racism. The Palestinians living in the territories occupied by Israel in 1967 also detest the Israeli claim of demographic threats; it does not engender images of peace. The Palestinians also have no great love for the idea of living together with the Jews. In the imaginary world that Jews and Palestinians create for themselves when they go to sleep, they see the land between the River and the Sea without the other people living on it.

Former Israeli President Yitzhak Navon used to say that Jews and Arabs were destined to live together in this land. Perhaps that is the most we can hope for—accepting our destiny. I have always tried to imagine something more than that—a sense that both sides have a lot to gain by having the other present on this land. I do believe that we will find the way, that we have to find the way. The continuation of this conflict is insane and totally futile, and there are ways to reach political agreements. Reconciliation and true peace will come later—the first step must be political agreements.

The Israeli occupation and control over the Palestinian people must come to an end. There is a need for clear political separation, including the demarcation of borders between the two states. Meeting this need will enable both sides to each have a territorial expression of their identity. They need to be masters of their own destinies on a piece of land they can call their own. Each side must know their borders will be recognized by each other and by the world. But even then there will be national minorities that will necessitate the development of expressions of shared societies both within Israel and within Palestine. On this small piece of land between the River and the Sea, there is no possible way to have the kind of divorce that is intended to prevent all future contact and engagement or that brings about total separation and ethnic cleansing. Physical separation between the two states may be necessary for a short time for stabilization and creation of mechanisms for security and border management, but eventually, and sooner rather than later, physical boundaries are going to have to be "soft" and permeable (in agreed upon legal ways) and that will allow people from both states to cross the borders with ease and with a welcome mat on the ground for each.

Perhaps if our geography was more like the United States, and "us here" meant New York and "them there" meant California, it could be possible, but not on the tiny piece of land between the Mediterranean Sea and the Jordan River. The space is too small to tolerate walls and barbed wire fences and to call that peace. Jerusalem is a shared city where Israelis and Palestinians will always live. Tulkarem and Netanya nearly touch each other. Our water comes from shared sources. The air we breathe is the same. We cannot separate by building walls that hide the other side and make believe that we are alone on this land. Not only is it not feasible in the long run, it does not inspire a vision of peace and will not create a reality of peace. Yes, in the short term, walls and fences can support the development of a security regime that will limit the damaging and deadly impact of terrorism against peace. But, ultimately, security cannot be secured by means of blocking peoples' movement; it can only be achieved in the long run by changing the consciousness of people and their desire to live in peace. That is a long-term process that must be a central dimension of any peace treaty, and its implementation must focus on changing peoples' lives. Peace treaties must become real and tangible for real people, for all those who live within the zone of peace, and not be only an agreement between governments and leaders.

In Israel and Palestine, it is not simply a reality that we share the same narrow land; the realization must come that two states, two peoples, living side by side, provide numerous blessings that enrich our lives and widen our horizons. This recognition is the place, the space, the time when a consciousness of peace begins. The simplest example is that the time will come when we will want to learn each other's language. That is an enormous blessing. Understanding languages opens numerous doors to enrichment and appreciation of the human experience. Hebrew and Arabic are so close to each other. Knowing one of the languages already provides the keys to unlocking the beauty of the other language. As someone who has studied both languages, it is an eye-opening experience, an uplifting awareness of the depth of the closeness between the two languages. Seeing the links between words, expressions, metaphors, and proverbs in Hebrew and Arabic is exciting and enriches my own understanding of my own language. If life was normal between Israeli Jews and Arabs, they would soon realize how much of each other's language they already know. But in the absence of peace, the other language is the language of the enemy, and the only reason to study that language is "to know the enemy," not the neighbor, friend, and partner. The study of Arabic in Israel is almost completely directed to serve the military and security needs of the Israeli intelligence community. The functionality of the Arabic language study in Israeli schools and in the Israeli Army demonstrates a complete lack of appreciation for the culture and civilization of the Arabic-speaking peoples. This phenomenon has been researched and documented in depth just this past year in Israel.[2]

We are blessed, even if we don't realize it, by having two peoples, two cultures, two societies living in the same land. A peace treaty will enable us to ensure that each side has their so desperately needed territorial expression of their identity. Each side has proven its readiness to fight and die and kill for a piece of land they can call their own. The peace treaty will enable us to end the struggle over who controls the land. It will also enable us to look at the other side with a new perspective, which should allow us to begin to see the positive side of each civilization. Rather than a "clash of civilizations," we will actually have the opportunity to begin to celebrate the diversity that exists within our midst. Conflict teaches us to fear diversity, even to hate what is different from ourselves. This has had a huge impact on Jews who originate from Arab and Muslim countries. Many have told stories of being ashamed of their parent's Arabic accent. Many would tell their parents to lower the volume of the radio when they listened to Arabic music. Many decided not to learn the Arabic language, a gift their parents could have given to them but they rejected. Some of that cultural rejection has transformed over the years as Mizrahi Jews, those whose parents or grandparents came from Arab or Muslim countries, have found a positive modern Israeli expression of their Eastern cultural roots, but it seems that this is largely on the margins—perhaps with the exception of Moroccan Israelis who have been more successful in preserving their Moroccan identity.

I remember one Passover several years ago when I was in Jerusalem's Old City. The Jewish holiday that year was also the same time as Easter and the Muslim Eid al-Adha. The Old City was the most crowded I have ever seen it. At one point the crowd was too much for me, and I stepped into a shop. I stood at the entrance to the shop and watched three civilizations all busy in their own worlds participating in the celebrations of the separate holidays. There were Jews running off to the Kotel—the Western Wall—to pray. There were parades of Christians carrying the cross in the path of Jesus. There were Muslims making their rounds to visit family members and to pray at al-Aqsa Mosque. To me it looked as if there were glass walls that separated the celebrating peoples as they went on to do their own thing. People were moving by each other, fast paced, charging forward in their own celebrations, in their own world. The others around them were almost invisible. It was quite an amazing scene. I stood in the entrance of the shop for almost thirty minutes, awestruck.

For a moment, I thought of how wonderful it would be if there were people walking across the lines, taking part not only in their own festivities but also celebrating with their neighbors in their rituals and feasts. That is how I imagine peace.

But peace also means more. Most Israelis and most Palestinians have connections to all parts of the land between the River and the Sea. There will be a political border between the two states, designating who is sovereign where. There will be separate legal jurisdictions. There will be minorities of each side living on the majority side of the other. There will continue to be deep economic ties, trade, sharing of natural resources, integration of infrastructure, and cooperation between the governments. There must also be free movement (or as close to it as possible) of people and goods across those borders. For one, all holy sites must be open and accessible to all people, regardless of what passport they hold. Ideally, holy sites would not have a national flag above them. They would remain in the domain of the divine. Each state would administer, protect, and guarantee free access to all of the holy sites, but they would not be "owned" by any country. As President Clinton once proposed, they would be under God's Sovereignty.

Palestinians and Israelis should be able to cross borders and to visit on the other side without fear and without limitations. Now under Israeli control, almost all Palestinians are suspect, and therefore their movements are controlled and their access into Israel is limited. In a reality of peace, almost all Palestinians would be allowed free movement and access except for the small number who have been excluded with good reason. As well, almost all Israelis would have free access and movement in and throughout Palestine; only a few who have violated the trust would be prohibited.

Tens of millions of people move across borders around the world every day with a relatively high degree of security. This movement is fast, efficient, and noninvasive. People are checked, their possessions are scanned, they are not humiliated, and security is still provided. That is what we should seek to achieve as well. Eventually we should reach a situation whereby people can apply for a permit or a visa (for as long as it will be required) online. They should be able to fill out a form and receive an answer back by text message or email. They should be able to print a document at home or in the office that will automatically appear on computer screens at border crossings. They should also be able to have a smartphone application to apply and to receive their permit/visa. They will be scanned along with their permit at border crossings and be able to move without unnecessary questioning or invasive checks.

This can be easy and efficient. People will still need to show legal identification documents at border crossings. Enabling people to move across borders and be welcomed on the other side would be a big step toward normalizing life between the two former enemies and opening possibilities for real cooperation.

Palestinians would be able to visit Israel, even places where they originated from before 1948, without having residency rights. They will be able to come to the beaches on the coast and enjoy the shopping and fine restaurants in Israel's towns and cities. Israelis will be able to visit all over Palestine, enjoying the fine restaurants and pubs of Ramallah, or the shopping in the Kasbah of Nablus, purchasing fresh "baladi" fruits and vegetables to bring home to their tables. Israelis will be able to experience the cultural events at Ramallah's Cultural Palace and in the new Palestinian Rawabi's amazing amphitheater, and Palestinians will be able to partake in the cultural events in all parts of Israel. Art galleries on both sides will be able to host exhibitions of artists from either side. Everyone will also be welcomed to visit historic heritage sites and holy places in Judea and Samaria even though those site might be under Palestinian sovereignty within the Palestinian state. There should be the possibility for a long-term and perhaps permanent place for Jews to be able to study and pray at Jewish holy places in the State of Palestine in places like Hebron and Nablus. Holy places would become sites of worship and mutual respect, not points of violent contention as they are today.

The opportunities for cultural exchange and cultural coproductions are endless. Various attempts at musical fusion between young people across borders are already taking place, and the results are astounding. Culture thrives most when it interacts with other cultures. The same can be said for food. The Israeli and Palestinian culinary worlds are already expanding at an amazing pace. The success of *Jerusalem: A Cook Book* by two chefs, one Israeli and one Palestinian—Yotam Ottolenghi and Sami Tamimi—is a living testament to the cross-pollination that is so natural between two schools of culinary culture. The results are delicious, and such cooperation inspires the imagination to consider other possible spheres of positive collaboration.

Peace is normalization. However, even today the concept of normalization is a political curse word and a condemned concept in Arab political culture. Israel desires normal relations with its Arab neighbors. The Arab neighbors refuse to grant Israel those normal relations until occupation of the Palestinian state ends and Palestinians can live in their own state with dignity. The Arab Peace Initiative of March 2002 promised Israel normal relations with all of the Arab world if it ended its occupation of lands captured in June 1967. The words in the Arab Peace Initiative sound dry and lack real incentives for Israelis when they view the reality in the Arab world today. The old dream of breakfast in Beirut and dinner in Damascus lacks appeal today, for obvious reasons. The core of normalization will be between Israelis and Palestinians. That normalization will enable Israelis to enjoy what the Arab world / Persian Gulf also has to offer. There is no real conflict between Israel and most of the countries of the Arab world. The center stage of the negative perceptions of Israel in the Arab world is the Palestinian issue. Every day, Arabs throughout the Arab world view the mistreatment of Palestinians by Israeli soldiers and settlers on their televisions screens, broadcast in real time by the Arab twenty-four-hour satellite stations. The pictures are not pretty, and the perception of Israel and Israelis is strongly tainted by what they see. If the Arab street—this is a common expression used to mean the peoples of the Arab world—hates Israel, it is because of what they see almost daily on those screens. This is not because the Arab world is so fond of the Palestinians. They are not, but they believe that it is their duty to be loyal to the Palestinian cause as long as Palestinians are under Israel's occupation. Most of the Arab world has come to terms with the existence of Israel, and largely they do not seek Israel's destruction. If the occupation were to end, those Arab states and the Arab street would find their way to normalize the relations with Israel, and Israelis would be welcome on the streets of the Arab world.

The key to normalization is with the Palestinians and the Israelis. A peace treaty is a prerequisite, but the real work of peacemaking will begin the day after the treaty is signed. Getting to the agreement is the easier part. Peacemaking will require not only the mechanisms designed for the many tasks to be undertaken within the agreement, it will also take a large amount of goodwill. Perhaps even more than the goodwill, it will take a large number of trained professionals who will serve as bridge-builders, facilitators, innovators, and reconcilers.

Peace and reconciliation are not the same. It will take even greater efforts to build reconciliation. South Africa invented its own "truth and reconciliation commissions" that were firmly based in the South African culture. Israel and Palestine will need to invent their own means of enabling people to reach out. People on both sides will need to tell their stories, to be heard, to have their pain and suffering acknowledged, to hear words of sorrow and maybe apologies. Israelis and Palestinians will have to come to terms with the possibility of visiting each other's national museums, each of which will tell their story—their side of the conflict narrative.

So what does the peace treaty look like?

The Palestinian state will be formally established and recognized on twenty-two percent of the land between the River and the Sea. This is the historic compromise that makes peace based on two states for two peoples possible. The exact delineation of borders is a complex matter because it will have to entail encompassing as many Israeli settlers as possible into the Israeli side of the border, on the minimum amount of land needed to be annexed to Israel. The so-called "settlement blocs," where the bulk of Israeli settlers reside, will be annexed to Israel, but the key to determining the size of the annexation will be the amount of available uninhabited land on the Israeli side of the border that can be transferred to Palestine in exchange for land annexed by Israel in the West Bank, on a one-to-one basis. There are those in Israel who would like to include Arab communities adjacent to the Green Line that are inhabited by Palestinian citizens of Israel, so that their towns and villages would become part of the Palestinian state. There is a certain sound logic to that idea—they are Palestinians, why shouldn't they live in the Palestinian nation-state? There would be no requirement for them to move from their homes. No one would be relocated. The border would move and the community that is today in Israel would tomorrow be in Palestine. The residents are Palestinians who have Israeli citizenship. They have been fully behind the struggle for Palestinian freedom and liberation. Why shouldn't they be glad to embrace the possibility of living in their own nation-state?

I believe it makes a lot of sense. I moved thousands of miles away from my home where I was born in New York in order to live in the nation-state of the Jewish people. These people wouldn't even have to move. The problem is that at this time they do not want to live in the Palestinian state; they prefer to remain in Israel. This is a great irony, almost a joke of history, but from a logical, rational viewpoint it is easy to understand. For one, from a point of view of heritage and history, both sides of the border are a part of historic Palestine. They don't have to move to Palestine; they are on Palestinian land that has been part of their heritage and identity for generations. Moreover, the economics of the issue make sense. Where would you choose to reside: in a place where the per capita income is more than $35,000, or where it is under $2,000? Even if you are on the lowest rung of the socioeconomic ladder, it makes sense to stay in the wealthier economy. Additionally, in Israel they have full health care and social security (which they pay for) in a very advanced and efficient system. The State of Palestine will not be able to provide anything like the Israeli health care and social security systems for many years to come. Finally, with all of its weaknesses and challenges, Israeli democracy seems a better political system to live in than the unknown system of governance that will develop in Palestine. So communities like Um el Fahem (a Palestinian city in Israel with some fifty thousand residents) will not be part of the equation of land swaps. If the government of Israel would propose to make a swap of land including an Israeli-Palestinian city like Um el Fahem, it would probably go to the Israeli Supreme Court, which would most likely contest the legality of removing a city of citizens from their natural right of citizenship. The residents of Um el Fahem would also most likely contest the decision, and democratic countries do not suddenly deny citizenship on a wholesale basis to entire communities that have been part of the state since its birth.

While the Israeli settlements in the West Bank have spread all over, trying to capture every hilltop (in the words of Ariel Sharon), in reality the entire "footprint" of all of the settlements is less than five percent of all of the land of the West Bank. This is not shown in the statutory maps (unilaterally determined by Israel) of the settlements, but rather the built-up areas of the settlements themselves. Israel continues to control sixty-two percent of the West Bank, which is area "c," designated by the Oslo agreements to be the areas under full Israeli control. Twenty-three years after Oslo, the Palestinians control less than twenty percent of the area designated as area "a" (the Palestinian cities that are supposed to be under full Palestinian control, according to the agreements, but Israel still enters those areas at its own discretion), and another almost twenty percent of the area that is designated as area "b" (the villages), which is under Palestinian civil control but Israeli military-security control. In reality, Israel controls all of the West Bank, regardless of the Oslo designations. Since the second intifada, Israel enters all areas of the West Bank when it wants and believes that it needs to for security reasons. Despite the security cooperation and coordination agreements with the Palestinian security forces, when the Israeli security forces enter area "a" to arrest someone, the Palestinian forces clear out of the area, giving the Israelis a free hand. This is part of the security cooperation. I call it the "Cinderella rule," meaning that at midnight the

Palestinian security forces disappear and the Israeli security forces appear in their place.

The forces in Israel against an agreement with the Palestinians are very strong—disproportionately strong in relation to their numbers, as can be witnessed by the success of the settlement movement throughout the years since 1967, with brief exceptions. So waiting until there is an agreement reduces the size of the possible swaps. An annexation of about 4.5 percent of the West Bank's settlement blocks would accommodate about 75 percent of the settlers remaining on the Israeli side of the border. These blocks include the largest settlements of Betar Elite and Modiin Elite—ultra-Orthodox settlements—and Ma'aleh Adumim. It would also include the Jewish neighborhoods built in East Jerusalem after 1967, including Ramat Eshkol, French Hill, Neve Yaacov, Pisgat Zeev, Ramot, Armon Natziv, and Gilo. It should also include Har Homa, but the Palestinians have so far objected to Har Homa's inclusion in the deal because it was launched and built after 1997, after the Oslo process began.

The settlers that remain beyond the Israeli border of sovereignty include some seventy thousand to eighty-five thousand people including Ariel, which is close to twenty kilometers inside the West Bank with about twenty thousand residents. Most of the residents of Ariel are not "ideological" settlers, but what we call "economic" settlers. They went to Ariel to find good quality housing with subsidized prices, mortgages, and tax benefits, and work in industrial zones constructed for their benefit. The university in Ariel also provides employment and a place for university students from the settlements to continue their education close to home. Ariel could become a city with a Jewish majority inside the State of Palestine. Difficult to imagine, but not impossible.

Many of the settlers east of the future border are the hard-core ideological settlers, including the "hilltop youth," who have demonstrated their propensity for violence against Palestinians and against Israeli soldiers and police. Some of the people left behind represent those who might be willing to use violence in response to their forced withdrawal. There would be a number of options available to them in the framework of a peace deal. They would be able to move back to the sovereign state of Israel. They would be able to move into parts of Judea and Samaria that will be annexed to Israel by agreement. For those religious settlers who believe that they answered God's call to settle the land of Israel by living in Judea and Samaria, they can continue to answer God's calling by remaining in the annexed areas.

There must also be an option and a real possibility for settlers to remain where they are and to become permanent residents or citizens of the State of Palestine. If they are willing to become citizens of Palestine, to recognize Palestinian sovereignty and Palestinian laws, and not to be armed militias, the State of Palestine should be willing to accept them. I have discussed this issue with Palestinian leaders, including President Abbas, and they agree. I have said to them that, if I were one of the Israeli negotiators, I would demand the right of Jews to live in the State of Palestine as a principle that cannot be compromised. Even for those who call the territory "the West Bank," and not "Judea and Samaria," there must be a recognition of the importance of that area to the Jewish people and to Jewish history. The land of the prophets of the Old Testament is there in the hilltops and valleys of Judea and Samaria, not on the beaches of Tel Aviv. I cannot imagine that the one place in the world where Jews would not be allowed to live, by agreement, is Judea and Samaria in the State of Palestine. Furthermore, as I have told my Palestinian friends, I think that it is very healthy for a democratic state to have a national minority. It challenges democracy and demands accountability—not for the rights of the majority, but rather for the rights of minorities.

There will probably be a significant number of ideological settlers who will refuse any of the above options and choose to fight their removal. This is a dangerous group of people who will very likely be prepared to use the weapons in their possession. If there is a future agreement with the Palestinians, it will only happen with the full support of the prime minister, who will bring the support of the majority of the cabinet, including the minister of defense. The agreement will not get a positive vote in the government without the full support of the entire leadership of Israel's security and military, meaning the backing of the army's chief of staff, the head of the Israel Security Authority, the head of the Mossad, and the chief of police. The agreement will be brought to the Knesset and will receive a majority of support there, and it is likely to be brought before the public as a referendum, where it will also most likely receive a majority of support from the people. If all of this happens, there will be a democratic decision taken by the State of Israel, supported by the people of Israel. If some groups of extremist settlers refuse to accept the democratic decision-making process of the State of Israel and choose to use violence against removal, the State of Israel is a state of law and knows how to use the law against people who chose to break it. The first soldier or policeman shot by an extremist settler in defiance of the democratic process will lead to a rapid demise in whatever popular support they may muster, and the army and the police will have a clear mandate to remove them.

THE SPECIAL CASE OF HEBRON

Hebron is a place where we can, without doubt, expect problems. In 1995, after the massacre committed by the Jewish terrorist Baruch Goldstein, there was a brief moment of opportunity for the Israeli government to remove the Jewish settlers from Hebron. There was a clear majority in the Israeli government in favor of removing the settlers, but Prime Minister Rabin was convinced by the late Prof. Ehud Sprinzak, an expert on Jewish right-wing groups, that in the case of forced evacuation, a group of settlers would be likely to commit suicide—blowing themselves up in a "masada"-type campaign. Sprinzak believed that the public outcry in Israel under those circumstances would bring down the Rabin government and the nascent peace process. Rabin decided not to bring the issue to the cabinet for a vote. Now, more than twenty years later, there are about five hundred fanatic messianic Jews in Hebron who continue to make life in Hebron a living hell for the 120,000 Palestinians in the city. This is a powder keg that could explode at any time.

Hebron is a very special city—no one doubts its religious importance as the city of the Patriarchs and Matriarchs. Hebron is also a special city because of its own bloody history in the conflict. For Jews, it has symbolized the barbarism of terrorism since the 1929 riots there. For Palestinians, the massacre of Baruch Goldstein "matches" the Jewish memories of horror. The Jewish settlers of Hebron have demanded special privileges in reclaiming the property of the Jews of Hebron from before 1929 because of and in the name of the massacre of 1929. Without tarnishing the memory of those who were brutally killed there, I suggest that there is nothing special about Hebron in the Israeli-Palestinian conflict. There are hundreds of places and dates that can be recalled from the one hundred years of conflict by both sides to invoke the memory of the fallen martyrs and the uniqueness and links to those places and dates. The massacre of 1929 does not grant any special privileges or rights to Jews to reclaim property in Hebron any more than it gives the rights to Palestinian refugees from Yaffa or any other of the hundreds of destroyed villages throughout the Land of Israel to reclaim their property rights. If one side of the conflict has the right to reclaim property rights from before 1948, then surely the other side must have the same right. The mutual claims on property rights must be addressed in the peace treaty, where a possible key to resolution and agreement may be found in a willingness to examine the difference between property rights and residence rights. But until that time, neither side has the right to unilaterally claim rights that are also unilaterally denied to the other side.

Hebron is also a special place because of its religious significance. The situation during the period of 1949 to 1967, when Jews were denied the possibility of praying in the Tomb of the Patriarchs, is not acceptable. Any peace must entail religious tolerance, a large degree of civility, and mutual respect for the holy places of all faiths. The religious claims of Jews regarding the holiness of Hebron and the Tomb of the Patriarchs cannot be denied by anyone or by any religious group that makes similar claims to that holy place or to any other. People of religion do not have to accept claims made by other religions as truth, but they must accept that the other religions' truths have equal value to their own.

If the Palestinians wish to remove the settlers from Hebron, it would be wise of them to propose a plan that recognizes the holiness of Hebron to the Jewish people and guarantees the religious rights of the Jewish people there. The issue of residency rights can and should be addressed in the framework of a peace agreement. If, in the post-conflict period, Jews would like to live in Hebron as peaceful citizens within the Palestinian state, there should be a Palestinian willingness to consider that possibility. During this period of continued entrenched conflict, I am afraid it is not possible for the group of the most fanatic and extremist right-wing messianic Jews to continue to reside in Hebron.

The agreement for Hebron should include a clear declaration that recognizes the holiness of Hebron to the Jewish people and the holiness of the same site to Muslims and Christians. There must be arrangements for Jews to pray on a regular basis in the Tomb of the Patriarchs as well as maintaining space for Muslim prayer—all by agreement. Jews should be able to establish a center of learning in one of the Jewish properties and to even have a museum of Jewish heritage there. Security arrangements should be made for convoys that would transport the Jews coming to pray into the city on a regular basis.

Palestinians have an opportunity to play a constructive role in assisting the Israeli government to resolve a very complex problem. It is more than likely that the settlers living in Hebron today would have to be evacuated against their will. A Palestinian initiative aimed at recognizing and guaranteeing Jewish religious rights in Hebron would be very helpful in building public support in Israel for removing the settlers as well as creating an international willingness to assist.

After the Baruch Goldstein massacre, when there was a threat of removing the settlers, the prosettler groups in Israel put out a bumper sticker that said, "Hebron—Now and Forever!" I wasn't surprised when I saw some Palestinian cars with the same sticker. Taking positive and constructive action now to relieve the difficult situation of Hebron could have a lasting and influential effect on renewing the political process. Hebron could explode into violence at any time—it has always been like that, but it also provides an opportunity for Israelis and Palestinians to begin to head toward better understandings and chances for reconciliation.

PREVENTING BREACHES

It is important to note that in any future agreement, implementation will be gradual, with significant time between phases for all who are affected to prepare to deal with the complex situations. One of the key lessons from the failure of the peace process must be that obligations and commitments taken by the parties upon themselves have to be fulfilled by both parties and an implementation assistance mechanism must be developed that includes full monitoring and verification by a trusted third party. The full implementation of obligations is crucial because of the history of breached agreements on both sides. The stakes are too high and the risks too great not to ensure that the agreements are fully executed. The process of implementation must be marked with clear and identifiable steps that must be completed before additional stages of implementation that contain additional risks to the parties are undertaken. A performance-based implementation process must be agreed upon to ensure that breaches do not lead to more failures, which usually end up with more violence. The timetable for implementation must be part of the agreement; however, that timetable will also be linked to full implementation, and the determination of full implementation will be in the hands of the implementation assistance mechanism headed by the third party.

The process must be viewed through the prism of risk mitigation with each party knowing that the best way to reduce the risks involved is by fulfilling their obligations. Furthermore, the implementation assistance mechanism, which will be in the hands of a trusted third party, most likely the Americans or a multilateral group led by the Americans, will include a monitoring and verification aspect that will determine when obligations have been met and when they have not. The implementation assistance mechanism will also include a dispute resolution team that will be empowered to deal with disputes as they arise in real time (and they will) and to propose solutions that will meet the needs and interests of both sides. It is essential that the monitoring and verification mechanism strive for maximum transparency because in the past, when there was a Road Map Monitor, his reports were kept secret from the public, which meant the officials in charge of implementing the Road Map were relieved of their accountability.[3] Accountability to the public is an essential aspect of peacemaking.

SECURITY—A PILLAR OF PEACE

Security will be one of the most important pillars of any future agreement. If there is no security, there will be no peace. One of the main reasons for the failure of Oslo is that the security situation worsened rather than improved. The peace process was based on the idea that disputes would be resolved around the table and not on the battlefield. Those opposed to the process did not "read the fine print" and did not agree to lay down their weapons. There were extremists on both sides who continued to use violence to demonstrate their dissatisfaction with the agreements. The Hamas and Islamic Jihad groups rejected the agreements from the outset and used violence from day one, repeatedly challenging Arafat and the Palestinian Authority. It took years before Arafat had the political resolve and determination to rein in Hamas, but much damage had already been done and large quantities of weapons and expertise in bomb manufacturing had been acquired.

After the violence of September 1996 when Israel opened the Kotel tunnels underneath the Muslim Quarter in the Old City, both Israel and the Palestinians began to ready themselves for the next round, should the peace process break down. In mid-September 1997, during the time of Prime Minister Netanyahu, Yasser Arafat gave an extended interview to Israeli Channel 2 News. That interview, which lasted about twenty minutes, was conducted in its entirety showing Arafat in "close-up." It was striking how ill he appeared. The camera focused on his quivering lower lip and his shaking hands. The local and international media was filled for weeks with guesses about what Arafat was suffering from, what medications he was taking, how the illness and medications effected his performance (or lack thereof), and how long he had left to live. All of a sudden everyone was asking what would happen in the post-Arafat era and who would take his place. I myself was interviewed more than forty times by journalists from all over the world on these questions. But more important than the questions of the journalists were the questions being asked by Palestinians themselves.

Many of the local West Bank and Gaza personalities were quickly dismayed as they saw the "Tunisians"—those who had come with Arafat from abroad—getting the top positions, the senior offices, the heads of ministries, while they were being given second or third chair in the orchestra that they thought they had created. More importantly, political "party" life, which had been the basis of the first intifada through the unified leadership of the main PLO factions, all but ceased to exist. The ideology of the Palestinian resistance and liberation movement seem to fizzle away with shortsighted, short-term private interests taking priority. One Palestinian intellectual and former Fatah activist described it as follows: "For me Palestine today ends at my door-step." The impact of that kind of thinking was the demise of the political parties—the PFLP, DFLP, Fida, PPP (Palestine People's Party—formerly the Palestinian Communist Party), and foremost, Fatah.

A short time after the Arafat interview, an informal meeting of former leaders of the first intifada from Fatah, some of them members of the Palestinian Legislative Council, was held in Ramallah. The discussion there focused on the question of what would happen when Arafat died. Most participants were in agreement that the two main bodies of Fatah, the

Fatah Central Council and the Fatah Revolutionary Council, would most likely play the critical role in selecting/electing a successor. Both of these bodies, the participants noted, were controlled by Arafat's Old Guard loyalists, mostly those who had come with the PLO leadership from abroad. The young indigenous leaders of the first intifada were not represented in those bodies. In fact, of the participants of the meeting in Ramallah, only one was a member of the Revolutionary Council and one was a member of the Central Committee. At that point, a decision was made to revive Fatah through grassroots activities and by taking a militant stand on central issues in the peace process—settlements, refugees, and, the first order of business, prisoner release. It is important to note that in September 1996 these Fatah leaders led the first days of violent demonstrations against the opening of the Kotel tunnel by Netanyahu. The success of those riots in gaining Palestinian public support signaled to them that the model of armed resistance against Israel was a real option for future confrontations. Thus a strategic decision was then taken to reconstitute the Fatah Tanzim (organization), which had been first established in 1983. The ultimate goal would be to "take control" of the Fatah organs of power and to revive the Palestinian struggle along the line of steadfastness to the Palestinian political goals of establishing a Palestinian state in all of the West Bank, Gaza, and East Jerusalem; removing all the Israeli settlers; preventing additional settlement expansion; and releasing all Palestinian prisoners from Israeli jails.

In the lead-up to the Wye River agreement in October 1998, Arafat declared a series of political actions throughout the Palestinian territories under the title "Days of Rage," in which Palestinians were instructed to demonstrate and march against Israeli settlements. All of these events, including the protests led by Faisal al-Husseini against Har Homa and Jabel Abu Ghneim, were failures. The people simply did not come. Arafat resorted to closing the ministries and ordering all PA workers and their families to board buses to go protest. In Jerusalem, it was even reported that people were paid to attend the demonstrations against Har Homa. Many might draw the wrong conclusion, that the Palestinian public was apathetic—they were not. They simply did not wish to answer Arafat's calls out of frustration, shame, and despair over what was becoming of their Palestinian dream. In a mass meeting held in Nablus prior to the Wye Agreement, a senior Palestinian security official who had come from Tunis called upon the people to "go to the streets and fight the occupation." One angry Nabulsi stood up and said, "We did our share during the intifada, we sacrificed our children and our lives. Now it's your turn to send your children." Everyone in the room knew that the children of the Palestinian security chief were all living and studying abroad.

While this was happening, the Fatah Tanzim began a process of democratic elections of new cadres of leaders throughout the West Bank and less so in Gaza where Arafat's Palestinian Security Forces had more influence and control. In every village, town, city, and refugee camp, Fatah was organizing. Soon they launched their very successful public campaign, which they called the "prisoners' intifada," with marches throughout the territories gaining wide public support. Fatah Tanzim was also amassing weapons. Between 1996 and 1999, Fatah held more than 122 conferences in the West Bank alone with more than eighty-five thousand people taking part. The stated aim of these conferences was to convene and elect a new Fatah Central Council and a new Revolutionary Council. These groups had not met in more than eleven years.

At Wye River, Israel (under Netanyahu), with firm American political and CIA support, pressured Arafat to disarm all of the militia in the West Bank, particularly the Fatah Tanzim. The Wye River Accord was signed on October 23, 1998. On October 25, 1998, the forces of Colonel Musa Arafat, the head of the Palestinian Military Intelligence Forces (and Arafat's nephew) forcibly entered the Fatah Tanzim office in Ramallah. Fatah Tanzim resisted and a shootout erupted in the middle of Ramallah. In the end, a young Palestinian, Wassim Tarifi (a nephew of PA Minister Jamil Tarifi) was killed. Downtown Ramallah was closed for several days, during which time a standoff developed between the Tanzim and Musa Arafat and his troops. In the end, Arafat ordered Musa Arafat to withdraw. The Tanzim had won their first strategic battle in the fight for Palestinian leadership. It was reported that following this incident the walls of Ramallah were filled with graffiti denouncing the "filthy collaborators of the Military Intelligence."

Three weeks later, there were riots in Balata refugee camp in Nablus where Tanzim activists stormed the local PA police headquarters in the camp, set it on fire, burned a police car, and only withdrew after being fired on by Palestinian police. The riots started after PA police prevented demonstrators from marching on Joseph's Tomb during the prisoners' intifada.

In May 2000, after completing the process of elections throughout the territories, the Fatah Tanzim decided the time had come to take the struggle to the streets. The final status negotiations with Israel did not begin. In their view, Prime Minister Barak was not taking the Palestinian issue seriously, preferring to seek an agreement with Assad in Syria as a way of weakening the Palestinians. Barak, insisting that it be part of the final status agreement, did not accept the third redeployment. Additionally, Palestinian prisoners were not being released; the committee dealing with the matter simply dragged its feet as Israel spoke about not being able to release prisoners with blood on their hands.

In a closed meeting organized by IPCRI in April 2000 between Israeli MKs from the ruling coalition and high-ranking Tanzim members, Marwan Barghouthi stated, "I feel ashamed that more than five hundred prisoners—some of whom killed Israelis—are still in Israeli jails. Before Oslo there was the Intifada and there was fighting between the two sides, between the PLO and Israel. Barak, who is now your Prime Minister—and we met with him personally—killed three leaders in Lebanon. But we sit down with Barak now because we have to start a new history between the two peoples."

During May 15 through 17, 2000, the Palestinian territories once again erupted in fire for three days of mass Palestinian demonstrations marking "Yom al-Nakba"—the day commemorating the catastrophe of 1948. This was not the first time the Palestinians had observed this day, but never before had so many thousands of them taken to the streets. Armed attacks took place at some of the major Israeli-Palestinian junctions in the West Bank and Gaza. The joint patrols, initiated to take action during times like this, ceased to work. The demonstrations and the military actions were all led by the Tanzim. It took Arafat three days to control the situation on the ground—and then only after grinding pressure from Israel and America. After the three days, Marwan Barghouthi said, "We used weapons against Israel, and, if we have to, we will use them again in the future." According to my analysis, at this time Arafat made a strategic decision to keep the Fatah Tanzim alongside of him. According to Arafat's thinking, if he reached an agreement with Israel, he would need the power of the Tanzim to carry the street, and if he didn't reach an agreement with Israel, he would need the Tanzim to lead the resistance. Shortly after the May 15–17 events, Arafat arranged a reconciliation meeting between the Tanzim and West Bank Preventive Security Chief Jabril Rajoub, whose relations had been strained about a year before when the Tanzim accused Rajoub of turning over several Palestinian prisoners to Israel after Israel demanded their extradition.

These were the events that led to the second intifada. The failure of the Camp David talks in July 2000 and other local and international events led to the outbreak of violence on September 28, 2000. After the horrendous suicide-murders, which peaked in 2002, Israel launched Defensive Shield, in which it retook total control of the West Bank and Gaza and left the Palestinian Authority in ruins. It took years to rebuild what had been destroyed. The trust that was destroyed was never rebuilt—it is much more difficult to rebuild than a building. Thousands were killed and many more thousands wounded. Lives and families were destroyed. The violence of the second intifada also killed the peace camps on both sides.

The primary lesson in the failure of the peace process and the violence of the second intifada is that there is very little reason for each side to trust the other. In peacemaking, that is not always a bad thing. It requires us to be a lot more careful. It forces us to plan for failure. And it should teach us to make much more intelligent agreements. Agreements that are based on a lack of trust or, even worse, on mistrust, can push us to ensure that we are more careful in taking risks and that we build in more mechanisms for dealing with breaches and breakdowns.

One primary security lesson for Israel puts its own security doctrine right out in front: Israel is correct in insisting that only Israel can provide security for Israel. The Palestinians cannot provide security for Israel—not alone. No third-party security forces can provide better security for Israel than Israelis themselves. There is no reason whatsoever why a NATO force should be deployed to protect Israel or Palestine or the peace treaty between them. There is no reason why young men and women from Kansas City, New Orleans, or Rochester should be sent to the Middle East to protect Israelis and Palestinians from each other.

Palestinians will never be able to protect themselves against the Israeli Army if the army is set on retaking control over their state. A Palestinian army would not provide security or protection for the Palestinian state. The State of Palestine will be a nonmilitarized state by agreement. It is true that an element of sovereignty is the right to have a standing army. Palestinian negotiators have intelligently understood until now that Palestine will be a state without an army. There will be a strong robust security force for keeping law and order and for countering terrorist threats, but the idea of the Palestinians investing the small amount of national resources that they have in an aggressive fighting force with artillery and fighter jets borders on the absurd. Not that it is not their right to do so, it is, but it would be an extremely foolish application of rights. The late Faisal al-Husseini, the great Fatah leader from Jerusalem, used to say in public speeches that the Palestinians would be crazy to spend their money on Palestinian tanks. He said that the Palestinians should use their resources to develop the Palestinian computer, not the Palestinian tank or the Palestinian gun. How right he was.

The great investment by Hamas in tunnels and rockets should be the clearest demonstration of wasted resources. Those tunnels and rockets did not protect a single Palestinian. Those investments made in rockets did not, and will not, liberate Palestine. The firepower of Israel and its ability to destroy all of Palestine cannot be challenged by anything that the Palestinians would be able to assemble. The only "achievement" for Palestine in their armed struggle has been in making Israelis feel the pain. At best, the armed struggle for Palestinian liberation creates a "lose-lose" scenario, which has essentially been what we have been facing for too long already. Security for Palestine is only possible when it is coupled with security for Israel. Israel will never be safe from Palestinian violence unless Palestinians are free from Israeli domination and control. There must be a symbiotic relationship between Palestinian freedom, dignity, and safety, and Israeli security. The tricky part of the equation is to find the proper balance between Palestinian sovereignty and Israeli security.

In the Israeli-Palestinian peace treaty, security is one of the main pillars of the agreement. The new relationship that will be developed between the two parties following the signing of the peace treaty must be based on real cooperation and on ending domination. Security must be undertaken by both parties with equal responsibility and through joint operations, shared intelligence, and collaboration. It will no longer be the kind of security co-ordination that has existed during past years, when Palestinians often felt that they were subcontracted by Israel to protect settlers and settlements and to sustain the occupation. During the past years, since Defensive Shield in 2002, Israel has had a free hand to move about in all areas of the West Bank. So as not to implicate themselves, and to avoid armed conflict between Palestinian and Israeli forces, Palestinian security forces would move out of the way whenever Israeli forces entered area "a," and the Israeli forces would do as they pleased. This cannot be the modus operandi after a peace treaty is signed.

Security arrangements must be based on cooperation and joint com-mand and control of forces. If the Israelis and Palestinians cannot agree on a joint security mechanism to protect themselves, each other, and the peace agreement, there will be no peace. This is one of the most fundamen-tal elements of any peace agreement. The most essential aspect of a real peace treaty will be the assurance that all violence is over and disputes are resolved at the table, not on the battlefield. This principle includes a full undertaking and commitment to root out all violence from within each side's own society toward the other. Each society must systematically and truly delegitimize the use of violence against the former enemy and must prosecute with the full force of law those who violate that mandate. This cannot be done by others; it can only be done by each side in its own so-ciety. It can only be done through the full cooperation of the security forces of both sides. It can only be done seriously and genuinely when each side sees it done on both sides of the border.

There is no room for mistakes, because we are dealing with real life and death. No foreign peacekeepers can replace the primary responsibilities of both of the parties for their own security. Third parties should only be in-volved in these issues as monitors, verifiers of implementation, and, if need be, facilitators of cooperation and dispute resolvers. This is a new concept and has not been part of the peace process until now.

The model of security coordination and cooperation that partially worked but ultimately failed during Oslo should not be repeated. The previous model failed for many reasons. Some of them were because the

Palestinians felt that they were providing security for the occupation, not for their own liberation, and because the structure of the coordination gave the impression that the Palestinians were subordinate to the Israelis.

When the security cooperation worked, it was based on Israel sharing intelligence information with the Palestinians, and the Palestinians taking action against terrorists based on that information. It worked at a time when agreements were being implemented and Israel was withdrawing from territories that had been transferred to the Palestinian Authority. When the Israeli withdrawal ended, coupled with the continuation of Israeli settlement building, the internal rationale of the security coordination imploded and its raison d'être became irrational in the eyes of the Palestinians.

The security of peace must be based on the full implementation of the peace treaty by both parties. Since the implementation will be performance based and monitored and verified by the implementation assistance mechanism, the element of security will be, certainly at the beginning, the most important element of the new relationship—along with Israeli withdrawals to what will eventually be the permanent border between the two states. The process of building, testing, and trying the security cooperation will proceed along with the first stages of an Israeli settlement freeze and initial withdrawals from areas that will become part of the Palestinian state—beginning with transferring area "b" (the Palestinian villages still under Israeli security control) and the bulk of area "c" to full Palestinian control. The idea that each side must have full control in their own sovereign areas is fundamental, yet the joint security mechanism will create specified places and roles for collaborative operations.

It is going to be very difficult to convince the Israeli security establishment to agree to this new relationship, but I maintain that without it there will be no security for Israel and no real peace. Overall, there should be a joint command headquarters that is actually *joint*—that is, sharing the same office, with parallel levels of commanders and full joint authority. It will probably be necessary for a senior US officer to be there at the beginning to help get the operation set up and running, but not as a commander of the Israelis and Palestinians, not giving orders, instead working with them so that they work together.

Intelligence sharing must be an inherent part of security cooperation. It is essential that this begin immediately so systems and intentions are put to the test. Israel could begin by defining a geographic area in which it will cease its incursions for the purpose of arresting suspected terrorists. Israel should provide Palestinian intelligence forces with information, and Palestinian security will bring in any suspected terrorists for questioning and, if need be, prosecution. The justice system and the penitentiary system are equal elements of importance in security cooperation. Israelis have claimed that Palestinian prisons are still centers with revolving doors and that not one Palestinian has been convicted of terrorism by a Palestinian court. This will have to be different in peace.

SECURITY—WORKING ASSUMPTIONS

Israel will always provide the best security for itself.

Palestinians must constantly demonstrate 100 percent effort in fighting terrorism.

Israel must demonstrate 100 percent effort and improved results against violent settlers who attack Palestinians.

The justice systems on both sides are a fundamental element in combatting terrorism—convicted terrorists and security violators must be brought to justice and serve reasonable terms in prison.

Binational (Israeli-Palestinian) security cooperation and joint mechanisms with international oversight (monitoring, verification, facilitation, and dispute resolution) is preferable to international or multinational peacekeeping forces.

The Palestinian state will be nonmilitarized (no offensive weapons), and its security forces will be armed with limited weapons.

Israel will continue to enjoy flyover rights above the Palestinian state while Palestinians will exercise their rights to civilian air corridors over their sovereign areas in accordance with international aviation laws and procedures.

Palestine will have control over its external borders (entry and exit points) and will determine who is allowed to enter and exit their state.

For a predetermined period, security along the Jordan River will be provided by coordinated forces, producing a Palestinian and Israeli presence on the west side of the border and Jordanian forces on the east side.

As a sovereign state, Palestine will control the entry and exit points of their external borders. For an agreed period of time (perhaps five years), there must be a verifiable third-party inspection mechanism that ensures that military equipment and unauthorized weapons, ammunitions, and so on, are not imported into the Palestinian state. The third-party mechanism must be able to carry out random spot checks of cargo and persons entering Palestine.

There is a strong need for a third-party mechanism for monitoring and verifiying the security arrangements that will be agreed upon. This mechanism must include:

- US senior military officers to assist in security coordination at command levels
- Third-party monitors overseeing processes of Israeli withdrawal and Palestinian force deployment
- Third-party monitors at designated formal border crossings between the two states for a predetermined period of time
- Third-party monitors and inspectors inside Palestine with free movement and the ability to have entry and access to any suspected location, particularly during the first couple of years, to verify prohibition of the production of weapons, rockets, ammunition, and so on

ADDITIONAL ISSUES

Security along the Jordan Border

A trilateral Israeli-Palestinian-Jordanian mechanism will be created that will include long-term physical stations at set locations along the border with joint command operations, including joint Palestinian-Israeli patrols along the western side of the border and Jordanian patrols on the Jordanian side. The joint patrols will continue for a period not less than ten years.

Palestine and Israel will operate a mechanism for rapid response in case of breaches along the border.

Israel will continue to operate electronic surveillance defenses along the border for a period not less than five years.

If joint patrols are unable to confront immediate threats, Palestinian forces should be deployed immediately to respond.

Rules of engagement must be defined and determined within the security annex and should be reviewed regularly to meet emerging threats if necessary.

Border breaches into Palestine are best prevented from the Jordanian side; Israel, Palestine, and Jordan will share intelligence information on the security of the border.

Israel will be allowed to use drone surveillance over the Jordan River area, flying west of the border; the intelligence information derived from such surveillance will be shared, in real time, with the two other parties.

Border Crossings

Both parties have the legitimate right to keep unwanted persons out of their territory. In general, all Israelis and Palestinians should have free access and movement to each other's territory on the basis of security parameters determined in the security annex. In a state of real peace, people from both sides should be able to gain entry into the other side. It is equally understood that people who are considered a threat to security will not be allowed entry into the other side.

There should be a double-tiered filtering system to determine who might be considered a threat. The first-level filter is the internal one—each side should determine who the people are from their own side who should be denied entry to the other side. Regarding others who have the right to apply for entry, the parties should determine equal and parallel criteria and rules for issuing various types of entry permits. This could include single-day visits, week-long, month-long, several-months-long, or longer. The permits could be for tourism, business, work, health care, and so on.

Systems should be established that would enable people to get a permit at the border at the time of crossing in the least amount of time possible. This should be the goal for the beginning of the process until the time, hopefully in the future, when restrictions on movement will be completely removed.

Systems should also exist to enable applications for entry permits online. Permits could be printed at home and be verified via encoded applications at the border crossing. Modern technologies, including the use of smart phone applications, should be employed to make the process as easy as possible. The basic goal is to facilitate movement efficiently while maintaining a high level of security. There does not have to be any contradiction between security and rapid and efficient movement through borders.

As soon as possible, the parties should agree to return access to Israel to Palestinian vehicles, taking into account all of the security precautions that are necessary for this to happen. The international community could help to facilitate this by providing additional assistance in the form of security scanners for vehicles, but even in the absence of international support for this purpose, Israel should place those scanners at the border crossing as soon as possible, even prior to the full implementation of the rest of the agreement.

Possibilities for double visa application should be available for foreigners entering Israel or Palestine who wish to visit the other side as well. It should be expected that once Palestinians have control of entry and exit points to the Palestinian states, large numbers of diaspora Palestinians and other Arabs and Muslims will be visiting Palestine regularly, and it can be easily assumed that many of them will wish to visit Israel, as well. A mechanism should be designed and made accessible for applying for a double visa. This should be a streamlined and efficient online process. Those requiring further attention for additional security checks could be referred to consulates and embassies.

Training and Deployment of Palestinian Forces

The US security assistance, in coordination with Jordan and Israel, should continue for a period of not less than five years while the Palestinian security forces take control of additional areas and additional authorities.

The security assistance and training should be upgraded to include intelligence gathering, including the uses of electronic surveillance.

SECURITY OFFENDERS

The legal regime for dealing with security offenders is an extremely sensitive issue, particularly in the immediate postagreement era. In an ideal situation, Palestinians who breach security in Israel should be able to be brought to justice within Palestine through cooperation with Israel in investigation, preparation of indictments and evidence, and so on. A court trial in Palestine and sentencing to Palestinian prisons according to the Palestinian justice system would reduce the animosity of Palestinians toward Israel. Likewise, Israelis who are security offenders in Palestine should be brought to justice in Israel with Palestinian cooperation in investigation, preparation of indictments, and securing evidence, with sentencing to Israeli prisons. The negotiators should take the various possibilities and potential implications of security under consideration for the different variables.

SPOILERS

We all remember Prime Minister Rabin's famous statement following several terror attacks in Israel that occurred after Oslo was signed: "We will fight terror as if there is no peace process and make peace as if there is no terror." That sounds good and might be possible if the chance of terror is very low. The past peace process was not capable of containing Baruch Goldstein and suicide bus bombers, and the political leaders could not sustain the process when the lack of security became so apparent. I don't think that anyone has good answers on how to deal with the issue of "spoilers." Spoilers are criminals working against the interests of their own side, state, and people, and must be treated as such. There will be spoilers. They will be on both sides. The failure to deal with them quickly and effectively can and will jeopardize the peace process.

Leaders and security apparatuses on both sides must demonstrate 100 percent effort and intent to deal with the spoilers harshly and quickly. Zero tolerance should be the policy, and explicit condemnation and statements ostracizing the perpetrators of violence against peace must be the uncompromising policy of both sides.

If and when there are victims of violence committed by these spoilers, they must not be termed "victims of the peace process." The appropriate terminology is "victims of terror, victims of hatred, and victims of war."

JERUSALEM

Jerusalem is the microcosm and nucleus of the entire Israeli-Palestinian conflict. Jerusalem is much more than a city, a physical space. It is a transcendental phenomenon encompassing the emotional energy that has propelled this conflict into violence for generations. Conventional wisdom throughout the years of the peace process has always been to leave Jerusalem until the end. Jerusalem is the issue on which the Camp David talks of July 2000 exploded. Jerusalem is where the second intifada erupted, where the latest round of violence began and was centered, and Jerusalem has been the constant source of strife in all of the past years. I have always believed Jerusalem should have been the first issue on the agenda. If we can resolve Jerusalem, everything else will be easier.

That is why in August 1989 I launched the first Israeli-Palestinian working group of experts on the future of Jerusalem. It was quite evident even then that Jerusalem would be a focal point of any future Israeli-Palestinian negotiations. Without finding a peaceful solution for Jerusalem that would enable both sides to have their national capital in the city, there could be no peace. That has not changed.

In 1992, after three years of intensive monthly meetings and an additional six long weekends together, we (IPCRI) published our first plan for sharing Jerusalem. It is important to note that I speak about sharing Jerusalem, not dividing it. The words in Hebrew are quite similar but their different meanings are diametrically opposed: לחלק את ירושלים–, to divide Jerusalem, as opposed to –להתחלק בירושלים, to share Jerusalem.

The plan was presented to Mayor Teddy Kollek a year before Oslo and still remains the most viable solution for the future of Jerusalem. As part of the exercise in our exploration for a solution, we prepared a map of the city, color-coded by population groups within the city. It was strikingly clear that Jerusalem is a very segregated city; I believe it is the most segregated city in the world. Israelis and Palestinians live in separate areas. There are no common areas in the city. This observation immediately led to the understanding that sovereignty in Jerusalem could be assigned to different neighborhoods on the basis of demography. We called this dispersed sovereignty. At the end of 2000, President Clinton, in the parameters for peace he presented to Israeli and Palestinian negotiators, created the terms of reference: "what is Jewish for Israel, what is Arab for Palestine."

Another principle that our 1992 plan shared with Clinton was that Jerusalem must remain one open city without physical boundaries—walls or fences—that would prevent free movement within the city. Jerusalem after all is an urban space where hundreds of thousands of people live, and walls and fences dividing the city into small pieces would kill the city and make it an impossible place to live and work. This obviously presents a lot of challenges because there is no peaceful solution for Jerusalem without dividing the sovereignty of the city, but both sides must at the same time guarantee that the city would remain physically united and open.

The separation wall that was built around the city in the south, east, and north was constructed to keep Palestinians out. The law of unintended consequences resulted in an influx of some sixty thousand Palestinians back into the city after its construction. These people, beginning in 1967, moved out of the city, mostly to the north where housing was available and cheaper than in Jerusalem. They moved back into the city out of fear of being cut off and possibly losing their rights to live there.

There are some 360,000 Palestinians living in Jerusalem, the overwhelming majority of whom are not Israeli citizens, but are residents of Jerusalem. According to Israeli law, inherited from the British, as residents they have the right to run in municipal elections and to vote in them. The Palestinians in the city boycott those elections, rejecting Israel's claim to sovereignty over the whole city. They are nonetheless subject to Israeli policies and laws, and enjoy some of the benefits of being residents of the State of Israel—mainly freedom of movement, national insurance, and access to Israel's health services. Despite the benefits, most Palestinians in Jerusalem demand to be part of the Palestinian state and for Jerusalem to be its capital. This is not only because Palestinians in Jerusalem suffer from significant discrimination. There are arguments regarding the statistics of how many of Jerusalem's Palestinian residents really would prefer to be part of the Palestinian state and how many would prefer to remain in Israel. What is clear is that none of them agree to Jerusalem being physically divided, and no one wants to have a second-class status in Jerusalem.

Since 1967, Israel has claimed that Jerusalem is the eternal, united, undivided capital of the State of Israel and the Jewish people. But Jerusalem is very divided, definitely not united, and is not recognized by any government in the world as the capital of Israel. There is not one country in the world that recognizes Israel's sovereignty over all of Jerusalem.

Before the establishment of the Palestinian Authority, Jerusalem was the center of Palestinian life—economically, culturally, educationally, religiously, and politically. Today, Jerusalem remains the center only in the area of religion. Jerusalem has been cut off from Palestinians, and Palestinians have been cut off from Jerusalem. The physical border established by Israel after Oslo cuts Jerusalem off from Palestinians in the West Bank and Gaza. Israel cynically exploited the Palestinian agreement to leave Jerusalem as a final status issue to prevent the Palestinian Authority from having any access to or input in Jerusalem. Israel refused to implement its obligations under the Road Map for Peace of President George W. Bush, which required Israel to reopen Palestinian national institutions in Jerusalem, primarily the Orient House and the East Jerusalem Chamber of Commerce. Palestinians have no official role in Jerusalem.

Since the death of Faisal al-Husseini in 2001, Jerusalem has been void of local leadership that could unite the people, and Israel has strongly enforced a "divide and conquer" mode of operation in the city to prevent the emergence of new leadership. Israel has ignored development in most of the Palestinian areas and even the police only enter those areas when engaged in antiterrorist activities, leaving largely lawless zones within Israel's allegedly eternal undivided capital. Jerusalem is not united, and there is no validity to the claim that united Jerusalem is the eternal capital of Israel.

Today both parties claim Jerusalem as their national capital. Israel asserts that Jerusalem is the cradle of Jewish civilization, the holiest city for Jews, and the focal point for Jewish existence. Jews all over the world turn toward Jerusalem in prayer, and those inside Jerusalem face the Temple Mount in the heart of Jerusalem's Old City.

The first direction of Muslim prayer was Jerusalem, but later changed to Mecca. It is from Jerusalem that the Prophet Muhammad ascended to heaven and met with the prophets before him. Jerusalem is spoken about in Islam as al-Aqsa (the distant mosque) and Beit al-Maqdas (the holy house), in reference to the Holy Temple. Jerusalem is the third most holy city in the world for Muslims, and, according to their tradition, the obligation of Haj (pilgrimage) is not complete until, after Mecca and Medina, the pilgrim completes the journey with a visit to Jerusalem.

THE POSITIONS BETWEEN THE PARTIES in Jerusalem are diametrically opposed and seem to be unbridgeable. The official policy of the Israeli government is that Jerusalem is and will always be the eternal undivided capital of the Jewish people and the State of Israel. Jerusalem will never be divided again, as it was for almost nineteen years, between 1949 at the end of Israel's war of independence and the Palestinian nakba (the catastrophe) and the June 1967 war. In March 1949, King Abdallah I of Jordan illegally annexed East Jerusalem and the West Bank of the Jordan River to the Hashemite Kingdom, and walls and barbed wire fences divided Jerusalem right through the middle of the city, cutting the Old City of Jerusalem and the Jewish holy places off from Israel and the Jewish world. After the lightning-fast Six-Day War in 1967, the Jewish state tore down the walls and fences and reunited the city, vowing that it would never be divided again. Israel then illegally annexed all of East Jerusalem and expanded its borders in the east, placing the entire city under Israel's sovereignty and law. Like the Jordanian annexation in 1949, Israel's annexation was rejected by the international community, who viewed it in contravention to International law.

The Palestinians' position is that all of East Jerusalem, the territory occupied by Israel in 1967, must become the capital of the State of Palestine. This position officially includes more than 250,000 Israelis who now live in that area in neighborhoods built by Israel on what Palestinians consider to be their land. The Palestinian position is that the entire Old City of Jerusalem, including the Jewish Quarter and the Jewish holy places, must be under Palestinian sovereignty in any peace agreement.

There are three concentric circles of issues in Jerusalem that need to be resolved. The closer to the center, the more difficult to resolve—nonetheless, there are solutions for all of them. The outer circle is the issue of the neighborhoods all around the city. The center circle is the Old City. The heart of hearts is the Temple Mount / Haram al-Sharif.

The neighborhoods, as already mentioned, are easiest to deal with because there are really no mixed neighborhoods. Every neighborhood is either Israeli or Palestinian, and the borders of the neighborhoods are equally clear. It is relatively easy to assign sovereignty to all of the neighborhoods. There are a few problematic areas that could be dealt with on an issue-by-issue basis—such as Palestinian enclaves on the French Hill; Gilo, a Muslim cemetery on Mount Zion; and Beit Safafa, where half of the neighborhood are Israeli citizens (although Palestinian) and the other half are Palestinians without citizenship. There are also the special cases of Israeli settlements that have been built inside Palestinian neighborhoods—such as in Ras al-Amoud and Nof Zion. Har Homa is also problematic because it was built after Oslo, and the Palestinians have not accepted that it will be included in the annexed areas by Israel (part of the 4–5 percent annexation), but today the situation in Har Homa is already too large to reverse. Palestine will be sovereign over all of the Palestinian neighborhoods, and Israel will be sovereign over all of the Israeli neighborhoods. This is perhaps unprecedented in the world, but Jerusalem is unique and requires unique solutions.

Municipal government in the city could be either through completely separate municipalities with coordination between them, or even one municipal council representing both cities. Other models have been examined from other parts of the world, including Brussels and even New York City with its borough system of government. The municipal governance issues are the easiest to resolve in Jerusalem, and, as in the Brussels model, adopting the principle of trial and error would be recommended—nothing etched in stone. The purpose of municipal government is to serve the day-to-day needs of the people within the municipality. In Jerusalem there must be coordination between both sides on issues of infrastructure, transportation, sewage, waste control and treatment, water and electricity supply, and of course on issues of economic development—tourism, antiquities, physical development, zoning, planning, and so on.

The Old City of Jerusalem is certainly the heart of the city and the focal point of conflict between Israel and Palestine. This area, less than one square kilometer in size, is a powder keg of nuclear proportions in terms of its volatility and potential for disaster. There are four quarters in the Old City: Armenian, Christian, Muslim, and Jewish. It could be possible to adopt the Clinton parameters in the Old City as well, so that the Jewish Quarter would be under Israeli sovereignty, and, based on demography, the other three quarters would be under Palestinian sovereignty. It could also be possible to adopt the kind of proposal Prime Minister Olmert offered in 2008, in which an international body composed of Israel, Palestine, the United States, Jordan, and Saudi Arabia would govern the Old City on behalf of its residents. Another similar proposal was made by a group of Jerusalem experts working with the University of Windsor in Canada in which an international management company would administer the Old City.[4]

In the center of the heart, the heart of hearts, is, of course, the Temple Mount / Haram al-Sharif (the Noble Sanctuary)—145,000 square meters of holy space. This is the most holy place in the world for Jews, the third most holy place for Muslims, and Palestinians see themselves as the protectors of al-Aqsa—mentioned in the Quran and referred to as the distant mosque. For Muslims, the entire mount, not only the buildings on the mount, is al-Aqsa, the place where they believe the Prophet Muhammad ascended to heaven on the Isra, the part of the journey of Muhammad from Mecca to Jerusalem. Once in Jerusalem, the second part of Muhammad's journey is the Mi'raj (an Arabic word that literally means "ladder"), where he toured the seven stages of heaven and spoke with the earlier prophets such as Abraham ('Ibrāhīm), Moses (Musa), John the Baptist (Yaḥyāibn Zakarīya), and Jesus (Isa). According to Islamic tradition, God instructed Muhammad that Muslims must pray fifty times per day; however, Moses told Muhammad that it was very difficult for the people and urged Muhammad to ask for a reduction, until finally it was reduced to five times per day. Moshe Dayan understood very well the potential volatility of the site when he ordered that an Israeli flag atop the Dome of the Rock be immediately removed. Israel understood that it would be very dangerous to change the status quo of continued Muslim presence and control on the Temple Mount.

In recent years, more Jews have combined deep religious beliefs with extreme nationalism and decided Jews should retake the Mount even before the Messiah comes, perhaps as a way of speeding up his coming. The demand of Jews to be allowed to pray there is understandable both from the position of religious importance and as an assertion of the rights of free access to all holy places. If there was no conflict between Israel and Palestine, it is even possible to imagine the day when it could happen peacefully. There is no prohibition in Islamic law (sharia) on people of other faiths praying on the Haram al-Sharif. But in the current situation, where the Muslims in Palestine and in the Muslim world are convinced that Israel's intentions are to remove the mosques, prevent Muslims from praying there, and rebuild the Temple, the Israeli-Palestinian conflict instantly becomes transformed from a political conflict into a religious war. This is the most dangerous scenario possible and too risky to tolerate. The status quo must be maintained, and, if it is to be changed, it should only be done through negotiations and agreements, not imposed by force.

The political solution for the Temple Mount / Haram al-Sharif is to formalize the current status quo whereby the Muslims (the Palestinians) control the Temple Mount / Haram al-Sharif on top and Israel controls the Western Wall below, which is outside of the Mount where Jews now pray to be as close to the Mount as possible. Both parties would agree to limit their sovereignty and control by not tunneling, constructing, digging, or damaging in any way the entire compound without mutual agreement.

If, after the Messiah comes, God should desire to change the arrangement, everything would be possible. For the time being, the makings of an agreement are possible.

CAN IT WORK?

So now we are left with two main questions: how can the city of Jerusalem be divided on the basis of demography and still function, and when should the issue be negotiated? The only way Jerusalem can survive as an urban space where real people live and work is for it to remain physically united and open. Jerusalem will die if it is torn to pieces with walls and barbed wire fences. The precondition for Jerusalem to be physically undivided and open is for there to be real personal security within the city. But this is a precondition for all aspects of Israeli and Palestinian life. Real security in Jerusalem will have to include three main components: (1) Each side's security and police forces will have to take full responsibility for security and law and order within the territory under its own domain. (2) There will be a need for very robust and active cooperation, including joint forces between the Israeli and Palestinian security and police forces in Jerusalem. (3) And finally, there must be a significant third-party monitoring component ensuring that both parties are fully meeting their obligations as well as building the trust necessary for the joint missions and providing a real-time, on-the-ground dispute resolution mechanism.

When should Jerusalem be negotiated: at the end or in the beginning of the negotiations? Going against conventional wisdom, I have always advocated putting Jerusalem on the table up front. Borders cannot be negotiated without resolving the issue of Jerusalem. Land swaps are meaningless without dealing with the delineation of borders of sovereignty in Jerusalem. Security arrangements have little validity without confronting security in Jerusalem, where the most terror attacks took place during the second intifada. National symbols and holy places cannot be dealt with anywhere in the area without dealing with Jerusalem. Jerusalem is the microcosm of the entire conflict and the most sensitive issue on the table. If the issues in conflict in Jerusalem can be resolved in negotiations, all other aspects of the negotiations will be easier. If Jerusalem cannot be resolved, there can be no Israeli-Palestinian peace.

Because most aspects of the Jerusalem issue have been negotiated in the past and there have been so many workable proposals designed for Jerusalem by Israeli and Palestinian experts who have worked together on finding them, it is more possible to reach an agreement on Jerusalem than most people believe. The solutions I have described enable both sides to have their national capitals in Jerusalem. Jerusalem will remain an open city, united for all to come and visit, while clearly designating separate sovereignties on maps and on the ground. Jerusalem's holy places will be open with free access to all, and each community will retain its control over its most sacred spaces while enabling dreams and future aspirations to remain within the realm of prayer.

Peace in Jerusalem is the key to Israeli-Palestinian peace—that key is on the table and waiting to be used. Jerusalem has the potential to become the one place in the world where civilizations do not clash but learn to appreciate each other through dialogue, through mutual respect, and through mutual and collective celebration.

Jerusalem's uniqueness lies in its spiritual calling and its rich human resources. The wealth of Jerusalem comes from those who hold it dear and from those who lives are connected to it. Fostering conflicts in the city and about the city through empty political slogans on billboards and on the sides of buses cheapens Jerusalem's value. The competition over Jerusalem's meager land resources increases the ugliness and the rudeness of the city's character and the face it presents to the world.

Jerusalem's history is a huge burden, a weight that has reduced Jerusalem's glory to a primitive tribal feud that has driven too many good people out of the city. When Jerusalem's present and its future potential outshines its past, without losing respect and appreciation of its past, then Jerusalem will be a magnet, instead of being a burden.

PALESTINIAN REFUGEES

When people speak about the unsolvable Israeli-Palestinian conflict, they usually end up focusing on the Palestinian refugee issue. According to the Final Report of the United Nations Economic Survey Mission for the Middle East published December 28, 1949, by the United Nations Conciliation Commission, 726,000 Palestinians became refugees as a result of the birth of the State of Israel and the war that began after the UN vote on partition on November 29, 1947. Today there are more than five million Palestinians registered with the United Nations as refugees.

First of all, it is important to note that Palestinian refugees are the only community of refugees in the world that have been granted multigenerational status. There are no second, third, and fourth generations of refugees from other communities who fled or were forced out of their countries. Secondly, the Palestinian refugees are the only refugee population who have their own UN-dedicated agency. All other refugees in the world are dealt with by the UN High Commissioner for Refugees. According to the UNHCR website, its mandate is to lead and coordinate international action to protect refugees and resolve refugee problems worldwide. Its primary purpose is to safeguard the rights and well-being of refugees. It strives to ensure that everyone can exercise the right to seek asylum and find safe refuge in another state, with the option to return home voluntarily, integrate locally, or resettle in a third country.

The United Nations Relief and Welfare Agency (UNRWA) is the body that deals exclusively with Palestinian refugees. Its mandate has never suggested that Palestinian refugees be resettled in other countries or that Palestinians who fled Palestine or who were forced to leave will not continue to be considered refugees for generations to come. UNRWA's mandate has been transformed into a mechanism that preserves the refugee status of the Palestinian decedents of refugees even though they may have been living in Palestine prior to 1948. The Gaza Strip has eight refugee camps and more than 1.2 million registered refugees. The West Bank has nineteen refugee camps and about 750,000 registered refugees. The refugee camps in Palestine and in Jordan are no longer refugee camps. They are mainly urban slums or densely populated inner-city areas of poverty. The refugees don't own the land in the camps, but they have built homes there, with funds allocated by the international community and that they earned over the years from their own labor. In the West Bank, only a small number of the 1.2 million registered refugees are still living in the camps. The majority of them are living in the main cities and large villages, but they keep a family home in the camps in order to maintain their status and their claims to the right of return.

Many former refugees have become very successful both inside and outside Palestine. Some 500,000 Palestinians live in Chile and another 250,000 in Costa Rica. Many of those people still consider themselves refugees from Palestine. Inside Palestine, many of the wealthiest Palestinians were refugees. Jamil Tarifi, for example, a former minister in Arafat's first government, is a refugee from Deir Tarifi—a village that was located where Ben Gurion Airport is today. I visited Jamil Tarifi in his home in June 2015. It is one of the most luxurious mansions in Ramallah. Jamil Tarifi and his children are registered refugees.

The Palestinian position on refugees is based on UN Resolution 194, whose operative clause on refugees (paragraph 11) states:

> Resolves that the refugees wishing to return to their homes and live at peace with their neighbors should be permitted to do so at the earliest practicable date, and that compensation should be paid for the property of those choosing not to return and for loss of or damage to property which, under principles of international law or in equity, should be made good by the Governments or authorities responsible; instructs the Conciliation Commission to facilitate the repatriation, resettlement and economic and social rehabilitation of the refugees and the payment of compensation, and to maintain close relations with the Director of the United Nations Relief for Palestine Refugees and, through him, with the appropriate organs and agencies of the United Nations.

On the basis of this resolution, Palestinians developed the term "right of return." The Palestinian position is that every Palestinian refugee and their descendants automatically have the right to return to their original homes. There are many problems with this position, which is completely understandable. The single most important thread of Palestinian identity and collective memory is the nakba—the tragedy that happened to the Palestinians with the birth of Israel. Keeping the memory of pre-1948 Palestine alive has been the fuel that crystalized Palestinians into a nation. Remembering what used to be almost seventy years ago is quite easy to identify with, especially for Jews who have kept their collective memory alive for two thousand years. Yet the possibility of return for most of the refugees is not even an option. Of the more than four hundred villages that used to exist in Palestine before 1948, almost nothing exists today. On top of those villages and towns are newer cities, villages, kibbutzim, and institutions—like Ben Gurion Airport, Tel Aviv University, and the Tel Aviv Hilton Hotel. Today there are Israeli

Jews who live in places where Palestinian refugees came from, and they have been living there for three and four generations. Justice is not done by doing injustice to others.

Furthermore, if Palestinian refugees were to come back to what is today the State of Israel, would they be willing to live as law-abiding, loyal Israeli citizens? Would they be able to identify with the State of Israel and agree to live in peace with their neighbors, as the UN resolution states?

Yet for Palestinians, the principle of the right of return is a holy right and an individual right. It is not a collective right, and it is not a right that is negotiable. For Israel, the implementation of the right of return would be a death blow to the idea of a Jewish nation-state with a clear Jewish majority. Millions of Palestinian refugees returning to the State of Israel would render the State of Israel a binational state and eventually one with a Palestinian majority and a large Jewish minority. This is a nonstarter for Israel. Statements made by Palestinian leaders, including Arafat and Abbas, that they would not nor could not ever give up the right of return, coupled with statements made by Israeli leaders, including Netanyahu and Tzipi Livni, that not one Palestinian refugee would be allowed to return, suggest that this problem is not resolvable, and therefore the conflict cannot be resolved.

On November 4, 2012, Abbas was interviewed on Israeli television Channel 2 and said, "Palestine now for me is the '67 borders, with East Jerusalem as its capital. This is now and forever. . . . This is Palestine for me. I am [a] refugee, but I am living in Ramallah. . . . I believe that [the] West Bank and Gaza is Palestine and the other parts [are] Israel." He also said that he does not have the right to go back to Safed. The statement created an uproar amongst Palestinians and struck a chord of hope with Israelis. Abbas was quick to restate that he has not given up the right of return for the Palestinian people, but only for himself. This is a very important distinction that actually provides the solution for the Palestinian refugee issue. There is no ability for any Palestinian leader to give up the right of return for Palestinian refugees. Giving up the right of return is an individual right, as Palestinians believe. I would prefer to say that deciding on the future for Palestinian refugees is the right of each Palestinian refugee.

Before presenting what I believe is the solution, I would like to add a comment about the anomalies of Palestinian refugee status. It is possible to complain and rant and rave about the multigenerational status of Palestinian refugees as opposed to all other refugees. It is possible to complain about UNRWA and its mission to keep the Palestinian refugee issue alive. All of this may be 100 percent correct and valid, but it does nothing to present a solution. We must accept the anomalies and move forward toward finding a solution. This proposal is based on one I originally suggested in a paper I wrote to Prime Minister Ehud Barak some ten days before he left for the Camp David Summit in July 2000.

This is what I wrote then, December 21, 2000:

1. The Parties recognize the validity of UNGA Resolution 194.
2. An international body will be established to provide international support for the resettlement of refugees, for the construction of homes, and for the development of employment opportunities for refugees.
3. The international body will also allocate funds for those countries that have hosted refugees since 1948.
4. The international body will allocate funds to individuals as well as to states.
5. Refugees will be granted the opportunity to choose between the following options:
   a. Return and (re)settlement within the State of Palestine.
   b. Remaining within the host country and receiving (or retaining) citizenship of the host country.
   c. Applying for resettlement and receiving citizenship of other countries.
   d. Applying for resettlement and citizenship within the State of Israel.
6. Following the final determination of the choice of the refugees, representatives of Palestine, Israel, and other countries willing to absorb refugees will convene to work out mechanisms for the best implementation of the requests of the refugees. There is no prior commitment by any of the parties to absorb all of those refugees who choose to relocate in any of the countries selected by the refugees, yet, with the signing of the Peace Treaty, the sides obligate themselves to act in good faith and to assume the maximal responsibility for cooperating with the international body in the absorption of all of the refugees and putting a final positive conclusion on the plight of the Palestinian refugees.

A more expanded version of this idea was sent to Yossi Beilin and Nabeel Shaath, who were in charge of the refugee file at the Taba negotiations in January 2001, where real progress was made, as opposed to Camp David where only six hours of talks were held on the refugee issue in two weeks.

In summary, the solution to the issue involves the following:

Every refugee will be given the choice between a number of options including: (1) return and citizenship in the Palestinian state—this option will be available to every Palestinian all over the world and forever, and strategic incentives will be added to those who select this option, including possibilities for financial assistance for housing and jobs; (2) a list of third countries willing to accept refugees—each country determining the number and the mechanism for applying for citizenship—this will include Israel; (3) the option of remaining in host countries (mainly relevant for Jordan).

An international fund will be established with an international legal panel for dealing with claims for financial compensation for property lost (Israel will participate in the fund). Settlements which are not included in the areas to be annexed by Israel within the territorial swap map will be left intact and applied for the use in the plan for the resettlement of refugees who choose the option to return to the State of Palestine. With the implementation of the peace agreement, there will no longer be a "refugee problem" and the organization of UNRWA will cease to exist. The resettlement of refugees in Palestine will be the responsibility of the government of the State of Palestine.

Every registered refugee would be given a specific time frame during which they must respond. With today's technologies available, this could easily be done online with international supervision and oversight. Every country offering to accept Palestinian refugees would determine the number of refugees and the terms under which they would be accepted. Every country has the sovereign right to determine its immigration and absorption policies. In September 2010, Prime Minister Ehud Olmert noted that President George W. Bush had agreed to accept 100,000 Palestinian refugees within a framework for an Israeli-Palestinian agreement. There will probably be at least twenty countries that will accept Palestinian refugees, including the State of Israel.

The last part of the solution is probably a "post peace" element involving deeper reconciliation. At some point, not too long after reaching a comprehensive agreement, there will have to be acknowledgement by Israel of its part of the responsibility for the creation of the Palestinian refugee problem. Israel does not bear full responsibility—there was more than enough to go around—including the Palestinian leadership itself, the Arab leaders, and the British. But Israel does bear significant responsibility, and there will be a need to own up to that. The acknowledgement can take many forms, including a public statement by the Israeli government. But deeper acknowledgment will involve the eventual learning about the nakba and the Palestinian history of what later became Israel within Israeli schools and civil society.

Palestinians will have their own owning up to do as well, taking responsibility for some of the horrific things that they have done over the years, and it will be important for them to be able to apologize, as well.

GETTING TO THE FINISH LINE

At the outset of the nine-month negotiation period allocated by Secretary of State John Kerry in July 2013, members of Kerry's team requested that I submit to them my ideas and recommendations. I drafted tens of pages of recommendations, including the following text. The sections that appear below deal primarily with issues that have not been elaborated previously.

Framework Document for the Establishment of Permanent Peace

This document is meant to serve the parties in the final stages of completing the negotiations for a permanent status peace agreement.

The government of the State of Israel and the PLO, representing the Palestinian people, reaffirm that it is time to put an end to decades of confrontation and conflict, recognize their mutual legitimate and political rights, and strive to live in peaceful coexistence and mutual dignity and security, and achieve a just, lasting, and comprehensive peace settlement and historic reconciliation based on the two-states-for-two-peoples solution.

ARTICLE ONE

Aim of the Agreement of Principles on Permanent Status

The aim of this Declaration of Principles is to provide a framework for negotiations on the detailed permanent status agreement of peace and end of conflict and all claims between the State of Israel and the State of Palestine that will be established based on these principles. This Declaration of Principles relates to all of the permanent status issues detailed in the DOP of September 1993 including: Jerusalem, refugees, settlements, security arrangements, borders, relations and cooperation with other neighbors, and other issues of common interest.

ARTICLE SEVEN

Water and Environment

Based on the Oslo II agreement in which Israel recognized Palestine's water rights, both sides agree to immediately increase the allocation of water to Palestine by twenty percent until a new water agreement is reached. The new water agreement in the full permanent status agreement will be based on the principle of equitable water rights and allocations. Both sides will work together for advancing infrastructure and development projects that will increase the amount of water available by all means including desalination, wastewater treatment, repair of water networks, etc.

Both sides undertake to work immediately on the advancement of environmental infrastructure projects that cause damage to the environment, especially those which have a cross-boundary nature.

Alternatively, a model of full joint water management could be adopted based on the creation of a bilateral public-private partnership company which is responsible for providing for all water needs for all peoples at reasonable prices. The company will run a closed budget and all revenues will be devoted to expanding and improving water delivery systems and increasing the quantity and quality of fresh water for all uses. Water allocation will not be determined by national identity. All users have exactly the same rights to receive as much water as they need. Water pricing will be differentiated based on how it is used and not by who uses it. Domestic water for basic human needs will be the lowest priced water and made available for all people between the River and the Sea for the same low price.

ARTICLE EIGHT
Creating a Culture of Peace, Education for Peace,
and Fighting against Incitement
With the signing of this Declaration of Principles the two sides undertake to work in partnership in a decisive way to foster a culture of peace including the undertaking of curricula review and modification of textbooks and the inclusion of education for peace within the school systems of both sides. The two sides also agree to make a concerted and decisive effort to eliminate all forms of incitement against the other sides in the public arena and in the media.

ARTICLE NINE
People-to-People Peacemaking
Both sides make a full commitment to advance comprehensive programs for people-to-people peacemaking activities at all levels of both societies. The governments of both sides declare their undertaking to provide full legitimacy for these activities and to allocate budgets for advancing them. The two sides call upon the international community to support the people-to-people peacemaking efforts with international donor support.

ARTICLE TEN
Ministers of Peace
Both sides will establish senior-cabinet-level positions of Ministers of Peace. The Ministries of Peace will be empowered to coordinate the implementation of all nonmilitary aspects of the peace treaty. The Ministries of Peace will coordinate the development of cooperation between all of the parallel government ministries on both sides. The Ministries of Peace will foster and

support the work of nongovernmental organizations supporting the development of peace and normalization of relations between the two peoples.

End of Conflict

Once a full agreement is reached which satisfactorily deals with all of the issues in conflict and there is an end-of-conflict and end-of-claims agreement, the United States and the other permanent members of the Security Council, with Israel's agreement, will sponsor a resolution in the Security Council for full statehood membership in the UN for the State of Palestine.

A second UN Security Council resolution will be sponsored by the United States and the other permanent members of the Security Council that grants the Israel-Palestine peace agreement the force of international law and legitimacy. The UN Security Council Resolution on Israeli-Palestinian peace will declare that a state of peace exists between Israel and Palestine. The resolution will declare that the Israeli-Palestinian peace agreement fulfills UNGA Resolution 181 with the establishment of a Jewish state and an Arab Palestinian state in the land between the Jordan River and the Mediterranean Sea. Furthermore, the Israeli-Palestinian peace agreement will constitute the full implementation of UNGA Resolution 194 and UNSC Resolutions 242, 338, and 1397.

The parties recognize Palestine and Israel as the homelands of their respective peoples. Israel and Palestine agree to adhere to principles of the UN Charter and to guarantee the full rights of minorities within their states regardless of race, religion, nationality, or gender, including the Palestinian minority in Israel and the Jewish minority in Palestine.

Final Thoughts

25 Throughout my life, as demonstrated in this book, there have been two constant themes: that the solution to the Israeli-Palestinian conflict is to be found in the formula of two states for two peoples, and that real peace will be established through the cooperation of people and institutions on both sides of the conflict lines. I continue to believe the roots of the conflict are in the desire and preparedness of both sides to fight, kill, and die so they can have a territorial expression of their identity. This has been a conflict over territory and its identity. That has not changed in the past one hundred years and seems that it will remain so for the coming decades. As such, there is no "one-state solution" because it is not a solution that provides the warring parties with that territorial expression for which they have been so willing to fight.

In the framework of the two-states-for-two-peoples solution, I have never supported the separation paradigm, which is based on walls and fences that prevent the interaction and cooperation I believe is cardinal to the development of real peace. The desire of both sides not to see the other side, whether through the imposition of walls, fences, and checkpoints, or through the senseless and damaging campaign against normalization, is easily understandable given all of the violence and suffering that both sides have experienced. Even Israelis on the left, who I believe truly want peace with the Palestinians, have become the loudest advocates of the separation model. There will never be peace, even with a peace agreement, that places people in cages and prevents or discourages interaction and cooperation. Of this I am sure. That is why it is essential to break down the myths of separation. The geography of fear has bred hatred and racism and has deepened the conflict for both Israelis and Palestinians, and this must be challenged by Israelis and Palestinians together.

An essential element of my thinking has changed over the past years. Throughout much of my work over the decades, I believed that the United States would assist us to make peace. The role of the third party has been central to most peace efforts since the creation of Israel. Israel and Palestine have grown to be dependent on the efforts of others to resolve our conflict. There was hope that the United States would come to the rescue when President Obama stated in his first days in the White House that the resolution of the Israeli-Arab conflict was a US national security interest. If that statement was true, then the old adage that "the parties have to want it more than us" was no longer true. But while the United States tried to get the parties back to the table during the eight years of the Obama administration, the United States was not prepared to apply pressure, or sufficient pressure, on the parties to reach an agreement. The United States has never made strategic use of its diplomatic toolbox of "carrots and sticks" when it comes to trying to resolve the Israeli-Palestinian conflict.

Today, I believe more strongly than ever before that peacemaking will have to come from within. The parties will have to do it for themselves. The United States and others will be prepared to assist, financially and otherwise, but change will be possible only when the parties decide to negotiate between themselves and, hopefully, by themselves. When the parties are close to agreement, the United States and others can provide some bridging proposals. There will be substantial roles for third parties, especially for the United States, at the implementation phases, particularly in monitoring, verification, and dispute resolution. Despite the asymmetry in the conflict, the best negotiations will happen when Israeli representatives and Palestinian representatives lock themselves in a room with the determination to reach agreement. The biggest favor that the United States and the international community can do for Israel and Palestine is to state that no one from outside Israel and Palestine will rescue Israel and Palestine from each other. We, Israelis and Palestinians, have to rescue ourselves, together, face to face. Our neighbors can and should help. Regional agreements, especially on security and economic and environmental cooperation in water and energy, will expand the benefits and create better agreements, but the core of this conflict is Israel and Palestine, and it is from the core that we must work.

Mutual recognition and acceptance will develop over time. We must learn each other's languages. We must reach out beyond the conflict lines. We must learn to cooperate in every aspect of life in this shared land between the Jordan River and the Mediterranean Sea. It is not only a matter of interests. The souls of our peoples and of our states are at hand. This I am sure of: Peace will come.

Notes

PREFACE

1. "Murder Video of Sasson Nuriel Released by Hamas Terrorists," September 2005. Available at *www.youtube.com/watch?v=CusTuiWlKSg*

2. The whole story of the secret back channel negotiations that I conducted can be read in my book *The Negotiator: Freeing Gilad Schalit from Hamas* (New Milford, CT: Toby Press, 2013).

CHAPTER 1

1. Nahum Goldmann speech at the Zionist Congress, August 1937. Qtd. in Simha Flapan, *Zionism and the Palestinians* (London: Croom Helm, 1979), 125.

2. Nahum Goldmann, *Memories: The Autobiography of Nahum Goldmann*, trans. Helen Goldmann Sebba (London: Weidenfeld & Nicolson, 1970), 284. Qtd. in Flapan, *Zionism and the Palestinians*, 126.

3. Flapan, *Zionism and the Palestinians*, 203.

CHAPTER 2

1. Joel Greenberg, "Press Bulletin" (State of Israel: Government Press Office, n.d.).

2. "Address by Prime Minister Yitzhak Rabin upon Signing the Israeli-Palestinian Declaration of Principles," September 13, 1993. Available at *www.rabincenter.org.il/Items/01100/signingoftheDeclationofPrinciples.pdf*

3. Israel Ministry of Foreign Affairs, "108 Declaration of Principles on Interim Self-Government Arrangements: Text and Speeches; The White House," Document #108, Israel's Foreign Relations, Vol. 13–14: 1992–1994, September 13, 1993. Available at *mfa.gov.il/MFA/ForeignPolicy/MFADocuments/Pages/Documents_Foreign_Policy_Israel.aspx*

CHAPTER 3

1. Yale Law School, "Biography of Allard K. Lowenstein," n.d. Available at *law.yale.edu/centers-workshops/orville-h-schell-jr-center-international-human-rights/lowenstein-clinic/biography-allard-k-lowenstein*

2. Young Judaea, 2017. Available at *www.youngjudaea.org*

3. *Aliya* means "to go up" and is used to refer to immigration to Israel, suggesting that immigrating to Israel puts you in a higher place.

4. The Green Line is the armistice line between Israel and the West Bank that designates the lines of deployment at the end of Israel's war for independence (1948–1949).

5. Flapan, *Zionism and the Palestinians.*

6. Partners for Progressive Israel, "In Memory of Rabbi Bruce Cohen, Interns for Peace," 2010. Available at *progressiveisrael.org/in-memory-of-rabbi-bruce-cohen-interns-for-peace*

CHAPTER 4

1. Zionist and Israel Information Center, "Zionist Quotes," n.d. Available at *www.zionism-israel.com/zionist_quotes.htm*

2. After Israel's war of independence from 1948–1949, there remained 156,000 Arabs in the territories under Israel's control. They were given Israeli citizenship, but as they were considered to belong to the enemy that fought against Israel's existence, they were placed under a military government until 1966.

3. Al-Ard (Arabic: الارض, "The Land") was a Palestinian political movement made up of Arab citizens of Israel active between 1958 and sometime in the 1970s, which attracted international attention. Ron Harris, *A Case Study in the Banning of Political Parties: The Pan-Arab Movement El Ard and the Israeli Supreme Court,* Working Paper 349, bepress Legal Series, August 2004. Available at *law.bepress.com/expresso/eps/349*

4. During this period, the government of Israel was planning to expropriate more Arab land in the Galilee. A plan for "Judaizing the Galilee" was discovered, which included building small Jewish settlements on hilltops throughout the area to prevent Arab expansion. Michael Omer-man, "This Week in History: The 1976 Land Day Protests," *Jerusalem Post,* March 25, 2012. Available at *www.jpost.com/features/in-thespotlights/this-week-in-history-the-1976-land-day-protests*

5. Adalah: The Center for Arab Minority Rights in Israel, "Discriminatory Laws in Israel," n.d. Available at *www.adalah.org/en/law/index*

CHAPTER 5

1. "Oasis of Peace," n.d. Available at *nswas.org*

2. The Van Leer Jerusalem Institute, n.d. Available at *www.vanleer.org.il/en*

CHAPTER 6

1. Hanns Seidel Stiftung, n.d. Available at *www.hss.de/english.html*

CHAPTER 7

1. The name comes from the 1921 essay written by Ahad Ha'am, the founder and spiritual leader of the movement for spiritual Zionism.

CHAPTER 8

1. *Encyclopedia Britannica*, "Said Hammami," 2008. Available at *www.britannica. com/biography/Said-Hammami*; *Encyclopedia Britannica*; "Issam Sartawi," 2008. Available at *www.britannica.com/biography/Issam-Sartawi*

CHAPTER 15

1. Sharm el-Sheikh, "Remarks by President Clinton and President Mubarak in Delivery of Joint Statements at the Conclusion of the Middle East Peace Summit; October 17, 2000," The Avalon Project, Yale Law School. Available at *avalon.law. yale.edu/21st_century/mid022.asp*

2. Sharm el-Sheikh, "Fact-Finding Committee Report: 'Mitchell Report,'" April 30, 2001. Available at *eeas.europa.eu/mepp/docs/mitchell_report_2001_en.pdf*

CHAPTER 21

1. "Reported Text of Draft UN Resolution on Palestinian Statehood," *Times of Israel*, December 30, 2014. Available at *www.timesofisrael.com/ reported-text-of-draft-un-resolution-on-palestinian-statehood*

2. Israel Ministry of Foreign Affairs, "The Clinton Peace Plan," Document #226, Israel's Foreign Relations, Vol. 18: 1999–2000, December 23, 2000. Available from *mfa.gov.il/MFA/ForeignPolicy/MFADocuments/Pages/Documents_Foreign_ Policy_Israel.aspx*

CHAPTER 24

1. Schlomo Avineri, "With No Solution in Sight: Between Two National Movements," *Haaretz*, September 27, 2015.

2. Yonatan Mendel, *The Creation of Israeli Arabic: Security and Politics in Arabic Studies in Israel* (Basingstoke, UK: Palgrave MacMillan, 2014).

3. US General Paul Selva, then a three-star general, now also a member of the Joint Chiefs of Staff with the rank of four-star general, served as special assistant to the Joint Chiefs of Staff and US Road Map Monitor from 2008 to 2011.

4. University of Windsor, "Jerusalem Old City Initiative," n.d. Available at *www1. uwindsor.ca/joci*

Index